# ERRING

Barry Moser. Untitled lithograph. Reproduced by permission of Barry Moser.

Mark C. Taylor

# ERRING

## A
## Postmodern
## A/theology

The University of
Chicago Press

*Chicago & London*

The University of Chicago Press, Chicago 60637
The University of Chicago Press, Ltd., London
© 1984 by The University of Chicago
All rights reserved. Published 1984
Paperback edition 1987
Printed in the United States of America

08 07 06 05 04 03 02 01 00 99 98    6 7 8 9 10

*Library of Congress Cataloging in Publication Data*

Taylor, Mark C., 1945–
    Erring: a postmodern a/theology.

    Bibliography: p.
    Includes index.
    1. Theology.   2. Deconstruction.   3. Death of God
theology.   I. Title.
BT83.8.T39   1984         230′.044         84.88
ISBN 0-226-79142-4 (paper)

♾ The paper used in this publication meets the minimum requirements of the American National Standard for Information Sciences—Permanence of Paper for Printed Library Materials, ANSI Z39.48-1992.

To

A A R O N   S T E A R N S   T A Y L O R

and

K I R S T E N   J E N N I E   T A Y L O R

_____

For teaching me the errors of my way

and the ways of their erring

# Contents

List of Figures     viii

Acknowledgments     xi

PART ONE · "DECONSTRUCTING THEOLOGY"

. . . Prelude     3

1. Death of God     19
      Mirror Play: Psychology of Mastery   19
      Utility and Consumption: Economy of Domination   25
      Narcissism and Nihilism   29

2. Disappearance of the Self     34
      Image, Identity, Imitation   34
      Naming: Propriety, Property, Possession   40
      Uncanniness of Presence: Representation and
        Repetition   46

3. End of History     52
      Shadows of Logocentrism: Types and Tropes   52
      Ariadne's Thread: Poetics of History   61
      Saving Presence   68

4. Closure of the Book     74
      Authorship: Mimesis and Poiesis   74
      Authority: Masterpieces and Tradition   87
      Heterography   90

PART TWO · Deconstructive A/theology

5. Writing of God                                          97
    Hieroglyphics   97
    Divine Milieu: A Middle Way    112
    Dissemination    118

6. Markings                                               121
    Dispossession, Impropriety, Expropriation   122
    Anonymity: Spending and Sacrifice    140
    Death, Desire, Delight    145

7. Mazing Grace                                           149
    Erring: Serpentine Wandering    149
    Aberrance: Carnival and Comedy    158
    Superficiality: Carnality    168

8. Erring Scripture                                       170
    Duplicity: Shiftiness and Undecidability    170
    Spinning: Tissue of Texts    177
    Wordplay: Pens and Needles    180

Interlude . . .                                           183

Notes                                                     185

Biblio Graphy                                             199

Index                                                     211

## List of Figures

Barry Moser, Untitled lithograph                    *Frontispiece*

Robert Morris, Groundplan of the Philadelphia Labyrinth        60

Hans Holbein the Younger, *The Bust of Terminus*, made for Erasmus   102

*The Parable of the Last Judgment*, a mosaic in Sant' Apollinare,
    Ravenna                                             124

Jan van Eyck, *The Madonna of Chancellor Rolin* and
    *The Goldsmith Jan de Leeuw*                        125

Diego Velázquez, *The Maids of Honor*                    126

Pablo Picasso, *Armchair Woman, No. 2*                   127

Barnett Newman, *L'Errance*                              128

# Acknowledgments

If authorship is never original but is always a play that is an interplay, then clearly "I" did not write this text. Or at least "I" alone did not write it. Like all works, this "book" (if it is a book) has been (and will continue to be) coauthored by many people and various institutions. To name any of these fellow writers is to attempt to bind a fabric that is boundless. One is, however, forever inscribed within and bound to the framework(s) that he or she struggles to subvert. And so we continue to sign and to acknowledge— even when such naming no longer rings true. Though here listed *hors d'oeuvre*, the others who are always already "within" the tangled lines of *Erring* include (among others) Thomas J. J. Altizer, Houston A. Baker, John W. Chandler, Donna Chenail, Stephen Crites, Jacques Derrida, Ray L. Hart, Toshihiko Izutsu, Thomas Krens, Rosemary Lane, Justus George Lawler, H. Ganse Little, John D. Maguire, John R. Miles, Eileen Sahady, Robert P. Scharlemann, Sara Suleri, Beryl C. Taylor, Dinny S. Taylor, Noel A. Taylor, Thelma C. Taylor, David Tracy, Lisken Van Pelt, and Charles Winquist.

If, as some critics have argued recently, the author is an "institution," then institutions can, in some sense, "author." Always parasitic, writing presupposes an economy, which it relentlessly interrogates. For their essential role in the genesis of this volume, I am deeply indebted to Williams College, the National Humanities Center, and the Fulbright Foundation.

And finally a special word of gratitude for Aaron and Kirsten, whose playful erring keeps me (sometimes) from the straight and narrow.

M.C.T.

Paris
May, 1983

Thinkers without final thoughts
In an always incipient cosmos,
The way, when we climb a mountain,
Vermont throws itself together.
—WALLACE STEVENS, "July Mountain"

# PART ONE

# "Deconstructing Theology"

# . . . Prelude

We must begin *wherever we are* and the thought of the trace . . . has
already taught us that it was impossible to justify a point of departure
absolutely. *Wherever we are*: in a text where we already believe ourselves
to be.

"We must begin *wherever we are* . . . *Wherever we are*: in a text where we
believe ourselves to be." But where *are* we? For many people today, there
seems to be no simple answer to this question. Individuals appear to be
unsure of where they have come from and where they are going. Thus they
are not certain where they are. Furthermore, the "texts" that have guided
and grounded previous generations often appear illegible in the modern and
postmodern worlds. Instead of expressing a single story or coherent plot,
human lives tend to be inscribed in multiple and often contradictory texts.
What makes sense and is meaningful in one situation frequently seems
senseless and meaningless in another setting. The resulting conflict creates
confusion that extends far beyond the pages of the book. In Yeats's well-
known words:

> Turning and turning in the widening gyre
> The falcon cannot hear the falconer;
> Things fall apart; the center cannot hold;
> Mere anarchy is loosed upon the world.[1]

This quandary is not, of course, particularly new. Though its sources are
complex, the confusion in the contemporary intellectual, cultural, social,
and spiritual landscape is closely tied to important developments in modern
philosophy and theology. Standing at the threshold of the twentieth century, Nietzsche, one of the greatest prophets of postmodernism, declared:
"God remains dead. And we have killed him."[2] The eclipse of belief in God
did not suddenly appear on the horizon. It emerged gradually over a period
of at least two hundred years. The critique of authority that arose during the
latter part of the eighteenth century was an important factor in the shift
away from traditional religious faith. Although rooted in Reformation
theology and the spiritualism of radical reformers, the heart of the Enlightenment critique of authority was the renewed confidence in human
reason. "*Sapere aude!*" declared Kant. "Have courage to use your own rea-

3

son!—That is the motto of enlightenment."[3] As Kant's own position makes clear, critique does not necessarily mean rejection. In Kantian philosophy, authority is maintained, though internalized. Heteronomy is translated into autonomy, as the word of one becomes the voice of all. From this point of view, the apparent universality of reason seems to provide a safeguard against relativistic historicism and to preclude the solipsism implicit in egalitarianism. While Kant believed his elaborate philosophical enterprise to be in the service of faith, the recognition of the inextricable relation between Author and authority led more radical thinkers of the era to be less optimistic about the possibility of reconciling religious belief and practice with the aims of emancipation and enlightenment. Many went so far as to argue that the chains of authority could be broken only by the death of the founding father. In many cases, rebellion became secular communion. The fraternal bond joining the sons of the Revolution was forged by common participation in the act of patricide and was sealed by the blood of the slain Father.

Although at odds with Kant's own perspective, the radicalism of post-Kantian thought was an understandable outgrowth of his critical philosophy. The Romantic veneration of creative individuality and preoccupation with historical process cast doubt on the purported universality of Kant's forms of intuition and categories of understanding. Throughout the nineteenth century, increasing sensitivity to the historical character of consciousness led to decreasing belief in apriori cognitive structures. This development had important consequences for the interpretation of religious belief. Having recognized the social, cultural, and psychological conditions of consciousness, thinkers like Hegel, Marx, Nietzsche, and Freud proceeded to examine religious behavior in efforts to discern its latent content. Though such hermeneutical suspicion led to analyses that differed widely, various interpreters agreed that what for centuries had been regarded as objective reality is, in fact, subjective projection. Inverting the traditional Creator/creature relation, God came to be regarded as the creation of human beings. This revolutionary reversal both called into question the actuality of the divine and rendered doubtful all forms of religious authority.

Typical responses to the disappearance of the divine Author and the corresponding demise of religious authority cover a wide, and usually predictable, range. In the wake of the criticism of belief, many people appear to have become completely indifferent to religious and philosophical questions. Totally engaged in everyday activities, they rarely feel the need to step back and reflect on their experience. Others seem deeply troubled by the implications of modernism and postmodernism for traditional religious faith. The reaction of these individuals often takes the form of a defiant rejection of every critique of foundational beliefs. The reassertion of traditional orthodoxies is presented as a bulwark against advancing infidelity. As I have suggested, still others receive the news of the death of God and the questionableness of authority with great enthusiasm. Like servants released from bondage to a harsh master or children unbound from the rule of a domineering father, such individuals feel free to become themselves. In addition to these contrasting points of view, there is a large, and I believe growing, group of people who find themselves caught in the middle of such extremes. Suspended between the loss of old certainties and the discovery of new beliefs, these marginal people constantly live on the border that both joins and separates belief and unbelief. They look yet do not find, search but do not discover. This failure, however, need not necessarily end the quest. Like Walker Percy's moviegoer, those who are betwixt 'n' between realize that "Not to be onto something is to be in despair."[4] It is to these marginal people (among whom I count myself) that this study is addressed.

Throughout the course of the twentieth century, Western philosophers of religion and theologians have addressed themselves in a variety of ways to those who find themselves between belief and unbelief. Some of the most thoughtful theological responses to modernity have been formulated by appropriating insights advanced in contemporary philosophy. Recent philosophers as different as Heidegger, Bloch, Wittgenstein, and Whitehead have provided the background for significant theological reformulations. In many cases this union of philosophy and theology has been very productive. Innovative developments in religious thought like process theology, liberation theology, theology of hope, existential theology, and hermeneutical theology would not have been possible without the contributions of contemporary philosophy. Nevertheless, in the face of the profound questions raised by postmodern experience, it is necessary to ask if any of these revisions has gone far enough.

In recent years there has been a philosophical development of major proportions that has yet to make a significant impact on philosophy of religion and theology. In France a "movement" of thought known as *deconstruction* has emerged. Although deconstruction is, in many ways, peculiarly French and distinctively postmodern, it is, nonetheless, closely related to critical developments in early twentieth-century philosophy, art, literature, music, linguistics, and psychology. Writers and artists like Heidegger, Joyce, Schoenberg, Saussure, and Freud must be counted among its precursors. Perhaps as important for deconstruction as any of these figures, however, are three major nineteenth-century thinkers: Hegel, Kierkegaard, and Nietzsche. Nowhere in twentieth-century thought have the insights of these pivotal philosophers been more thoroughly absorbed and reworked than in deconstruction. This is especially evident in the writings of the leading deconstructive philosopher—Jacques Derrida. Derrida actually goes so far as to suggest that "We will never be finished with the reading or rereading of Hegel, and, in a certain way, I do nothing other than attempt to explain myself on this point."[5] In his reading and rereading of Hegel, Derrida repeatedly, though rarely explicitly, relies on the writings of Kierkegaard and Nietzsche. This is not to imply that Derrida attempts to synthesize the insights of those who have preceded him. Though clearly parasitic on Hegel, Kierkegaard, and Nietzsche, Derrida's deconstruction is not Hegelian, Kierkegaardian, or Nietzschean. It falls somewhere *in between* all three of these positions. By simultaneously drawing together and pulling apart the works of such seminal writers, deconstruction opens new perspectives on the perplexing worlds of postmodernism.

In many ways, deconstruction might seem an unlikely partner for religious reflection. As a form of thought it appears avowedly atheistic. Derrida speaks for others as well as himself when he adamantly maintains that deconstruction "blocks every relationship to theology." [6] Paradoxically, it is just this antithetical association with theology that lends deconstruction its "religious" significance for marginal thinkers. By reflecting and recasting the pathos of so much contemporary art, literature, and philosophy, deconstruction expresses greater appreciation for the significance of the death of God than most contemporary philosophers of religion and theologians. Though anticipated in Hegel's speculative philosophy and Kierkegaard's attack on Christendom and proclaimed by Nietzsche's madman, the death of God is not concretely actualized until the emergence of the twentieth-century industrial state. And yet, as Nietzsche realized, "This tremendous event is," in an important sense, "still on its way, still wandering; it has not yet reached the ears of men." [7] This deafness is all too evident among many contemporary philosophers of religion and theologians. Too often they attempt to solve difficult religious problems by simply trying to recapture a past that now seems decisively gone. This attitude is no longer defensible.

Postmodernism opens with the sense of *irrevocable* loss and *incurable* fault. This wound is inflicted by the overwhelming awareness of death—a death that "begins" with the death of God and "ends" with the death of our selves. We are in a time between times and a place which is no place. Here our reflection must "begin." In this liminal time and space, deconstructive philosophy and criticism offer rich, though still largely untapped, resources for religious reflection. One of the distinctive features of deconstruction is its willingness to confront the problem of the death of God squarely even if not always directly. The insights released by deconstructive criticism suggest the ramifications of the death of God for areas as apparently distinct as contemporary psychology, linguistics, and historical analysis. In view of its remarkable grasp of the far-reaching significance of the dissolution of the Western theological and philosophical tradition, it would not be too much to suggest that *deconstruction is the "hermeneutic" of the death of God*. As such, it provides a possible point of departure for a postmodern a/theology. Given the marginality of its site, an a/theology that draws on deconstructive philosophy will invert established meaning and subvert everything once deemed holy. It will thus be utterly transgressive.

The failure (or refusal) to come to terms with the radical implications of the death of God has made it impossible for most Western theology to approach postmodernism. This shortcoming results, at least in part, from the lack of a clear recognition that concepts are not isolated entities. Rather, they form intricate networks or complex webs of interrelation and co-implication. As a result of this interconnection, notions mutually condition and reciprocally define each other. Such thoroughgoing corelativity implies that no *single* concept is either absolutely primary or exclusively foundational. Clusters of coordinated notions form the matrix of any coherent conceptual system. It would, of course, be a vast oversimplification to insist that all Western theology can be made to fit a single system. Efforts to totalize the tradition inevitably leave a remainder and consequently always negate themselves. It is, nonetheless, possible to identify a set of inter-related concepts that have been particularly persistent in theological reflection. This network includes at least four terms: God, self, history, and book. In order to anticipate the course of the argument that follows, it might be helpful to indicate briefly the interplay of these important notions and to suggest some of the assumptions and consequences of the closely knit network that they form.

According to the tenets of classical theism, God, who is One, is the supreme Creator, who, through the mediation of His divine Logos, brings the world into being and providentially directs its course. This Primal Origin (First Cause or *Archē*) is also the Ultimate End (Final Goal or *Telos*) of the world. Utterly transcendent and thoroughly eternal, God is represented as totally present to Himself [*sic*]. He is, in fact, the omnipresent fount, source, ground, and uncaused cause of presence itself. The self is made in the image of God and consequently is also one, i.e., a centered individual. Mirroring its Creator, the single subject is both self-conscious and freely active. Taken together, self-consciousness and freedom entail individual responsibility. History is the domain where divine guidance and human initiative meet. The temporal course of events is not regarded as a random sequence. It is believed to be plotted along a single line stretching from a definite beginning (creation) through an identifiable middle (incarnation) to an expected end (kingdom or redemption). Viewed in such ordered terms, history forms a purposeful process whose meaning can be coherently represented. Page by page and chapter by chapter, the Book weaves the unified story of the interaction between God and self. Since the logic of this narrative reflects the Logos of history, Scripture, in effect, rewrites the Word of God.

God, self, history, and book are, thus, bound in an intricate relationship in which each mirrors the other. No single concept can be changed without altering all of the others. As a result of this thorough interdependence, the news of the death of God cannot really reach our ears until its reverberations are traced in the notions of self, history and book. The echoes of the death of

God can be heard in the disappearance of the self, the end of history, and the closure of the book. We can begin to unravel this web of conceptual relations by plotting the coordinates of a new a/theological network.

The Western theological tradition, in all its evident diversity, rests upon a polar or, more precisely, a dyadic foundation. Though consistently monotheistic, Christian theology is repeatedly inscribed in binary terms. The history of religious thought in the West can be read as a pendular movement between seemingly exclusive and evident opposites.

| | |
|---|---|
| God | World |
| Eternity | Time |
| Being | Becoming |
| Rest | Movement |
| Permanence | Change |
| Presence | Absence |
| One | Many |
| Sacred | Profane |
| Order | Chaos |
| Meaning | Absurdity |
| Life | Death |
| Infinite | Finite |
| Transcendent | Immanent |
| Identity | Difference |
| Affirmation | Negation |
| Truth | Error |
| Reality | Illusion |
| Certainty | Uncertainty |
| Clarity | Confusion |
| Sanity | Madness |
| Light | Darkness |
| Vision | Blindness |
| Invisible | Visible |
| Spirit | Body |
| Spiritual | Carnal |
| Mind | Matter |
| Good | Evil |

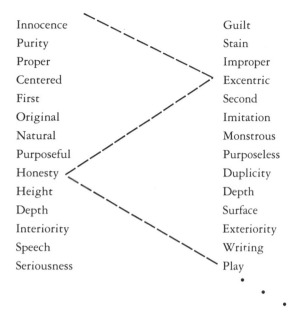

| Innocence | Guilt |
| Purity | Stain |
| Proper | Improper |
| Centered | Excentric |
| First | Second |
| Original | Imitation |
| Natural | Monstrous |
| Purposeful | Purposeless |
| Honesty | Duplicity |
| Height | Depth |
| Depth | Surface |
| Interiority | Exteriority |
| Speech | Writing |
| Seriousness | Play |

Like its intellectual twin, philosophy, theology does not regard these opposites as equivalent. It refuses to allow the possibility that oppositional
terms can coexist peacefully. Invariably one term is privileged through
the divestment of its relative. The resultant economy of privilege sustains an asymmetrical hierarchy in which one member governs or rules the
other throughout the theological, logical, axiological, and even political
domains.

It is against just this hierarchy that so many modern thinkers rebel.
Indeed, modernism might be described as the struggle to overturn this
structure of domination upon which Western thought and society traditionally have rested. Many theologians who have taken up the challenge of
modernism have been inevitably driven to revolutionary radicalism. The
theological radical learns from modern politics, painting, music, and literature that "true revolution is not simply an opening to the future but also a
closing of the past. Yet the past which is negated by a revolutionary future
cannot simply be negated or forgotten. It must be transcended by way of a
reversal of the past, a reversal bringing a totally new light and meaning to
everything which is manifest as the past, and therefore a reversal fully
transforming the whole horizon of the present. Modern revolutionary as-
saults upon the whole movement of a profane or secular history can now
serve not only as models but also as sources for a revolutionary theological
assault upon the history of faith."[8] Even revolutionary thought, however,
runs the risk of being *insufficiently* radical. If hierarchical oppression and

repression are to be overcome, it is necessary to *pass through* a phase of inversion. But reversal can remain caught within the dyadic economy of conflictual opposition. Merely "To put a minus sign instead of a plus sign before the elements of Western culture is not to liberate oneself from them but to remain entirely bound within their net. To define God as the supreme evil is as much an act of homage and belief as to define him as the supreme good."[9] In place of a simple reversal, it is necessary to effect a dialectical inversion that does not leave contrasting opposites unmarked but dissolves their original identities. Inversion, in other words, must simultaneously be a perversion that is subversive. Unless theological transgression becomes genuinely subversive, nothing fundamental will change. What is needed is a critical lever with which the entire inherited order can be creatively disorganized. It is at this point that deconstruction becomes a potential resource for the a/theologian.

Deconstructive criticism unravels the very fabric of most Western theology and philosophy. When subjected to a deconstructive critique, the structure of relationship that both joins and separates opposites is reformulated in such a way that contraries are not merely reversed but are recast to dissolve their original propriety and proper identity. Deconstruction, therefore, both affects specific concepts within a dyadic economy and calls into question the entire network of notions that traditionally have grounded theological reflection. Once terms undergo deconstructive analysis, they cannot simply be reinscribed within an oppositional system that previously had defined and constituted them. It is important to stress that this critique does not approach the theological network from without and thus does not involve a disjunctive epistemological break. Like any parasite, deconstruction attacks from within, using "the strengths of the field to turn its own stratagems against it, producing a force of dislocation that spreads itself throughout the entire system, fissuring it in every direction and thoroughly *delimiting* it."[10]

Deconstruction is irrevocably liminal or marginal. Its liminality marks an unstable border along which marginal thinkers wander. This novel and admittedly controversial form of criticism seems to me to be particularly well suited to address many of the issues that preoccupy people caught *between* belief and unbelief. Deconstruction itself is at one and the same time inside and outside the network that it questions. On the one hand, deconstruction's uncanny criticism pervades and subverts the hierarchical system of theological concepts. On the other hand, the survival of this parasitic discourse presupposes the continuing existence of its host. Hence deconstructive writing is always paradoxical, double, duplicitous, excentric, improper, . . . errant. Calling into question the very notion of propriety, the language of deconstruction can possess no final or proper meaning. It remains transitional. Its words cannot be completely fixed, mastered, or captured in the net of either/or. Instead, deconstructive criticism constantly errs along the / of neither/nor. Forever wavering and wandering, deconstruction is (re)inscribed betwixt 'n' between the opposites it inverts, perverts, and subverts. Consequently, deconstruction can be written only on the boundary, a boundary that, though always the "middest," knows no bounds. The time and space of this border form a middle age or middle kingdom that is not, in any ordinary sense, intermediate. The ceaseless play of opposites renders transition permanent and passage absolute. This interval is the medium or mean within which all extremes cross. While not reducible to or expressible in a traditional oppositional logic of extremes, this milieu is the "nonoriginal origin" of everything that is—and that is not.

In the following pages I shall be asking whether the scriptural network graphed in deconstruction can be read as the eternal cross(ing) of the word that repeatedly inscribes and reinscribes the infinite play of the divine milieu. In a sense, this query implies the possibility of deconstructing deconstruction. As I have noted, proponents of deconstruction insist that their practice blocks every relationship to theology. Insofar as theology remains bound to or caught in its traditional systematic form, this claim of deconstructive critics is, of course, correct. I have, however, briefly suggested that deconstruction calls into question the coherence, integrity, and intelligibility of this network of oppositions. By inverting and subverting the poles between which Western theology has been suspended, deconstruction reverses itself and creates a new opening for the religious imagination.

Thought that wanders into this interstitial space will, of necessity, be unsettled and unsettling. Repeatedly slipping through the holes in the system within which it must, nevertheless, be registered, such thought is perpetually transitory and forever nomadic. It is neither simply this nor that, here nor there, inside nor outside. To follow the ways of such vagrant thought is inevitably to err. Writing that attempts to trace the border and retrace the margin can, therefore, be described as *erring*. *Err* is an uncommonly rich word whose many (perhaps bottomless) layers suggest multiple dimensions of the argument I shall be developing. By roaming through the labyrinth of this word, we catch an initial glimpse of the wiles and ways of postmodern a/theology.

*Err* appears to derive from the Latin *errāre* (whose "prehistoric" form is *ersāre*) by way of Middle English *erre*, French *errer*, Provençal and Spanish *errar*, and Italian *errare*.[11] *Errāre* ("to wander, or stray about, to rove") is cognate with the Gothic *aírzjan*, which means "to lead astray." To err is to ramble, roam, stray, wander, like Chaucer's "weary ghost that errest to and fro." Such wandering inevitably leads one astray—away from one's path or line of direction. To err, therefore, is to "fail, miss, go wrong in judgment or opinion; to make a mistake, blunder, or commit a fault; to be incorrect; to go astray morally"; even "to sin." *Err* drifts toward: *Errable* ("fallible, liable to error"); *Errabund* ("random"); *Errancy* ("the condition of erring or being in error"); *Errand* ("a message, a verbal communication to be repeated to a third party; a petition or prayer presented through another; a short journey on which an inferior—e.g. a servant, a child—is sent to convey a message or perform some simple business on behalf of the sender"); *Errantly* ("wandering, prone to wander; wandering from place to place, vagrant, nomadic; irregular or uncertain in movement, having no fixed course; irregular or eccentric in conduct, habit, or opinion"); *Erratum* ("an error in writing or printing"); *Erre* ("wound, scar"); *Erre* ("wrath"); *Erroneous* ("wandering, roving, moving aimlessly, vagrant; straying from the ways of wisdom or prudence; misguided; of doctrines, opinions, statements: incorrect, mistaken, wrong"); *Error* ("the action of roaming or wandering; hence a devious or winding course, a roving, winding; chagrin, fury, vexation; extravagance of passion; the condition of erring in opinion; holding of mistaken notions or beliefs; a delusion, trick; something incorrectly done through ignorance or inadvertance; a departure from moral rectitude; a transgression"); and, of course, *Errant*. "Errant" subdivides into three branches. I. Old French *errer*, which is from the Latin *iterāre* ("to journey, travel"): "Itinerant, traveling; said of knights who traveled about in quest of adventure; in chess, a traveling pawn, one that has been advanced from its original square; and *Errant juif*—the Wandering Jew." II. "The primary notion of branch II is uncertain: "A notorious, 'common' thief." III. French *errēr*, which is from the Latin *errāre* ("to stray, wander, err"): "Astray, wandering, roving; straying from the proper course or place; having no fixed course." *Erring*, then, is "wandering, roaming; deviating from the right or intended course; missing the mark." The semantic branches of *err* spread to errancy, erratic, erratum, erre, erroneous, and errant.

The erring a/theologian is driven to consider and reconsider errant notions: transgression, subversion, mastery, utility, consumption, domination, narcissism, nihilism, possession, uncanniness, repetition, tropes, writing, dissemination, dispossession, expropriation, impropriety, anonymity, spending, sacrifice, death, desire, delight, wandering, aberrance, carnival, comedy, superficiality, carnality, duplicity, shiftiness, undecidability, and spinning. In view of these preoccupations, it should be clear that erring thought is neither *properly* theological nor nontheological, theistic nor atheistic, religious nor secular, believing nor nonbelieving. A/theology represents the liminal thinking of marginal thinkers. The / of a/theology (which, it is important to note, can be written but not spoken) marks the *limen* that signifies *both* proximity and distance, similarity and difference, interiority and exteriority. This strangely permeable membrane forms a border where fixed boundaries disintegrate. Along this boundless boundary the traditional polarities between which Western theology has been suspended are inverted and subverted. Since it is forever *entre-deux*, a/theology is undeniably ambiguous. The a/theologian asks errant questions and suggests responses that often seem erratic or even erroneous. Since his reflection wanders, roams, and strays from the "proper" course, it tends to deviate from well-established ways. To traditional eyes, a/theology doubtless appears to be irregular, eccentric, and vagrant. At best it seems aimless, at worst devious. Within this framework, a/theology is, in fact, heretical. For the a/theologian, however, heresy and aimlessness are unavoidable. Ideas are never fixed but are always in transition; thus they are irrepressibly transitory. For this reason, a/theology might be labeled "Nomad Thought."[12] The erring nomad neither looks back to an absolute beginning nor ahead to an ultimate end. His writing, therefore, remains unfinished. His work is less a complete book than an open (perhaps broken) text that never really begins or actually ends. The words of a/theology fall in between; they are *always* in the middle. The a/theological text is a tissue woven of threads that are produced by endless spinning. This vertiginous wordplay points to the paradoxical nonbinary (a)logic of the cross. I am persuaded that along the middle way traced by deconstruction there lies a revolutionary reading of writing that reveals scripture anew. The way of the word, of course, is also the tortuous path to Golgotha. As the threshold of absolute passage, the cross marks the intersection of ascent and descent that is the "marriage of heaven and hell."

The course that I will pursue in the following pages, as one might easily infer, will not be straight and to the point. It will inevitably be serpentine. To avoid needless confusion, it might be helpful to cast an anticipatory glance at the erratic boundary along which I will be wandering. The study is divided into two major parts: Deconstructing Theology and Deconstructive A/theology. In the first, I shall explore the implications of deconstruction for four notions essential to the Western theological network: God, self, history, and book. By following deconstructive procedures, I seek to solicit the inherent instability and covert contradictions of these foundational concepts. The second part of my inquiry is devoted to a deconstructive reformulation of each of these notions. I shall attempt to interpret God as writing, self as trace, history as erring, and book as text.

I "begin" my analysis of the theological network by considering the way in which the death of God comes to expression in the humanistic atheism that is typical of modern (as opposed to postmodern) critiques of religious belief. The humanistic atheist denies God in the name of self by transferring the attributes of the divine Creator to the human creature. This shift results in the undialectical inversion of classical theology into modern anthropology. Humanistic atheism expresses a psychology of mastery in which self-assertion is a function of the attempt to negate the other in whose specular gaze the self sees itself reflected. This struggle for domination embodies the interrelated principles of utility and consumption which lie at the heart of technological consciousness. The psychology of mastery and the economy of domination represent efforts to deny death. This labor proves to be both narcissistic and nihilistic. Such self-assertion is finally *self*-defeating. The death of God, ironically, culminates in the disappearance of the self.

In the second chapter I explore the intricate relation between Western images of God and self. I argue that the epoch of selfhood spans a period that extends roughly from Augustine's *Confessions* to Hegel's *Phenomenology of Spirit*. Within these bounds, knowledge of self is mediated by knowledge of God. Through the presentation of a consistent narrative of personal experience, the subject seeks to establish individual identity and to secure personal property. Such self-presentation is inseparable from recollection, representation, and repetition. This insight suggests that the self is thoroughly temporal. The temporality of the subject, however, subverts the identity, propriety, presence, and property of selfhood. This subversion effectively dispossesses the subject.

While autobiography presents an ordered account of an individual self made in the image of God, historical narrative strives to uncover the coherence of time as a whole. History, envisioned as plotted along a line that stretches from a definite beginning through an identifiable middle to an expected end, is bound to the notion of a providential creator God. Within the Christian tradition, this view of history can best be described as Logocentric. Christ is the Logos who forms the center through which beginning and end join to form a unified totality. The implicit unity of apparently disparate events is made explicit through typological and tropological interpretation. In my third chapter, I maintain that these closely related interpretive strategies are actually efforts to master temporality by comprehending human activity as a meaningful historical totality. But this undertaking fails; Chronos reasserts itself in the very effort to negate it. With the death of God and the disappearance of the self, history comes to an end.

The book re-presents personal and social history. Whether understood mimetically (as representing the work of the Author) or poetically (as representing the work of the author), the book remains caught in a closely knit web of signification. The network of signs articulated in the book presupposes a closure that is intended to render experience intelligible. When interpreted in this way, the book is most fully realized in its encyclopedic form. Just as Augustine's *Confessions* points to Hegel's *Phenomenology*, so the Western notion of the book achieves completion in the Hegelian *Encyclopedia of the Philosophical Sciences*. A work that successfully "rationalizes" experience is regarded as a masterpiece. Masterpiece and tradition stand in a circular relationship in which each establishes and is established by the other. And yet neither masterpiece nor tradition can ever completely control experience. They inevitably include within themselves the disruptive other that they try to exclude.

The deconstruction of the Western theological network discloses the recurrent effort of human beings to achieve a position of domination. This struggle appears to grow out of the conviction that mastery results from the ability to secure presence and establish identity by overcoming absence and repressing difference. The battle for mastery, however, is always self-defeating. The supposedly vanquished slave inevitably returns to haunt the apparently victorious master. This return of the repressed simultaneously unravels the web of traditional theology and makes possible the writing of postmodern a/theology.

In part two I begin to develop a deconstructive a/theology by arguing that the death of God can be understood in terms of a radical christology that prepares the way for reinterpreting the notion of the divine. From an a/theological perspective, Jesus is manifested as word, and word is read as writing. Writing, in this context, is not to be understood in the ordinary sense of the term. In developing my analysis of writing or scripture, I extend the insights advanced in deconstructive criticism. I argue that writing is the interplay of presence/absence and identity/difference that overturns the polar opposites of classical theology. Though scripture neither properly is nor is not, it is the nonoriginal "origin" of all being and nonbeing. Everything is always already inscribed within the generative/destructive play of (the) word(s). When understood in this way, writing can be read as the divine milieu. Along this middle way, writing of God repeatedly appears as the unending dissemination of the word.

The analysis of divine scripture discloses the interiority of exteriority; this ruptures the integrity of identity and the propriety of person. In the sixth chapter I explore the possibility that the dissolution of the individual self gives rise to anonymous subjectivity, in which care-less sacrifice takes the place of anxious mastery and unreserved spending supplants consuming domination. The expropriation of personality presupposes the appropriation of death. This loss of self is not, however, simply nihilistic. The disappearance of the subject is at the same time the emergence of the trace. The trace concretely embodies the ceaseless interplay of desire and delight.

According to the argument that I develop in the seventh chapter, the death of God, erasure of self, and end of history open the possibility of mazing grace. When human experience no longer can be graphed along a line that has a definite beginning, middle, and end, life becomes serpentine wandering. Though such erring is purposeless, it does not necessarily represent desperate exile. Profitless play can overcome the unhappy consciousness of the historical agent. The excentricity of erring leads to the aberrance of carnival. In the festive dance of the carnival, individual identities dissolve and social oppositions break down. Here the levity of comedy replaces the gravity of tragedy. In the absence of transcendence, interiority and depth give way to a labyrinthian play of surfaces. When nostalgia is gone and waiting is over, one can delight in the superficiality of appearances.

The unending play of surfaces discloses the ineradicable duplicity of knowledge, shiftiness of truth, and undecidability of value. Since there is no transcendental signified to anchor the activity of signification, freely floating signs cannot be tied down to any single meaning. Everything inscribed within the divine milieu is thoroughly transitional and radically relative. Inasmuch as signs are always signs of signs, interpretations are inevitably interpretations of interpretations. This infinite interrelationship of interpretations cannot be captured in a closed book; it must be written in an open text. Texts point beyond themselves to other texts. In view of this intertextuality, it becomes apparent that writing is a ceaseless process in which writer is already reader and reader necessarily becomes writer. Endless wordplay is the everlasting play of the word that enacts the death of the A/author and subverts every final authority. When writing is understood as divine scripture, it appears to be unfinished and ever erring. In an unconcluding Interlude, "I" underscore the impossibility of ending in a world that has no End. The eternally recurring play of scripture marks and re-marks our unending *Inter Ludus*.

This cursory overview of my errant course suggests that it might also be helpful to offer a few preliminary comments about the style of the text that follows. The extraordinary analysis of writing that has been developed by deconstructive critics raises the question of the relationship between form and content in an acute way. If, after the death of God, it no longer is possible to write theology in a traditional way, it is also impossible, in the wake of deconstruction, to write books in a customary manner. No critic, of course, is ever completely free. One always remains bound in, to, and by the network one is trying to unravel. For example, the writer who attempts to raise the question of the meaning and significance of the book is still caught within the form he is criticizing. One can, of course, attempt to turn the book against itself. But such an undertaking is always parasitic. Accordingly, the continuation of successful criticism presupposes partial failure. It is possible, however, that the unavoidable failure of writing will eventually disclose the end of the book and of all that the book implies.

Writing, in deconstructive terms, is never purely original; it is *always* secondary and derivative. Like God, self, history, and book, the idea of origin or absolute beginning is a theological notion that arises from a human need that can never be totally fulfilled. Writing does not express the individual intention of an original author. To the contrary, writing stages a play of repetition in which apparent production is actual reproduction. All writing, in other words, is rewriting. For this reason, there often seems to be something improper and transgressive about writing. It is not insignificant that Hermes, son of Zeus and messenger of the gods, is both a thief and the discoverer of writing. The words of the writer are always stolen. This (inevitable) theft establishes the writer's ineradicable secondariness and deprives him of originality. In writing, "I" discover my perpetual entanglement in a net or a web, which both surpasses and encompasses me. As I write, it becomes clear that "my" text is not my own. I slowly learn that a work is never the product of a single author but is always the work of many coauthors. The text is a fabric woven and stitched from multiple texts. The names of the authors are not always evident in the lines of the work and the thread of the argument. Usually their voices sound anonymously through seemingly empty white spaces of the text.

In the following pages, I attempt to embody such an understanding of the text. In the course of rereading the word by writing about writing, form becomes content, and content form. As I have indicated, this rereading and rewriting always take place within the web I am trying to unravel. This situation creates a double bind, which repeatedly forces me to turn to tropes. Irony, humor, metaphor, paradox, pun, and parable are not mere rhetorical embellishments but are necessary to the act of writing. Furthermore, many authors appear namelessly in the text. Some of these names I know, others I do not recognize. Some are noted, others go unnamed. This style (if that is what it is) inevitably creates confusion and surely involves loss. With proper names absent or erased, proper meaning is elided. When dispossession, impropriety, and expropriation replace possession, propriety, and property, univocality, stability, and certainty give way to duplicity, shiftiness, and undecidability. For many people, these developments provoke considerable anxiety and are, therefore, passionately attacked and vigorously resisted. For the a/theologian, however, the resulting bewilderment creates seminal openings—openings that make it possible to reexamine and reformulate established assumptions and presuppositions.

*Erring* extends to the reader an invitation to participate in a "thought experiment." By rereading notions that have long formed the very basis of the Western theological network from perspectives advanced by deconstructive criticism, I shall attempt to uncover new resources for the postmodern religious imagination. Insofar as others join with me in my undertaking, they will, I believe, gradually come to recognize themselves as both readers and writers. When this happens, the lines of the text not only stretch back to formative precursors but also extend beyond the pages of the book to entangle the readers-writers to whom it is addressed. (A) Work is ever unfinished, even though it is always being refinished in unending textual activity.

"We must begin *wherever we are* . . . *Wherever we are*: in a text where we believe ourselves to be." Wherever we are: Death of God, Disappearance of Self, End of History, Closure of the Book. *Our* problem is how to count all of this not only as loss but as gain.

\*         \*         \*         \*

A Prelude is usually considered an *hors d'oeuvre*—mere *Prae Ludus* or fore-play, which whets the appetite by at once promising and denying consum-mation. It attempts to sketch a circle that joins beginning and end in a self-contained semantic totality. This totality, however, must (impossibly) point beyond itself, for the Prelude always remains secondary to and in the service of the words whose way it prepares. Preludes, along with prefaces, forewords, introductions, preambles, prologues, and prolegomena, "have always been written, it seems, in view of their own self-effacement. Upon reaching the end of the *pre-* (which presents and precedes, or rather fore-stalls, the presentative production, and, in order to put before the reader's eyes what is not yet visible, is obliged to speak, predict and predicate), the route which has been covered must cancel itself out." [13] The Prelude, in other words, is really a para-site. "Properly" speaking, it is neither inside nor outside the work. Always bordering (on) (a) text, the Prelude is per-petually liminal.

If played freely, the ceaseless oscillation and uncanny duplicity of the Prelude eventually invade the book itself. Within the ambiguous space of liminality, hierarchies crumble and boundaries dissolve. As a contagious parasite, the Prelude infects interiority with exteriority and exteriority with interiority. The unending play of inside and outside inscribes a margin that "displaces the opposition of the pre-text and text. It complicates the boun-dary line that ought to run between the text and what seems to lie beyond its fringes, what is classed as the real." [14] By pointing to the inversion, perversion, and subversion of opposites, the boundary delimits the liminal space of writing. Writing is ever errant. Wandering between an Origin that never was and an End that never is, writing has always already begun and never finally ends. The writer, therefore, remains liminal—a trickster, a joker, a clown—perhaps mad, probably a fool, who, in his "sounddance," is usually "unbewised again."

The Prelude "begins" by attempting to frame the work and "ends" by dislocating the frame itself. Like a postmodern painting, the Prelude ren-ders the frame invisible by placing it behind the back of both viewer/reader and artist/author. In this way, author and reader are drawn into the play of (the) work. When boundary becomes boundless, the *hors d'oeuvre* is no longer *hors d'oeuvre* and the *Praeludus* is no longer foreplay. On the thresh-old, we discover that we are "middle men" who are forever marginal. Though we have no fixed or certain pre-scription to offer, we are inscribed within a script in which our "foreplay" is the play itself. But with this we have, as always, already begun.

# 1

## Death of God

DANS

FLETS　　CE

RE　　MI

LES　　ROIR

SONT　　JE

ME　　SUIS

COM　　EN

NON　　Guillaume Apollinaire　　CLOS

ET　　VI

GES　　VANT

AN　　ET

LES　　VRAI

NE　　COM

GI　　ME

MA　　ON

I

### Mirror Play: Psychology of Mastery

" 'Whither is God?' he cried: 'I will tell you. *We have killed him*—you and I. All of us are his murderers. But how did we do this? How could we drink up the sea? Who gave us the sponge to wipe away the entire horizon? What were we doing when we unchained this earth from its sun? Whither is it moving now? Whither are we moving? Away from all suns? Is there still any up or down? Are we not wandering [*Irren wir nicht*] as through an infinite nothing? Do we not feel the breath of empty space? Has it not become colder? Is not night continually closing in on us? Do we hear nothing as yet of the noise of the gravediggers who are burying God? Do we smell nothing as yet of the divine decomposition? Gods, too, decompose. God is dead, God remains dead. And we have killed him." [1] The death of God is not tragedy passively suffered by hapless and helpless servants but an event enacted and embraced by rebellious and self-confident human beings. But when? How? Why?

With the death of God, a dark shadow falls over the light that for centuries illuminated the landscape of the West. Released from any fixed center, everything is left to wander through seemingly infinite space, erring "backward, sideward, forward—in all directions." Paradoxically, this eclipse begins during the period known as the "Enlightenment" and marks the dawn of what usually is labeled "the modern era." Modernism, I have suggested, involves the effort to overturn the hierarchical structures of domination upon which Western thought and society traditionally have rested. As such, it represents a contest both for and against mastery. Within the sphere of religion, the result of this struggle can be seen in the death of God. This critical event in Western history carries implications for the entire theological network, implications that only now are being realized. To fathom its meaning and significance, it is necessary to recognize that, since the Enlightenment, the death of God has been decisively articulated in at least two contrasting ways. While the modern form of the death of God comes to expression in humanistic atheism, the postmodern form points toward a posthumanistic a/theology. By denying God in the name of man, humanistic atheism inverts the Creator/creature relationship and transforms theology into anthropology. Posthumanistic a/theology, by contrast, maintains that this inversion, though it is necessary, does not go far enough. The humanistic atheist fails to realize that the death of God is at the same time the death of the self. Despite this important difference, these two points of view are inextricably bound together. Carried to completion, humanistic atheism negates itself and leads to posthumanistic a/theology. We can begin to trace the unraveling of the intricate web of Western theology by exploring the formation and dissolution of humanistic atheism.

While humanistic atheism constitutes a significant philosophical and religious departure, it remains closely related to critical developments in theology, science, and philosophy. In some ways, recent humanism reflects and elaborates important elements of Renaissance humanism. Although modern statements of humanism no longer are completely preoccupied with classical culture, they do continue to focus on noteworthy expressions of "the human spirit" such as history, language, literature, and art. The goal of the modern as well as the Renaissance humanist continues to be moral progress toward some form of human perfection.

Less evident, but no less important, is the close tie between modern humanistic atheism and its apparent opposite, Reformation theology. Profoundly distressed by the abstraction and universality of medieval theology and deeply impressed by the concreteness and particularity of nominalist philosophy and theology, Luther started a religious and social revolution by directing his theological attention to the individual believer. Plagued by dread, doubt, and despair, Luther constantly sought the certainty afforded by a *personal* relationship with God, mediated by Christ. He believed that faith in the free grace of God could provide the security for which believers long. The conclusion of this quest for salvation is summarized succinctly in the theological doctrine implied by the phrase *pro nobis*. The significance of Christ, Luther argued, lies in the "fact" that he lived and died *"for us."* Luther himself never lost sight of the overriding ascendancy of divine purpose. Moreover, he always insisted that a person never really possesses faith. Belief and doubt continually contend with each other for the mind and heart of the individual. For many people who were less dialectical than Luther, however, the notion that Christ is always *pro nobis* signaled a significant shift toward the centrality of the self. From this point of view, the emphasis on individual salvation suggested that *human* concerns lie at the center of divine, and therefore of cosmic, purpose. As will become increasingly apparent, this anthropological preoccupation grew considerably in the years following the Reformation.

While early modern science was directed to very different ends, it shared many of Luther's concerns. Equally suspicious of metaphysical speculation and theological abstraction, early scientists joined in the effort to explore concrete experience. In its initial phase, modern science was also strongly influenced by late medieval nominalism. The empiricism and experimentalism that were necessary for the emergence of modern science were, in fact, direct outgrowths of the nominalist emphasis on the significance of the individual and the nominalist insistence on the essential role of sense experience in the knowing process. As important as this individualism and empiricism, however, was what seemed to some thinkers to be a scientific analogue to Luther's doctrine of *pro nobis*. Early scientific investigators argued that all of nature is potentially "for us." In order to realize this potential, the searching scientist had to put nature "to the rack and compel her [*sic*] to answer our questions."[2] From this point of view, the world is intended to respond to human probing and to serve *man's* purposes.

Early modern philosophy expanded these theological and scientific developments. The modern period in philosophy is generally acknowledged to have begun with Descartes's decisive turn to the subject. This Cartesian revolution initiated an era of extraordinary intellectual, cultural, and social upheaval, which culminated in the French Revolution and the Reign of Terror. During the period extending from Descartes to Robespierre, the foundations of Western thought, culture, and society began to fissure. Though ostensibly a revolt against irrational belief and repression, the Enlightenment actually rested on faith and became repressive. Belief in man supplanted belief in God as oppressed servants battled harsh mas-

ters for intellectual and political freedom. Throughout this period, freedom was identified with autonomy. The explicit goal of the fight for
mastery and against domination was independent selfhood. Through free
self-legislation, humanity, it was believed, could achieve the goals of Li-
berté, Egalité, Fraternité. In the course of this revolutionary struggle,
religion and politics became patricidal. Sons struggled against primal,
personal, and political fathers. As the result of an unforeseen reversal,
however, "absolute freedom" turned into "absolute terror."

Social rebellion reflects and is reflected by intellectual revolution. Descartes, like his theological precursor, Luther, suffered nearly pathological
doubt. Descartes's entire philosophical enterprise can be understood as an
effort to overcome the insecurity brought by uncertainty and to reach the
security promised by certainty. Suspecting that the hand that inflicts the
wound holds the cure, Descartes radicalized doubt. He doubted everything
until he discovered that which is unconditionally indubitable—the *cogito*.
Then, in a move destined to change the face of the earth, Descartes identified truth with certainty. Truth, in other words, is *pro nobis*. This modern
form of truth "expresses the fact that truth concerns consciousness as a
knowledge, a representation which is grounded in consciousness in such a
way that only knowledge is valid as knowledge which at the same time
knows itself and what it knows as such, and is certain of itself in this
knowledge. Certainty here is not to be taken only as an addition to knowledge in the sense that it accomplishes the appropriation and the possession
of knowledge. Rather, certainty is the authoritative mode of knowledge
that is 'truth,' as the consciousness of itself, of what is known. The mere
having of something in consciousness is, in contrast, either no longer
knowledge or not yet knowledge."[3]

The identification of truth and certainty is, in effect, a *reductio ad hominem*. When fully developed, the Cartesian philosophy of the *cogito* leads to
the "theory of the subject," which "lies at the heart of humanism"[4] and
forms the basis of humanistic atheism. Within the framework outlined by
Descartes, "The ego has put everything in doubt, and has defined all
outside itself as the object of its thinking power. *Cogito ergo sum*: the
absolute certainty about the self reached by Descartes' hyperbolic doubt
leads to the assumption that things exist, for me at least, only because I
think them. When everything exists only as reflected in the ego, then man
has drunk up the sea. If man is defined as subject, everything else turns into
object. This includes God, who now becomes merely the highest object of
man's knowledge. God, once the creative sun, the power establishing the
horizon where heaven and earth come together, becomes an object of
thought like any other. When man drinks up the sea, he also drinks up
God, the creator of the sea. In this way man is the murderer of God."[5] This
murder marks a critical event in the development of self-consciousness. To

"enlightened" eyes, the shadows of superstition can be dispelled only by the death of God.

Though assuming multiple guises, the God the enlightened seek to slay is essentially the transcendent Christian Creator God. "Master of the exclusions and restrictions that derive from the disjunctive syllogism,"[6] this God rules (and is ruled) by the nondialectical "logic of simple negation, which is the logic of repression."[7] Omnipotent, omniscient, and omnipresent, God is the *causa sui*, the Unmoved Mover who is both the origin of all motion and the source of all rest. "The God who alone is God" is "an identity which is only itself."[8] Such a transcendent deity appears to be completely self-enclosed, totally self-identical, and absolutely self-present. This powerful sovereign forms "the primary embodiment of a solitary and isolated self-hood."[9] The ultimate subjectivity of God does not, however, establish a continuum between divinity and humanity. As the full realization and original ground of selfhood, God is wholly other, is absolute alterity.

From the perspective of individuals who are struggling to establish their autonomy, the wholly other is manifest as the shadow of death—eternal death. "God is thus the proper name of that which deprives us of our nature, of our own birth; consequently he will always have spoken before us, on the sly. He is the difference which insinuates itself between myself and myself as death."[10] "The death of God," therefore, signifies not only the death that God suffers but also the death that is God's or that God is. *God is death, and death is absolute master.*

Since God is experienced as death rather than life, the death of God enacted in humanistic atheism actually represents an effort to deny death. God and self, master and slave, engage in a life-and-death struggle that is inspired by the "absolute fear" that grows out of "the first encounter of the other as *other*."[11] This meeting establishes a "specular relation" in which the "eyes" of the other initially appear to dispossess the "I" of the self. The penetrating gaze of the other seems improper, for it disrupts self-identity. In the mirror play of self and other, the self sees itself reflected in the *other*. This duplication brings self-alienation. The confrontation with the other as other leads to the encounter with the *self* as other. Facing the all-powerful master, the self realizes that "it has lost itself, for it finds itself as an *other* being."[12] The slave remains "outside of himself (insofar as the other has not 'given him back' to himself by recognizing him, by revealing that he has recognized him, and by showing him that he [the other] depends on him and is not absolutely other than he)."[13] By forcing the self outside of itself, the disruptive stranger discloses the subject's estrangement.

In an effort to overcome alienation and gain self-possession, slave rebels against master and son turns against father. The subversive activity of the subject has as its goal mastery of the master. By overthrowing the lord, the subject hopes to establish identity, maintain integrity, and protect pro-

*how do we experience God?*

priety (as well as property). This struggle for mastery joins affirmation and negation. The self asserts itself by negating the other, which it regards in thoroughly negative terms. Consequently, the rebellious subject embodies a form of negation in which identity secures itself by *excluding* difference. Instead of subverting the "logic" of mastery, this negative activity merely turns it to its own ends. The self remains caught in the logic of simple negation and bound to the noncontradictory logic of identity, which establishes the noncontradictory identity of logic. Within this "structure of exclusion," every "entity is what it is, the outside is out and the inside in." [14] The servile subject tries to master the terror that absolute alterity provokes by negating the wholly other and enclosing the self within the secure "solitude of solidity and self-identity." [15]

It should be clear that the slave's offensive assertion is undeniably defensive. Aggressive action is actually a reaction that grows out of impotence. "The slave revolt" is not "a triumphant affirmation" but a reaction that "from the outset says No to what is 'outside,' what is 'different,' what is 'not itself'; and *this* No is its creative deed." [16] The "reaction formation" that constitutes the subject's rebellion against the omnipotent sovereign reveals the deepgoing *ressentiment* that incites and sustains the agon of the slave. An uncommonly ambiguous sentiment, *ressentiment*, combines affirmation and negation, acceptance and denial, and attraction and repulsion. *Ressentiment* is never simply hostile. It carries within itself latent admiration of, and attraction for, the other against whom one, nonetheless, reacts negatively. *Ressentiment* always harbors *envy*. Never responding to the other in a merely negative way, the envious person yearns to possess what belongs to the other. The source of the slave's discontent is not only the condition of bondage. Though distressed by subservience, the subject resents not being master and envies the master's mastery. The lord's exercise of power simultaneously manifests his own strength and discloses the weakness or impotence that seems to define the slave. In this way the other introduces a lack, and this opens a gap or creates a void in the subject. The reaction of servant to master is not only intended to upset the sovereign's rule; it also seeks to usurp his power. With newly acquired power, the bondsman hopes to be able to overcome the lack, close the gap, and fill the void, which disrupts identity and unsettles the sense of self. However, the struggle in which the subject attempts to assert itself by negating other and tries to secure identity by excluding difference inverts itself and becomes an act of identification with and incorporation of the other. This reversal uncovers yet another face in the play of mirrors.

Whereas the slave provisionally suffers dispossession when he sees himself reflected in the eyes of the other, he gradually comes to realize that this self-duplication is itself duplicitous. By recognizing self in *other*, the self also discovers *self* in other. The subject "does not see the other as essential being, but in the other sees its own self." [17] Contrary to expectation, the specular relation culminates in *"Pure* self-recognition in absolute otherness."[18] No longer seeing the master merely as his own opposite, the slave recognizes the master as the independent and integral self that he (i.e., the slave) seeks to be. In trying to unseat the master, the subject attempts to become master. If *the* master is God and the slave man, then man's murder of God is an act of self-deification. It seems that the son always follows in the footsteps of Oedipus by attempting to take the place of the father. Though usually not recognized, "The essence of the Oedipal complex is the project of becoming God . . . , *causa sui."*[19]

This reversal of divinity and humanity is the distinctive mark of humanistic atheism. Instead of simply denying the reality of God, the humanistic atheist transfers the attributes of the divine subject to the human self. From this point of view, religious faith represents an inverted awareness. In the object of worship, the believer "becomes acquainted with himself; consciousness of the objective is the self-consciousness of man. We know the man by the object, by his conception of what is external to himself; in it his nature becomes evident; this object is his manifest nature, his true objective *ego."*[20] Since the consciousness of God is really human self-consciousness, all theology is actually anthropology. In order to get back on his feet, the believer need only invert this inversion. The humanistic atheist insists that "when it is shown that what the subject is lies entirely in the attributes of the subject; that is, that the predicate is the true subject, it is also proved that if the divine predicates are attributes of human nature, the subject of those predicates is also human nature."[21] This reversal reveals the slave's struggle *against* the master to be a struggle *for* mastery. By transferring the predicates of divinity to the human subject, the humanistic atheist inverts, but fails to subvert, the logic of repression. With this inversion, the problem of mastery and slavery is relocated rather than resolved. The death of the sovereign God now appears to be the birth of the sovereign self.

## Utility and Consumption: Economy of Domination

The psychology of mastery realizes itself in an economy of domination, which grows out of the interplay of utility and consumption. The inversion of divinity and humanity that results from humanistic atheism issues in a ceaseless quest for total control and sovereign domination. Faced with the absolute fear brought by the encounter with the wholly other, "man precisely as the one so threatened, exalts himself to the posture of lord of the earth. In this way the impression comes to prevail that everything man encounters exists only insofar as it is his construct . . . . It seems as though man everywhere and always encounters only himself."[22] The translation of the encounter with other into a meeting with self has significant implications, which do not become apparent until the emergence of modern technological society. "The industrialization and urbanization of man mean the progressive transformation of the world. Everything is changed from its natural state into something useful or meaningful to man. Everywhere the world mirrors back to man his own image, and nowhere can he make vivifying contact with what is not human. Even the fog is not a natural fog, rolling in from the sea, but is half soot and smoke. The city is the literal representation of the progressive humanization of the world. And where is there room for God in the city? Though it is impossible to tell whether man has excluded God by building the great cities, or whether the great cities have been built because God has disappeared, in any case the two go together. Life in the city is the way in which many men have experienced most directly what it means to live without God in the world."[23]

These remarks imply a close relationship between humanism and utilitarianism. Not radical enough to reject completely the notions of center and centeredness, the humanistic atheist removes one center, God, in the name of another, humanity. We have already noted that, by extending the Reformation notion of *pro nobis* and the early scientific interpretation of knowledge as power, Descartes is able to identify truth and certainty. This revolutionary identification carries with it the possibility of "man's determining the essence of certainty by himself in accordance with the essence of certainty in general (self-assurance), and thus of bringing humanity to dominance within what is real."[24] The humanist pushes to its conclusion the Cartesian *reductio ad hominem* by attempting to humanize the entire world. Freed from the Creator God, the creative subject engages in "calculative thinking," which views "the world as our own, our private property, designed according to our needs and readily domesticated."[25]

The enlightened lord of the earth who attempts to humanize the world is continually guided by the principle of utility. Utility can be defined as "the truth which is equally the certainty of itself." For the utilitarian, the object is neither independent nor possesses being-in-itself. Quite the opposite, the object is only to the extent that it is *for* the subject. No longer subservient to absolute alterity, the subject is free to see *self* in other. In the notion of utility, this "insight achieves its realization and has itself for its *object*, an object which it now no longer repudiates and which, too, no longer has for it the value of the void or the pure beyond." "The useful," in other words, "is the object insofar as self-consciousness penetrates it and has in it the *certainty* of its *individual self*, its enjoyment (its *being-for-self*); self-consciousness sees right into the object, and this insight contains the *true* essence of the object (which is to be something that is penetrated [by consciousness], or to be *for an other*)."[26] This understanding of utility discloses its close relationship to consumption. Taken together, utility and consumption form an economy of domination.

In order to come to terms with this economy, it is important not to confuse need and desire. In general, need and desire can be described as "the presence of an *absence*." Since neither exists "in a positive manner in the . . . spatial Present," both represent a lack that is "like a gap or a 'hole' in Space: an emptiness, a nothingness."[27] Curiously, this absence, gap, hole, emptiness, or nothingness can assume various shapes. Need and desire designate two different forms of lack. Recalling the well-established distinction between fear and anxiety, it can be argued that as fear is to anxiety, so need is to desire. Need has a degree of specificity that desire does not share. While need is always related to a particular object, desire remains perpetually indeterminate and "free-floating." Unlike desire, need is not a primordial lack but is experienced as a "negated presence." Insofar as need appears to be deficiency, it represents "an *emptiness* greedy for content, an emptiness that wants to be filled by what is full, to be filled by *emptying* this fullness, to put itself—once it is filled—in the place of this fullness, to occupy with *its* fullness the emptiness caused by overcoming the fullness that was *not* its own."[28] The needy subject longs for plenitude. The quest for satisfaction is the search for the useful object that "contents, fills, grants euphoria."[29] The experience of satisfaction arises when the negated presence that generates need is itself negated through the presentation of the absent object. The effort to fulfill need embodies the logic of simple negation that characterizes the struggle for mastery. Satisfaction involves the assimilation of otherness that occurs when difference dissolves in identity. For this reason, need inevitably leads to consumption.

Having emerged victorious from the play of mirrors involved in the struggle for mastery, "the mirroring ego" proceeds to swallow up the whole world, until "everything exists inside the looking glass."[30] When one follows the "acquisitive" logic of need rather than the "productive"[31] logic of desire, "the core of the economic problem becomes not production but consumption."[32] To consume is "to take up completely, make away with, devour, lay hold of, burn, or reduce to ashes." The consumer seeks to possess, appropriate, and incorporate otherness wherever it is encountered. Given free reign, "the circuit of reproductive consumption"[33] tends to extend itself until "the world no longer offers any resistance to man's limitless hunger for conquest."[34]

The sovereign subject who seeks total mastery joins utility and consumption to form utilitarian consumerism. The result of this union is an economy of domination based on the principle of ownership. Ownership, in turn, presupposes both propriety and property. The accumulation of property is intended to secure the identity and insure the propriety of the hoarding self. When needy subjects seek satisfaction by consuming useful objects, the struggle for mastery expands into the economic domain. Like insurgent servants who take over the palace and equally divide the king's property, rebellious sons universalize the principle of ownership by offering the dismembered body of the father for general consumption.

It would be a mistake, however, to restrict the economy of domination to the "money complex." The principle of ownership pervades all realms of life. In the "public" sector the economy of domination takes the form of political colonialism or totalitarianism; in the "private" sphere it issues in "phallocentric sexuality." The modern struggle for autonomy is a search for self-possession that leads to a "totalitarianism"[35] or "imperialism of the same."[36] Domination equalizes the unequal by erasing the difference of the other. "Blinded to the point of madness by the sight of whatsoever will elude its rule,"[37] sovereign power is driven to domesticate the strange and colonize the alien. Like the imperial lord, colonial power constantly thrusts outward and always expands. In an economy of domination, needs are satisfied by continually extending economic manipulation to new markets and political control to new territories. Eventually the entire public domain reflects "the organization of a lack."[38] With this development, it becomes clear that mastery, utility, consumption, ownership, propriety, property, colonialism, and totalitarianism form a seamless, though seamy, web. In the shadow of the death of God, humanism tends to become inhuman.

The link between the political and sexual economy of domination is patriarchy. "The cement which binds the wider collection together is the same which binds the family: 'kinship.' The patriarchal family supplies the primal model for political government: the first form of government is kingship, 'because families are always monarchically governed'; the essence of government is domination, 'rule'—in the family the domination of male over female, parent over child, master over slave."[39] The death of the Father God does not, of course, end the regime of patriarchy. The humanistic inversion of divinity and humanity leads to a worldly representative of the omnipotent Father. Utilitarian consumerism expresses a psychology of possession, which, historically, has tended to be masculine. Insofar as the sexual economy is also organized by a lack, it is phallocentric. When the subject is driven by the need to close gaps and fill holes, the phallus becomes the focus of the sexual relation. From the phallocentric perspective, "The obscenity of the feminine sex is that of everything which 'gapes open.' It is an *appeal to being*, as all holes are. In herself, woman appeals to a strange flesh which is to transform her into a fullness of being by penetration and dissolution."[40] In the economy of domination, consumption is consummated in war and rape, two acts that are finally inseparable. Wars of conquest, however, invariably founder. Despite its offensive character, the phallus (or its substitute, the sword) remains the "signifier of a lack." The effort to fill the hole without discloses a hole within. This gap eventually becomes gaping.

We have seen that the economy of domination, which is a product of the interrelation of utility and consumption, has satisfaction as its goal. Satisfaction emerges when previously servile subjects achieve sovereignty by discovering self in other. If the other fails to mirror the self, its territory must be invaded and colonized. In this way, the quest for satisfaction brings a "revolutionary transformation of the world."[41] The aim of this radical change is the creation of a domestic economy. No longer disturbed by unsettling otherness or upset by troubling strangers, sovereign subjects feel thoroughly satisfied with themselves and at home in the world.

There is, nonetheless, something uncanny (cf. *unheimlich*) about such domesticity. The economy of domination carries within it the seeds of its own negation. Eventually consumption becomes all-consuming. The satisfaction of need appears to overcome emptiness and fill lack by rendering the self totally present to itself. But complete satisfaction is indistinguishable from death. In other words, "the establishment of a pure presence, without loss, is one with the occurrence of absolute loss, with death."[42] Inasmuch as total satisfaction brings death, the end of utility and consumption appears to be nihilism.

### Narcissism and Nihilism

The psychology of mastery and the economy of domination are different masks of Narcissus. For Narcissus, the entire world becomes a mirror in which he sees his own face reflected. Unable to enjoy without possession, the narcissist insists that "human perfection consists in an expansion of the self until it enjoys the world as it enjoys itself."[43] The effort to possess the other represents an indirect attempt to possess one's own self. As the foregoing argument implies, one who struggles for self-possession relates to otherness in two seemingly contradictory ways. On the one hand, the subject is attracted to the other and thus seeks identification and/or incorporation. On the other hand, the agent is repulsed by the other and hence attempts to negate or exclude difference. Within these two rhythms lurk the contrasting forces whose paradoxical union gives birth to Narcissus: *Eros* and *Thanatos*.

Aggression is the death instinct turned outward. Through this extroversion, the death drive inverts itself and becomes the denial of death. The aggressive subject attempts to preserve its integrity by negating the other, whose presence portends dispossession. Self-assertion, which aims at securing self-identity, is mediated by the domination or even the destruction of the other. Violence, however, is inextricably related to eros. Thanatos no more can be separated from eros than eros can be torn from thanatos. Successful aggression not only masters but actually consumes the other. While initially intended to be an act of exclusion, aggression entails both identification and incorporation. "The individual *appropriates* the object in such a manner as to deprive it of its peculiar nature, convert it into a means for itself, and give its own subjectivity for its substance. This assimilation accordingly coincides with the individual's reproduction."[44] From this perspective, the consummation of aggressive action is manifestly erotic. Eros seeks to overcome otherness by establishing the identity of subjectivity and objectivity. In love, self and other appear to be one rather than two. This union translates affection into "auto-affection" and overt love into covert self-love. Love, as well as aggression, is narcissistic.

Inseparably bound to the psychology of mastery and the economy of domination, humanistic atheism is irrevocably narcissistic. The foregoing analysis leads to the suspicion that the hidden goal of Narcissus is the denial of death. I have argued that for revolutionary subjects, who seek autonomy and self-possession, God is the absolute master who is the figure of death. If God is death, then the murder of God seems to be the denial of, or flight from, death. The sovereign subject regards the death of God as the death of death—a death that is necessary for its own birth. The primal scene depicts the resentful reaction of the son against the omnipotent founding father, who, as Alpha and Omega, is *causa sui*. This hostile rebellion gives rise to the son's/sons' own *causa sui* project. Since the narcissist is too weak to accept dependence, acknowledge loss, and affirm death, he is driven to pursue the elusive goal of self-determination. By negating the transcendent *causa sui*, the narcissistic subject hopes to become *causa sui*. This aim of self-possession can be fully realized only if the self becomes the father of itself. If, however, the son is to become father, the father *must* die. Just as the son identifies with and tries to take the place of the father through deeds of aggression, so the humanistic atheist identifies with and tries to take the place of God through the act of deicide. Self-deification is, of course, the extreme expression of narcissism. This narcissism is finally nihilistic.

Carried to its conclusion, the pursuit of self-possession actually dispossesses the searching subject. When consumption becomes all-consuming, self-affirmation is transformed into self-negation. Through an unanticipated twist, the riotous subject discovers that, in turning everything upside down, it also turns everything outside in. The struggle for mastery in which the self seeks to preserve itself by denying death proves to be the circuitous path by which the subject pursues its own death.[45] The twofold course of this pursuit conforms to the dual rhythm that governs the life of Narcissus.

As we have seen, the self that labors to establish its identity tries to surmount the threat that the other poses to its autonomy by dissolving alterity and assimilating difference. The act of aggression is simultaneously hostile and erotic. In order to secure its propriety, the Napoleonic self attempts to expropriate the other by appropriating its propert(y)ies. In the course of battle, however, the imperious subject unintentionally conquers itself. Apparent success is really failure. The appropriation of the other expropriates the self. Instead of achieving self-possession by possessing the other, the subject becomes possessed by the other. This reversal reveals that the other is not really without but is actually within the struggling subject.

This outside that is inside is experienced in two different ways: as a repressive master and as a seductive demon.

The realization of autonomy does not overcome the psychology of mastery. To the contrary, the progression from heteronomy (*hetero*, other + *nomos*, law) to autonomy (*auto*, self + *nomos*, law) marks a movement from a situation in which the subject is given the law by an other to a condition in which one gives oneself the law. The struggle against the sovereign other results in the *internalization* of the other and the *inwardization* of mastery. Autonomy is, in effect, *self-mastery*. The difference between the heteronomous subject and the autonomous subject is that the former has his "lord outside of himself, while the latter carries his lord in himself, yet at the same time is his own slave."[46] In other words, the slain father invariably returns to haunt the murderous son. The "emotional ambivalence" that is typical of the father-son relationship manifests itself in a complex interplay of attraction and repulsion, eros and thanatos, love and hate. This conflict finally leads to the son's consumption of the father. The communion of rebellious sons takes the form of a symbolic totem meal in which the dead father is incorporated. In contrast to mere expropriation of paternal properties, the assimilation of the father to the son(s) also involves the dispossession of the son(s). The "dead" father proves to be as strong as or even more powerful than the living patriarch had been. The struggle for mastery therefore leads to self-mastery, in which the aggression that had been directed toward the other turns inward. In different terms, through the internalization of aggression, the superego forms and gradually comes to dominate the ego. Since aggression represents the extroversion of the death instinct, the introversion of aggression is the transformation of the denial of death into the affirmation of death. From this perspective, self-affirmation is at the same time self-negation.

The repression exercised by the superego reveals a second way in which otherness is "present" within the subject. The interiority of exteriority is not only experienced as the omnipresence of a harsh taskmaster. The wholly other against which the subject rebels is neither fully known nor completely knowable. Consequently, the internalization of absolute alterity disrupts the self-conscious subject by "revealing" the presence/absence of an unconsciousness that can never fully enter consciousness. The unconscious can be interpreted as "the discourse of the Other"[47] that brings man face to face with his own radical 'extraneousness to himself.'"[48] Since this outside is *always inside*, the self is, in some sense, *forever outside* itself. The gap, hole, emptiness, or nothingness "within" is not merely a need that can be filled by the possession of a useful object. The discourse of the other signifies insatiable desire. Such desire desires not satisfaction but desire itself.

The repressive master and seductive demon join forces to split the subject. Suffering the victimization it had sought to inflict, the subject becomes "un corps morcelé" rather than an integral self. The disruption and distension imposed by the inner other render self-possession impossible and reveal the unattainability of total satisfaction. The divided subject is left to err between the extremes it both joins and separates. As will become clear in the next chapter, the splitting of the subject leads to the disappearance of the self. Narcissus, after all, eventually loses himself in his mirror.

It has become apparent that the pursuit of self-possession not only takes the form of the incorporation of otherness within the self, but also finds expression in the self's effort to exclude difference from identity. In order to secure its integrity, the sovereign subject is convinced that it must protect itself from the invasion, violation, and pollution of the other. Offensive gestures are defensive strategies through which the self asserts itself by negating the other. But this action (or reaction) is self-contradictory. In negating the other, the self finally negates itself. "Narcissus needs a pool, a mirror, in which to see himself." [49] Without the other, the self not only cannot *see* itself; it cannot *be* itself. Thus "by making the other disappear, I also make myself disappear." [50] What the narcissistic subject "beholds is that whatever assumes the form of essentiality over against it is instead dissolved in it—in its thinking, its existence, and its action—and is at its mercy." This dissolution represents the return of everything "into the certainty of [the self,] which, in consequence, is [the] complete loss of fear and of essential being on the part of all that is alien." [51]

Such self-certainty is, of course, the goal of enlightened modernism. As we have noted, the Cartesian revolution points toward *the* modern revolution, which is enacted in the name of liberty, equality, and fraternity. Though undertaken for the sake of freedom, the rebellion of the sons culminates in the Reign of Terror. Absolute self-certainty turns out to be "absolute terror." "The sole work" of this "*fury* of destruction" is "*death*, a death which has no inner significance or filling, for what is negated is the empty point of the absolutely free self. It is thus the coldest and meanest of all deaths, with no more significance than cutting off a head of cabbage or swallowing a mouthful of water." [52] The effort to master "absolute fear" leads to "absolute terror." In fleeing death, the self unknowingly rushes into its arms. The psychology of mastery and the economy of domination issue in a radical form of consumption that reduces everything to ashes by igniting flames that spread to become a (the) holocaust (ὄλος, whole + καυστός, burnt).

The nihilistic implications of modernism are already evident in humanistic atheism. Nihilism can be defined as "the nothingness of consciousness when consciousness becomes the foundation of everything. Man the murderer of God and drinker of the sea of creation wanders through the infinite nothingness of his own ego." [53] As a result of the death of God, "*the highest values devalue themselves.*" [54] This axiological shift faults the foundation of Western thought and society. In its initial stage, the devaluation of the highest values really amounts to the reversal of high and low. We have seen that the humanistic atheist simply inverts the traditional values against which he reacts. By laboring to convert "lovers of God" to "the love of man," the humanist hopes to transform *"otherworldly truth"* into *"the truth of this world."*[55] This inversion of heaven and earth effectively shifts value from the divine to the human subject. Far from suffering the disorientation brought by the loss of center, modern humanism is self-confidently anthropocentric. While denying God, the humanist clings to the sovereignty of the self. The humanistic critique of values never reaches the extreme point of questioning the function of truth and the value of value. As a result of this shortcoming, the nihilism of modern humanistic atheism is incomplete and thus inadequate.

Nihilism remains partial until it is realized that the *reductio ad hominem*[56] is actually a *reductio hominis.* "The night brought on by the death of God is a night in which every individual identity perishes. When the heavens are darkened, and God disappears, man does not stand autonomous and alone. He ceases to stand. Or, rather, he ceases to stand *out* from the world and himself, ceases to be autonomous and apart. No longer can selfhood and self-consciousness stand purely and solely upon itself: no longer can a unique and individual identity stand autonomously upon itself. The death of the transcendence of God embodies the death of all autonomous selfhood, an end of all humanity which is created in the image of the absolutely sovereign and transcendent God."[57] For the devout humanist, such loss of self is but another form of dehumanization to be vigorously resisted. The humanist, therefore, refuses to repeat the confession of the writer:

> The meandering word dies by the pen, the writer by the same weapon turned back against him.
> "What murder are you accused of?" Reb Achor asked Zillieh, the writer.
> "The murder of God," he replied. "I will, however, add in my defense that I die along with him."[58]

Nihilism can be a sign of weakness or a mark of strength. Unable to accept loss and anxious about death, the partial nihilism of the modern humanistic atheist is a sign of weakness. For the writer who suffers the crucifixion of selfhood, nihilism is the mark of the cross. On Golgotha, not only God dies; the self also disappears.

# 2

## Disappearance of the Self

I beseech You, God, to show my full self to myself.

In the life of the individual the task is to achieve an ennoblement of the successive within the simultaneous. To have been young, and then to grow older, and finally to die, is a very mediocre form of human existence; this merit belongs to every animal. But the unification of the different stages of life in simultaneity is the task set for human beings.

Once I produce, once I write, it is the Text itself which (fortunately) dispossesses me of my narrative continuity.

My work, my trace, the excrement that robs *me of* my possessions after I have been *stolen from* my birth, must thus be rejected. But to reject it is not, here, to refuse it but to retain it. To keep myself, to keep my body and my speech, I must retain the work within me, conjoin myself with it so that there will be no opportunity for the Thief to come between it and me: it must be kept from falling far from my body as writing. For "writing is all trash." Thus, that which dispossesses me and makes me more remote from myself, interrupting my proximity to myself, also soils me: I relinquish all that is proper to me. Proper is the name of the subject close to himself— who is what he is—and abject the name of the object, the work that has deviated from me. I have a proper name when I am proper.

### Image, Identity, Imitation

To be a self is to possess and to be possessed by a name. For every self, the primal scene is the scene of nomination—a scene of naming and being named. This nomination is a vocation, a call that is both a blessing and a curse. A name awakens identity by calling forth, setting apart, establishing difference. Only by a name can the slumberous innocence of anonymity be overcome. This "gift" is not, however, a simple given. Vocation poses a task—the task of a lifetime. Thus "the difficulty begins with the name." [1] The identity bestowed by naming opens rather than closes the drama of

34

selfhood. By marking the paradoxical coincidence of freedom and fate, the name forces each self to decide "How One Becomes What One Is."[2]

Within the Western theological tradition, the "original" scene of nomination involves God and man. The relation between God and self is thoroughly specular; each mirrors the other. In different terms, man is made in the image of God. This *imago* is an imitation, copy, likeness, representation, similitude, appearance, or shadow of divinity. The *imago dei* confers upon man an identity; this establishes a vocation that can be fulfilled only through the process of imitation. The specularity of the God-self relation forges an inseparable bond between the name of God and the name of man. "God is the name of names, the source of names."[3] It is, therefore, necessary to speak "His name to name ourselves. For the God whom we have been given has 'named' Himself in us, and named Himself in such a manner that we cannot dissociate His identity from our own."[4]

The recognition that man is believed to be the *imago dei* suggests that the self is a "theological conception."[5] It is not often realized that the notion of the self is a relatively "recent invention." "Indeed, it was not until that period in Western history when God was fully manifest as being wholly isolated and apart that man discovered himself as an absolutely unique and autonomous being."[6] The epoch of selfhood spans a period that extends roughly from Augustine's *Confessions* to Hegel's *Phenomenology of Spirit*. Although the roots of the distinctively Western interpretation of subjectivity lie in the Letters of Paul, it is Augustine who must be credited with the discovery of personal subjectivity. Augustine's relentless self-reflection leads to the creation of a new literary genre—autobiography. In the course of presenting what eventually becomes the dominant view of God in the West, the *Confessions* elaborates a genuinely new vision of personal identity. It was left for Hegel to flesh out the self-portrait initially sketched by Augustine. Hegel's completion and fulfillment of the subject, however, also represent a surpassing and sublation of Augustine's insights. If portraiture and self-portraiture were impossible *before* Augustine, they are no longer possible *after* Hegel. In the *Phenomenology of Spirit*, Hegel in effect joins the *Confessions* and the *City of God* to form an all-inclusive *Bildungsroman* that simultaneously recapitulates the emergence of individual identity on both a personal and a cultural scale and inscribes the end of self-consciousness. By so doing, the *Phenomenology* concludes the epoch of selfhood and marks the "end of man." We shall see that this closure creates a seminal opening.

Our consideration of the multiple dimensions of the death of God has already suggested some of the complexities involved in the interplay between theology and anthropology. We have noted that throughout most of the Western tradition God is believed to be the supreme Creator, who, through the mediation of his divine Logos, brings the world into being and providentially directs its course. In order to establish more completely the correlation between the images of God and self, it is necessary to examine carefully some of the most significant attributes traditionally predicated of God. More specifically, we must explore the intricate interrelationship of God's being, eternity, transcendence, unity, identity, substantiality, essence, and subjectivity.

As the supreme Creator, God is the source, ground, and cause of all that is. In the ontotheological tradition of the West, God is virtually indistinguishable from the power of Being or Being-itself. To the extent that Being is interpreted as presence, God is viewed as absolutely present and thus totally self-present. Insofar as being is associated with the present, God is regarded as always present and hence eternal. God, who is the original source, groundless ground, and uncaused cause, is both "spatially" and temporally omnipresent. In most cases the identification of God with Being and presence does not lead to belief in divine immanence. To the contrary, God is consistently regarded as radically transcendent. The Creator is other than, and separate from, the creation over which He exercises omnipotent rule. As the result of this transcendence, divinity is, in some sense, inaccessible to humanity. Though completely self-present, the Creator is never totally present to the creature or in the created order. God possesses a hidden inwardness or unapproachable interiority that never becomes outward or exterior. Revelation, therefore, is *necessarily* incomplete and forever partial. Despite divine omnipresence, the mysterious God always manages to escape one's grasp.

This transcendent God is not only the *supreme* Creator; He is also the *sole* Creator. From its earliest days, orthodox theology has rejected the polytheism that was typical of both many ancient Near Eastern religions and Roman paganism and has refused to accept the principle of divine hierarchy that characterized various forms of Gnosticism and also informed Neoplatonic speculation. For the Christian, God is one. To claim that God is one is to insist that God is centered in Himself and is the center of everything else. This self-centered center that is inwardly unified forms the founding principle of all cosmic and personal unity. God's unity is indissociable from His eternity and immutability. Since plurality is always subject to change, the immutable *cannot* be many and *must* be one. It is important to note in this connection that God's unchangeability requires His omniscience. Unable to suffer any change whatsoever, God's knowledge cannot develop and therefore must always be perfect or complete. The divine eye views everything *sub specie aeternitatis*.

The transcendent unity of God points toward the identity of the divine. Identity, which derives from the Latin *idem* (same), means "The quality or condition of being the same in substance, composition, nature, properties, or in particular qualities under consideration." Identity can also refer to: "The sameness of a person or thing at all times or in all circumstances; the condition or fact that a person or thing is itself and not something else;

individuality, personality." In sum, identity includes two closely related elements: self-sameness at a particular time and continuity through time. In the eternal life of divinity, these aspects of identity merge to form a structure of absolute self-relation. "Self-relation in essence is the form of identity or reflection-into-itself."[7] God is the absolute self-identity that resounds in "I AM THAT I AM."

It would be a mistake, however, to hear these words merely as the representation of *simple* equality-with-self. Absolute self-relation establishes a self-identity that "is in its self-sameness different from itself and self-contradictory, and that in its difference, in its contradiction, is self-identical, and is in its own self this movement of transition of one of these categories into the other. . . . In other words, identity is the reflection-into-self that is identity only as internal repulsion, and is this repulsion as reflection-into-self, repulsion which immediately takes itself back into itself. Thus it is the identity as difference that is identical with itself."[8] When God is understood as the absolutely self-identical, which in-itself is complex, He is grasped as substance. Substance (*substantia*: *sub*, under + *stare*, to stand) is traditionally associated with the Greek *ousia* or essence. The notion of substance designates what "underlies phenomena; the permanent substratum of things; that which receives modification." Though substance itself is never a mode, accidents inhere *in* and are modifications *of* substance. The asymmetry of this relationship implies that "substance is power, and power that is *reflected into itself* and not merely transitory, but that posits *determinations* and *distinguishes them from itself*. As self-relating in its determining, it is *itself* that which it posits as a negative or makes it into a *positedness*." This all-powerful substance "is the *absolute*, the actuality that is in and for itself—*in itself* as the simple identity of possibility and actuality, absolute essence containing all actuality and possibility *within itself*; and *for itself*, being this identity as absolute *power* or purely self-related *negativity*."[9]

Since substance is essential nature or "absolute essence," it must always be present. The omnipresence of substance discloses the critical link between *Wesen* (substance or essence) and *Anwesenheit* (presence; *Anwesen*, property). Essential substance or substantial essence is *always* present—present not only to itself but also in its *own* "other." Consequently, otherness is merely apparent; it is actually illusory being (*Schein*). Essence, by contrast, "is the self-subsistent, which *is* as self-mediated through its negation, which negation essence itself is; it is, therefore, the identical unity of absolute negativity and immediacy."[10]

Substance, which is essential, is at the same time subject (*subjectus*: *sub*, under + *jacere*, to throw). "The concept of a (conscious or unconscious) subject necessarily refers to the concept of substance—and thus of presence—out of which it is born."[11] Subjectivity both grows out of and takes up into itself each of the divine predicates previously considered. In the briefest terms possible, subjectivity is "*Pure* self-recognition in absolute otherness." The subject "*relates itself to itself* and is *determinate*, is *other-being* and *being-for-self*, and in this determinateness, or in its self-externality, abides within itself; in other words, it is *in and for itself*." [12] With the articulation of the structure of the subject, it becomes clear that divine subjectivity is essentially reflexive. Throughout the theological tradition, this reflexivity has been repeatedly illustrated by two primary examples: love and knowledge or, more precisely, auto-affection and self-consciousness. Absolute subjectivity comes to completion in loving and knowing itself.

It was Augustine who first recognized and defined the principle of subjectivity. Plagued by doubt and uncertainty not unlike that which Luther and Descartes would suffer centuries later, Augustine turned inward and reflected upon his own personality. The world within, however, proved to be as perplexing as the puzzling world without. Rather than a simple individual or singular substance, Augustine found the self to be complex and inwardly divided. In an effort to interpret the insights derived from his self-analysis, Augustine argues that, since man is created in the image of God, the structure of selfhood must mirror the structure of the divine. From the time of the early church councils, Christian orthodoxy had insisted that, though God is one, He is triune. Augustine's genius lay in interpreting the doctrine of the trinity in terms of subjectivity. By means of this important theological innovation, Augustine provides what seems to be a reasonable account of the relationship between God and self. Inasmuch as it is a reflection of the divine subject, human subjectivity is triune. "We both exist, and know that we exist, and rejoice in this existence and this knowledge. In these three, when the mind knows and loves itself, there may be seen a trinity, mind, love, knowledge; not to be confounded by any intermixture, although each exists in itself, and all mutually in all, or each in the other two, or the other two in each." [13]

Although Augustine's account of the specular relation between God and the self was highly influential throughout the tradition, its full implications were not realized until Hegel formulated his speculative philosophy. By drawing directly and indirectly on the insights of Augustine, Hegel developed a reinterpretation of the concept of subjectivity that proved to be nothing less than revolutionary. In order to grasp the distinctive features of Hegel's analysis, it is necessary to recognize its relation to certain theological and epistemological principles. As will become increasingly apparent, Hegel's account of reflexive subjectivity forms a significant chapter in the appearance and disappearance of the self.

According to Hegel, the notions of self-love and self-consciousness combine to form the identity of God. For the Christian, God *is* love. The speculative significance of this claim emerges with the recognition that "love implies a differentiation between two who are, however, not merely different from one another. Love is this feeling of being outside of myself, the feeling and consciousness of this identity. I have my self-consciousness not in myself, but in another in whom alone I am satisfied and am at peace with myself—and I am only insofar as I am at peace with myself, for if I do not have this, I am the contradiction that sunders itself."[14] The love relation provides a representation (*Vorstellung*) of God that points toward the more complete expression of divine subjectivity disclosed in the structure of self-consciousness. God's self-love is, of course, impossible apart from His self-knowledge. The self-consciousness of God involves an "act of distinguishing or differentiation which at the same time gives no difference and does not hold this difference as permanent. God beholds Himself in what is differentiated; and when in His other He is united only with Himself, He is there with no other but Himself, He is in close union only with Himself, He beholds *Himself* in His other."[15]

If God is best understood in terms of auto-affection and self-consciousness, divine subjectivity must be interpreted as "self-relating negativity that remains internal to itself."[16] Subjectivity, in other words, is thoroughly *reflexive*. In order to grasp the nature of reflexivity, it is necessary to distinguish cognition, reflection, and reflexion. Quite clearly, consciousness is always intentional. Consciousness invariably is consciousness *of* something and hence is always related *to* an object. Cognition, reflection, and reflexion are distinguished by contrasting interpretations of objectivity. In the movement from cognition through reflection to reflexion, subject and object become ever more closely united.

The gaze of the cognitive subject is directed outward, toward an object that appears to be other than the knowing self. The aim of cognition is knowledge of the external object. By contrast, the reflective subject turns inward. The object of reflection is, in fact, cognition. In reflection, the subject thinks about itself thinking about an object that seems to be different from itself. Reflexion deepens this inwardness by taking reflection as its object. The reflexive subject thinks about thinking about thinking. The relation of cognition, reflection, and reflexion can be summarized as follows:

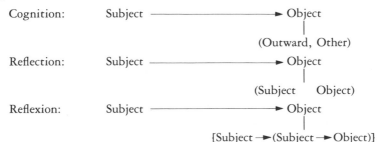

The reflexive relation is "an 'absolute' one inasmuch as the experienced phenomenon (reflection) is of the same kind as are the experiencing act (reflecting) and the origin of the experience (self-reflection)." [17] The unity of subject and object in reflexive subjectivity provides the most complete expression of the structure of absolute self-relation that is definitive of God. Thoroughly reflexive and completely self-related, the divine subject is fully self-sufficient, totally self-present, and absolutely self-conscious.

Created in the image of God, the human subject reflects divine subjectivity. The self, therefore, can be defined in terms of self-relation. The activity of self-relation culminates in the reflexivity of self-consciousness. The self-conscious individual mirrors the self-conscious God. Such self-consciousness is not, of course, immediately given. It poses a task that constitutes the self's vocation. *Imago* (which is related to the same root as *imitari*) invites *imitatio*. The image that the self is called to imitate is not at all obvious. The transcendent God, who can never be fully known in Himself, must be known indirectly, through a mediator. For the Christian, the divine Logos, Christ, effects this mediation. By representing the presence of God to humanity, the Logos reveals the self to itself. Christ, who is the perfect image of God, is also the figure of "a complete man." To actualize "mature manhood," the self must attain "to the measure of the stature of the fullness of Christ." [18] In this way, the self transforms itself into Christ's "very image." [19]

Since the human subject's full realization of the *imago dei* necessarily entails the *imitatio christi*, the self is actually an image of an image, an imitation of an imitation, a representation of a representation, and a sign of a sign. By becoming a copy of a copy, the self paradoxically becomes *itself*. In struggling to relate itself to itself, the human subject attempts to enact the complex movement of repetition that would fulfill the divine mandate: "Become what you are!" [20] The aim of this imitative repetition is self-appropriation. By means of the activity of self-relation, the subject attempts to take possession of itself and to secure its identity. The interplay of image, imitation, and identity reveals that the stages on life's way that comprise the believer's journey to selfhood repeat the stations of the cross marked by Christ.

## Naming: Propriety, Property, Possession

To be a self, I have suggested, is to possess and to be possessed by a name. But not just any name will do. The self-identity of the subject presupposes that one possesses the property of a *proper* name. The self in search of identity is forced to confess: "I have a proper name when I am proper." The relation of naming, propriety, property, and possession raises a host of questions: What does it mean to be proper? What constitutes propriety? Is propriety appropriate? Or is it inappropriate? What is impropriety? Is impropriety appropriate? Or is it inappropriate? Can one avoid impropriety? Should one avoid impropriety? What is property? Is propriety a property? Or should property be seen as propriety? What is expropriation? Can property be expropriated? Can property be protected from expropriation? Should property be expropriated? Should property be protected from expropriation? What is possession? What are possessions? Are possessions possessed? Or do they possess? Are properties possessions? Or are possessions properties? Are possessions proper? Can one possess? Should one possess? Is possession possession? What is dispossession? Can one dispossess? Should one dispossess? . . . What exactly *does* it mean to possess (or be possessed by) a (proper [or improper]) name?

*Proper* derives from the Latin *proprius*, which specifies that which is one's own, special, particular, peculiar, not held in common with others. Accordingly, proper means "Belonging to oneself or itself; (one's or its) own, owned as property; that is, the, or a, property or quality of the thing itself, intrinsic, inherent; distinctive; characteristic; opposed to common; private possession, private property, something belonging to oneself." Proper can also mean "excellent, admirable, commendable, capital, fine, goodly, of high quality; of good character or standing; honest, respectable, worthy; adapted to some purpose or requirement, fit, apt, suitable, appropriate to circumstances or conditions; what it should be, or what is required; such as one ought to do, have, use; right, in conformity with social ethics or with the demands and usage of polite society; respectable." In French, *propre* not only means "own, very, same, selfsame, proper, peculiar, appropriate, fitted, suitable, good, right, and correct" but also denotes "neat, tidy, and clean." The German *eigentlich* is cognate with *eigen* ("proper, inherent, own, characteristic, specific, peculiar, individual") and can be defined as "proper, true, real." But *eigentlich* also means "authentic."

A proper name, therefore, is peculiar, characteristic, and individual. It is one's own, a private possession or private property that one owns. One who has a proper name is not common but is distinctive, correct, of high quality and good character . . . respectable, never soiled, stained, or blemished, always neat, tidy, and clean. To have a proper name is to be true, real—in short, authentic.

Possession of a proper name is not only the aim of sojourning subjects; it is also the goal of Western philosophy and theology. "A noun is proper only when it has a single sense. Better, it is only in this case that it is properly a noun. Univocity is the essence, or better the *telos*, of language. No philosophy, as such, has ever renounced this Aristotelian ideal. This ideal is philosophy."[21] When one moves from philosophy to theology, it becomes clear that monotheism extends beyond the narrow confines of religion "proper" to encompass selves and the uni-verse as a whole. From a monotheistic perspective, to be is to be one. In order to be one, the subject cannot

err and must always remain proper. By following the straight and narrow
course, the self hopes to gain its most precious possession—itself. The
questions of propriety, property, and possession are inseparable. "I am what
is mine. Personality is the original personal property . . . 'By property I
must be understood here, as in other places, to mean that property which
men have in their persons as well as goods.' Here is the psychological root of
private property. Every man has a 'property' in his own person."²² The
property of personality suggests that owning is oneing and oneing is
owning.

The interplay of oneness and ownness implies the inextricable relation
between propriety and proximity. Propriety requires ownership of private
propert(y)ies. To own something is to possess, appropriate, seize, or lay
claim to it. Ownership draws near (*proximare*) and, by so doing, establishes
propriety. "The near," consequently, "is the proper; the proper is the
nearest (*propre, proprius*)."²³ Insofar as propriety presupposes proximity, it is
clear that "Proper is the name of the subject close to himself—who is what
he is." Proper subjectivity requires self-proximity. Propriety, in other
words, is impossible apart from self-presence.

Far from being lost in the past, the scene of nomination is always (the)
present. Naming realizes the "eschatology of the *proper* (*prope, proprius*, self-
proximity, self-presence, property, own-ness)"²⁴ by announcing "the *parousia*, the presence in the present."²⁵ The proper name necessarily entails
presence and/in the present. Self-presence is most fully realized in self-
consciousness. In becoming conscious of itself, the self becomes present to
itself. "The *I am*, being experienced only as an *I am present*, itself presupposes the relation with presence in general, with being as presence."²⁶ The
adequation of subject and object in reflexive subjectivity erases error and
inscribes proper knowledge, i.e., ideas that are clear and distinct or that are
univocal rather than equivocal. With this self-awareness, the self is freed
*from* the anxiety of uncertainty and *for* the enjoyment of certainty. The self-
presence of the self-conscious subject reflects the self-presence of absolute
subjectivity.

Such self-presence is possible, of course, only in the present. In self-
consciousness, the subject "is itself self-present in the fullness of its life, its
living present."²⁷ The identification of propriety and presence implies an
interpretation of time that in effect absolutizes the present. In order to
speak "of the present as the absolute form of experience, one *already* must
understand *what time is*, must understand the *ens of the praes-ens*, and the
proximity of the *Being of this ens*. The present of presence and the presence of
the present suppose the horizon, the precomprehending anticipation of
Being as time. If the meaning of Being has always been determined by
philosophy as presence, then the *question of* Being, posed on the basis of the
transcendental horizon of time . . . is the first tremor of philosophical
security, as it is of self-confident presence."²⁸ The ontotheological tradition

recognizes an essential relation between subjectivity and time. Within this framework, however, time is understood in terms of the present. "The present alone is and ever will be. Being is presence or the modification of presence."[29] Insofar as any thing that is must be present, it is, in principle, nominal. Proper names indicate what is by specifying substantives that represent both objects and subjects. Since presence and the present are indissoluble, the subject cannot appear apart from the verb. Furthermore, the verbal form of the subject is always in the present tense. This intricate relation between time and the self deserves closer examination.

From their earliest days and in a variety of ways, Western philosophy and theology have consistently, even if usually implicitly, expressed the importance of time for being. It was not, however, until Augustine's penetrating self-analysis that the full scope of the problem of time was appreciated. It would not be too much to say that Augustine's discovery of the subject would have been impossible apart from his recognition of the subjectivity of time. In the course of his confession, Augustine asks: "When then is time? I know what it is if no one asks me what it is; but if I want to explain it to someone who has asked me, I find that I do not know. Nevertheless, I can confidently assert that I know this: that if nothing passed away there would be no past time, and if nothing were coming there would be no future time, and if nothing were now there would be no present time."[30] Further reflection discloses deeper complexities. In a certain sense, neither the past nor the future exists. Since "the past no longer is, and the future has not yet come to be,"[31] Augustine concludes that the present alone is actual. He recognizes, however, that while only the present is, the present is not simple. He insists that it is "perfectly clear that neither the future nor the past are [sic] in existence, and that it is incorrect to say that there are three times—past, present, and future. Though one might perhaps say: 'There are three times—a present of things past, a present of things present, and a present of things future.' For these three do exist in the mind, and I do not see them anywhere else: the present of things past is memory; the present of things present is sight; the present of things future is expectation. If we are allowed to use words in this way, then I see that there are three times and I admit that there are."[32] Contrary to common sense, time is not made up of three separate tenses or three discrete moments. There is but one tense of time, the present. The present, moreover, is comprised of three inseparable modalities. Memory and expectation join in the present.

The complexity of the present complicates the presence of the self. The self-conscious subject is not immediately present to itself but must become self-present through the process of self-presentation. In different terms, the identity of the self is synthetic rather than simple. Although the self is one, it is at the same triune—a unity that is a trinity. The activity of self-presentation constitutes a process of self-appropriation through which the subject comes into possession of itself. By relating itself to itself, the subject realizes itself as self-present subjectivity. Only with this "parousia of the self"[33] does the subject assume its proper name.

Due to the *internal* distension of the present, the realization of the self's full presence to itself necessarily involves a process of re-membering or re-collection. Augustine already recognized the close connection between *cogo* ("to drive together to one point, collect, compress, crowd, bring or urge together, assemble, gather together") and *cogito*. Building on his Platonic and Neoplatonic heritage, Augustine went so far as to argue that to know *is* to re-collect. In the act of knowing, the subject re-members or re-collects what previously had been dismembered or dispersed. Insofar as the object of consciousness is the self itself, self-knowledge inevitably entails self-recollection. Such recollection must not be confused with the simple act of recalling. As the word in German (*Erinnerung*) and Danish (*Erindring*) implies, recollection and inwardness are closely related. Recollection involves interiorization or internalization. This process of inwardization draws sustenance from memory. Instead of merely retrieving "facts" that have been stored in the "belly of the mind," recollection inwardizes the rich diversity of experience. Through this interiorization, sequential succession gives way to coherent interrelation. Apart from or prior to recollection, events and/or things seem fragmented and unrelated. Recollection joins what apparently is disjoined and connects what seems to be disconnected. When thought turns on itself, recollection enables the self to become present to itself by comprehending, gathering together, and unifying the three modalities of the present. The complex self-presence that results from self-recollection mirrors the intricacy of the present itself. Self, as well as time, is *one* substance with *three* modes.

The necessary interplay of self-appropriation and recollection points to the importance of autobiography for self-realization. Recollection *graphs* the self or plots the stages of the subject's journey to selfhood. The activity of remembering re-presents the story of its own becoming to the self-conscious subject. According to its "founder," the aim of autobiography is the establishment of personal identity through the integration of the personality. In order to achieve this coherence, it is necessary to relate the multiple experiences the self has undergone in such a way that they constitute a comprehensive and comprehensible totality. The meaning of any particular event or experience is a function of its place within the total life of the individual. Since the meaningful totality for which the autobiographer searches is not immediately given, it must be constructed. By means of the synthetic power of the imagination, the subject attempts to weave the various strands of experience into a unified whole. Instead of merely chronicling experience, the autobiographer *narrates* the story of the self becoming itself. "[E]very narrative combines two dimensions in various proportions, one chronological and the other nonchronological. The first may be called the episodic dimension, which characterizes the story as made out of events. The second is the configurational dimension, according to which the plot construes significant wholes out of scattered events."[34] The relationship between narrativity and meaning is so close as to suggest that absence of the former leads to lack of the latter. Conversely, meaning emerges when episodes are narrated so as to form a plot. The coherence of any plot requires an identifiable center to provide the organizing focus of the narrative.

In Augustine's autobiography, for example, the conversion experience serves as such a meaningful center. Reflecting on this pivotal episode in his life, Augustine becomes convinced that it is the "intelligible event which makes all other events intelligible."[35] Prior to this experience, he is a "sick soul" or an "unhappy consciousness" who suffers interminable conflict brought on by inward dismemberment. With self set against self, Augustine is unable to find the peace and rest for which he longs. But all of this changes suddenly when he hears a *voice* in the *garden*, which calls: "Take it and read it. Take it and read it." Augustine reports what followed: "I snatched up the book, opened it, and read in silence the passage upon which my eyes first fell: *Not in rioting and drunkenness, not in chambering and wantonness, not in strife and envying: but put ye on the Lord Jesus Christ, and make not provision for the flesh in concupiscence.* I had no wish to read further; there was no need to. For immediately I had reached the end of this sentence it was as though my heart was filled with a light of confidence and all the shadows of my doubt were swept away."[36] This experience in the *garden* is, in effect, Augustine's scene of nomination. It constitutes nothing less than a revelation that illuminates his entire inner history. After years of apparently pointless erring, Augustine at last "finds himself." Following in the footsteps of the prodigal son, he finally comes home, not to his father—who, as usual, is absent—but to himself. Homecoming, however, remains incomplete until the sojourner offers a narration of his travels.

The necessary role of narration in the correlative processes of self-presentation and self-realization carries significant implications for the notion of the self. In view of the imaginative coherence of autobiography, the centered self appears to be more a literary creation than a literal fact. "The 'subject,'" in other words, "is not something given, it is something added and invented and projected behind what is there."[37] As the product of the literary imagination, the self assumes the form of a fictive text. From this perspective, "The 'subject' is only a fiction."[38] The inversion of this insight further clarifies human selfhood. Insofar as the self is a function of narrative, it can also be understood as a "narrative function." The self is present to itself as a character, usually the leading character, in a story. Autobiography, therefore, is really the subject's auto-graph. In order to be a self in the "proper" sense of the word, every subject must tell and retell its tale. But to whom is this story addressed?

Augustine's autobiography offers a possible answer to this important question. The *Confessions* is actually a confession addressed to God. Augustine presents himself to himself by presenting himself to the omnipresent God. As the sovereign Creator, God is the ground and source of all presence. From Augustine to Hegel, "God is the name of the element of that which makes possible an absolutely self-present self-knowledge."[39] For Augustine, this full presence comes to complete expression in *speech* or *voice*. His confession is really an extended prayer *spoken* to God. Untainted by extraneous marks and unsoiled by exterior signs, voice permits the self to become transparent to itself by becoming visible to God. Speech is the element of self-presence, the medium in which presence becomes fully present. "To speak of God is finally to speak of speech itself," and to speak of speech itself is finally to speak of God. "[T]he voice of 'I AM' is heard in the voice of 'I am.'"[40] God is the absolute "self-presence, pure auto-affection,"[41] that is reflected in all presence and in every present. Since "God is the name of names, the source of names,"[42] the self cannot name itself without at the same time speaking the name of God.

Augustine's confession is, of course, also the *Confessions*. His prayer is not only spoken; it is also written. In its written form, the confession constitutes a book. This book is an auto-bio-*graphy*—a *writing* about the life of the self. Although not often recognized by the author, writing actually subverts the proper name by disclosing the uncanniness of both presence and the present. Intended to establish my identity, writing really "dispossesses me of my narrative continuity."[43] Like its discoverer, Hermes, writing is a thief "which dispossesses me and makes me remote from myself, interrupting my proximity to myself."[44] Every auto-graph turns out to be improper, for writing "soils me" and forces me to "relinquish all that is proper to me."

## Uncanniness of Presence: Representation and Repetition

To catch a glimpse of the improper space of writing, it is sufficient to conduct a simple thought experiment. The least-complicated instance of naming appears to be the denomination of something that is present-at-hand. For the sake of argument, let us call the object of nomination a "This."[45] Every "This" is made up of a temporal and spatial component. The "This," in other words, is "Here and Now." To grasp "This," both of these elements must be considered. It is, first of all, necessary to ask: "'What is Now?' [L]et us answer, e.g. 'Now is Night.'" In order to test the truth of this claim, we can *write* it down. "A truth cannot lose anything through our preserving it. If *now, this noon*, we look again at the written truth, we shall have to say that it has become stale. The Now that is Night is *preserved*, i.e., it is treated as what it professes to be, as something that *is*;

but it proves itself to be, on the contrary, something that is *not*. The Now does indeed preserve itself, but as something that is *not* Night; equally, it preserves itself in the face of the Day that it now is, as something that also is not Day, in other words, as a *negative* in general. This self-preserving Now is, therefore, not immediate but mediated; for it is determined as a permanent and self-preserving Now *through* the fact that something else, viz. Day and Night, is *not*." The same, of course, "will be the case with the other form of the 'This,' with 'Here.' 'Here' is, e.g., the tree. If I turn round, this truth has vanished and is converted into its opposite: 'No tree is here, but a house instead.' 'Here' itself does not vanish; on the contrary, it abides constant in the vanishing of the house, the tree, etc. and is indifferently house or tree."

This analysis applies not only to the named object but also to the naming subject. "I, *this* 'I,' see the tree and assert that 'Here' is a tree; but another 'I' sees the house and maintains that 'Here' is not a tree but a house instead." Whether taken objectively or subjectively, the *hic et nunc* is "dissolved, deleted, dispersed the very moment I express it in language." "The Now that *is*, is another Now than the one pointed to, and we see that the Now is just this: to be no more just when it is. The Now, as it is pointed out to us, is Now that *has been*, and this is its truth; it has not the truth of *being*. Yet this much is true, that it has been. But what essentially *has been* is, in fact, not an essence that *is*; it is not, and it was with *being* that we were concerned." [46]

In order to clarify this crucial point, "let us consider the extreme case of a 'statement about perception.' Let us suppose that it is produced at the very moment of the perceptual intuition: I say, 'I see a particular person by the window' while I really do see him. It is structurally implied in my performance that the content of this expression is ideal and that its unity is not impaired by the absence of perception here and now. Whoever hears this proposition, whether he is next to me or infinitely removed in space and time, should, by right, understand what I mean to say. Since this possibility is constitutive of the possibility of speech, it should structure the very act of him who speaks while perceiving. My nonperception, my nonintuition, my *hic et nunc* absence are expressed by that very thing that I say, by *that* which I say and *because* I say it. This structure will never form an 'intimately blended unity' with intuition. The absence of intuition—and therefore of the subject of the intuition—is not only *tolerated* by speech; it is *required* by the general structure of signification, when considered *in itself*. It is radically requisite: the total absence of the subject and object of a statement—the death of the writer and/or the disappearance of the objects he was able to describe—does not prevent a text from 'meaning' something. On the contrary, this possibility gives birth to meaning as such, it gives it out to be heard and read." [47]

The "This" with which we started no longer seems simple. The consideration of writing discloses that every "This" is "compound and complex":

Here is a "plurality of Heres," and Now is a "plurality of Nows." Nomination, therefore, is not a simple act of presentation, it is, instead, the complex activity of representation. Always hurrying to grasp the fleeting here and now, representation can only re-present a presence/present that never is and never can be fully realized. Since representation invariably opens the gap it seeks to close, it is always "tied to the work of spacing."[48] Spacing, however, "'is' the index of an irreducible outside, and at the same time the index of a *movement*, of a displacement which indicates an irreducible alterity."[49] Inasmuch as all presentation is representation, the subject's struggle to secure identity and establish a proper name *inevitably* fails. "We are dispossessed of the longed-for presence in the gesture of language by which we attempt to seize it."[50] Like Alice gazing into the looking glass, the reflective/reflexive subject discovers an uncanny hole, through which it disappears.

We have seen that, though the self is made in the image of God, the *imago* presents the task of *imitatio*. Through imitation of the image, the self seeks to achieve identity or to become what it is. In order to come into possession of the property of a proper name, the subject must *become* present to itself by presenting itself to itself. But now we discover that presentation is actually re-presentation. In other words, there is no identity without repetition. Something can be itself only by doubling itself. "What is is not what it is, identical and identical to itself, unique, unless it *adds to itself* the possibility of being *repeated* as such. And its identity is hollowed out by that addition, withdraws itself in the supplement that presents it."[51] "This hollow space is not an opening among others. It is opening itself, the opening of opening, that which can be enclosed within no category or totality, that is, everything within experience which can no longer be described by traditional concepts."[52] This opening forms the "exit from the identical into the same."[53]

Identity, we have observed, is usually defined in terms of same, and same in terms of identity. This direct identification, however, proves to be misleading. Identity encompasses a synchronic element (identity at any particular moment) and a diachronic factor (continuity over time). While it is tempting to view the former component as spatial identity and the latter as temporal identity, this would obscure the space within time and the time of space. The notion of the *same* captures the play of time and space by pointing to the representative character of all presence and every present and by underscoring the repetitiousness of all identity. The same is not a simple identity; it is, rather, a "structure of iterability" that includes *both* identity and difference. The self that becomes what it is becomes the same. In becoming the same, however, the self does not merely become itself but simultaneously becomes other. The repetition involved in self-becoming embodies iterability, which joins identity and difference. Instead of establishing propriety and assuring purity, naming marks or inscribes the end of all identity that is only itself. "For we can evoke an actual or real identity only by embodying difference, a real and actual difference, a difference making identity manifest, and making it manifest as itself. Only the presence of difference calls identity forth, and calls it forth in its difference from itself." With the name, or in the word, "every identity is other."[54] Here lies the duplicity of all self-presentation. There is always difference *within* identity and absence *within* presence. Through an unexpected inversion, repetition and re-presentation turn out to involve a "de-presentation" that disrupts presence and dislocates the present. Contrary to common sense, the interior doubling through which presence and the present appear also makes them disappear. Presence/present and identity are forever fugitive—they disappear in the very act of appearing. If, however, something can appear only by disappearing, it would seem to be undeniably temporal and unquestionably mortal.

We have observed that throughout the Western tradition there has been a very close relationship between being and time. Being has been consistently interpreted as presence and hence constantly regarded in terms of the present. While apparently establishing the essentiality of time, this customary view of the relation between being and time actually serves to *repress* the inevitable temporality of selfhood. This repression becomes apparent when one recognizes some of the hidden implications of Augustine's extraordinarily influential interpretation of time and self. While Augustine's self(-)analysis leads to the related discoveries of the subject and the subjectivity of time, his argument remains bound to the traditional identification of being and presence. For this reason, he insists that, since the present alone exists, the self *is* only to the extent that it is (or becomes) *present* to itself. To be is to be present, and to exist fully is to be present totally. Unlike his predecessors, however, Augustine recognizes that the present is complex, not simple. Instead of being an isolated point or a punctual Now, the present is constituted by three modes, which, though distinguishable, are, nonetheless, all present. This is the basis of his conviction that the present consists of a present of things past, a present of things present, and a present of things future.

Viewed from a slightly different angle, Augustine's provocative examination of time leads to significantly different conclusions. The "omnipresence" of past and future within the present uncovers an "original" nonpresence at the very heart of the present. Past and future are not modalities of the present but signify irreducible absence. As identity possesses and is possessed by difference, so presence necessarily involves absence. As a matter of fact, "only the alterity of past and future presents permits the absolute identity of the living present as the self-identity of non-self identity."[55] Given this insight, one "sees quickly that the presence of the perceived present can appear as such only inasmuch as it is *continuously compounded* with a nonpresence and nonperception, with primary memory

and expectation (retention and protention). These nonperceptions are neither added to, nor do they *occasionally* accompany, the actually perceived
now; they are essentially and indispensably involved in its possibility." [56]
This conclusion recalls our earlier discovery of the inseparability of Now
and not-Now. The absence of presence opens the gap through which the
space of time appears. Time not only transpires "in" space, but space
"indwells" time. The spacing of time creates a hole that can never be
completely filled and engenders a desire that cannot be totally satisfied.

Due to the everlasting interplay of identity and difference and of presence
and absence, the present is "present not as total presence, but as *trace*."
Rather than a *nunc stans*, time is ceaseless transition, perpetual motion, and
constant movement (*momentum*). So understood, temporality is passage,
"absolute passage." Irreducibly transitional, time is always the "middest,"
ever errant, irrevocably liminal. As we shall see in more detail in a later
chapter, the trace marks the liminality of temporality. "The concepts of
*present*, *past*, and *future*, everything in the concepts of time and history
which implies evidence of them—the metaphysical concept of time in
general—cannot adequately describe the structure of the trace. And deconstructing the simplicity of presence does not amount only to accounting
for the horizons of potential presence, indeed of a 'dialectic' of pretention
and retention that would install [itself] in the heart of the present instead of
surrounding it with it. It is not a matter of complicating the structure of
time while conserving its homogeneity and its fundamental successivity, by
demonstrating for example that the past present and future present constitute originarily, by dividing it, the form of the living present." [57] Unmasterable by the logic of identity and noncontradiction, the trace marks
the place where identity and difference, presence and absence, constantly
cross.

Insofar as time and selfhood are inextricably related, the self is nailed to
this cross. Although Augustine discerned the subjectivity of temporality,
his reduction of the absence of past and future to the presence of the present
obscures the temporality of subjectivity. Had Augustine been more critical
of the Western ontotheological tradition, he might have seen the radical,
indeed revolutionary, implications of his insight. "The real presence of
Time in the World is called *Man*. Time *is* Man, and Man *is* Time." [58] But
time appears to be a trace. If man is time and time a trace, then "the self of
the living present is primordially a trace." This insight leads to an unexpected conclusion: "The trace is the erasure of selfhood, of one's own
presence." [59]

In the effort to secure its identity and establish its presence, the self
discovers its unavoidable difference and irrepressible absence. Though we
struggle to deny it, "There is nothing in a name." [60] The search for self-
presence in self-consciousness leads to the discovery of the absence of the
self. Once again self-affirmation and self-negation prove to be indivisibly

bound. Apparent "selving" is actual "unselving." The journey to selfhood turns out to be a dangerous voyage—nothing less than the way of the cross. "In its representation of itself, the subject is shattered and opened." The shattering of the subject is registered by the trace. The trace "is the opening of the first exteriority in general, the enigmatic relationship of the living to its other and of an inside to an outside: spacing."[61] The absence that is always "present," the outside that is always "inside," is *death* itself. "The living present is always marked by death."[62] And this death, this eternal death, is the uncanniness that forever haunts presence. Within the space of the trace is inscribed a cross that marks the site of the disappearance of the self.

# 3

## End of History

. . . the end of history and the death of God are not only simultaneous but identical movements. The end of history is the self-negation of self-consciousness, an ending which is fully and openly embodied in the twentieth century, and an ending which is eschatological in the sense that it is an absolute end of everything which is here manifest and real as history itself. So it is that the end of history has, indeed, occurred, and not simply the history of metaphysics, but the history of the West as a whole, for the 'metaphysical' identification of being as presence is simply the philosophical voice of the Western consciousness itself.

Here I stand in the midst of the surging of the breakers [this is an untranslatable play on words: *Hier stehe ich inmitten des Brandes der Brandung. Brandung* is related to the conflagration expressed in *Brand*, which itself also signifies the mark left by a burning branding iron. It is the seething surf, the waves rolling back over themselves as they crash against the rocky shoreline or break on the reefs, the cliffs, the *éperons*], whose white flames fork up to my feet [so I too am an *éperon*];—from all sides there is howling, threatening, crying, and screaming at me, while in the lowest depths the old earth shaker sings his aria [*seine Arie singt*, beware, Ariadne is not far away] hollow like a roaring bull; he beats such an earth shaker's measure thereto, that even the hearts of these weathered rock-monsters tremble at the sound. Then, suddenly, as if born out of nothingness, there appears before the portal of this hellish labyrinth, only a few fathoms distant,—a great sailing ship [*Segelschiff*] gliding silently along like a ghost. Oh, this ghostly beauty!

### Shadows of Logocentrism: Types and Tropes

After these things God tested Abraham, and said to him, "Abraham!" And he said, "Here am I." He said, "Take your son, your only son Isaac, whom you love, and go to the land of Moriah, and offer him there as a burnt offering upon one of the mountains of which I shall tell you." [1]

For it is written that Abraham had two sons, one by a slave and one by a free woman. But the son of the slave was born according to the flesh, the son of the free woman through promise. Now this is an allegory: these women are two covenants. One is from Mount Sinai, bearing children for slavery; she is Hagar. Now Hagar is Mount Sinai in Arabia; she corresponds to the present Jerusalem, for she is in slavery with her children. But the Jerusalem above is free, and she is our mother. For it is written,

> Rejoice, O barren one that does not
>     bear;
> break forth and shout, thou who are
>     not in travail;
> for the desolate hath more children
> than she who hath a husband.

Now we, brethren, like Isaac, are children of promise. But as at that time he who was born according to the flesh persecuted him who was born according to the Spirit, so it is now. But what does the scripture say? "Cast out the slave and her son; for the son of the slave shall not inherit with the son of the free woman." So, brethren, we are not children of the slave but of the free woman.[2]

Once upon a time there was a man who as a child had heard the beautiful story about how God tempted Abraham, and how he endured temptation, kept the faith, and a second time received a son contrary to expectation. When the child became older he read the same story with even greater admiration, for life had separated what was united in the pious simplicity of the child. The older he became, the more frequently his mind reverted to that story, his enthusiasm became greater and greater, and yet he was less and less able to understand the story. At last in his interest for that he forgot everything else; his soul had only one wish, to see Abraham, one longing, to have been witness to that event. His desire was not to behold the beautiful countries of the Orient, or the earthly glory of the Promised Land, or that godfearing couple whose old age God had blessed, or the venerable figure of the aged patriarch, or the vigorous young manhood of Isaac whom God had bestowed upon Abraham—he saw no reason why the same thing might not have taken place on a barren heath in Denmark. His yearning was to accompany them on the three days' journey when Abraham rode with sorrow before him and with Isaac by his side.[3]

"Once upon a time. . . . And. . . . They lived happily (or not so happily) ever after." Beginning . . . Middle . . . End. Between the "tick" of Genesis and the "tock" of Apocalypse, the history of the West runs its course.[4] The line that joins beginning, middle, and end traces the plot that defines history. History, as well as self, is a theological notion. "To be a self is to have a God, to have a God is to have a history, that is, events connected in a meaningful pattern; to have one God is to have one history."[5] Within the Christian West, history is not merely theocentric; it is, more importantly, *logocentric*. Since the sovereign God creates and rules through the divine

*Logos*, His creation is rational rather than chaotic. To acknowledge that history is a theological notion is no more to imply that history is always *explicitly* theocentric or logocentric than it is to insist that the bond between anthropology and theology transforms every centered self into an overt religious believer. The principle of unity and organizing center through which time assumes coherence can be expressed in many ways. Nevertheless, it is important to recognize that the conviction that a temporal course of events is plotted along a single line, which extends from a definite beginning, through an identifiable middle, to an expected end, is linked to particular notions of God and self. As we shall see, this relationship is of more than "historical" interest. If God, self, and history are so closely bound, then the death of God and the disappearance of the self would seem to spell the end of history. But since time "clearly" continues, what can it possibly mean to say that history is over? To ask the same question from a different perspective: What does it mean to *write after* the advent of Absolute Knowledge?

Whether or not one agrees that there is something like an "Axial Period," during which "Man, as we know him today, came into being,"[6] it does seem clear that history, like the self, is a relatively recent invention. Indeed, there can be no individual self apart from history and no history without the individual subject. In addition to having provided one of the most influential formulations of the Western concept of God, discovered the personality, and created the genre of autobiography, Augustine also developed the first *full-blown* theology of history. The rudiments of his vision can be found both in earlier Western theology and in the Gospels. Augustine repeatedly acknowledged his debt to his predecessors and freely drew on their writings. The *City of God*, however, surpasses prior works to which it might be compared. Augustine integrates the insights of previous authors to form a comprehensive interpretation of history, stretching from the original creation, through the confusion of the city of man, to the fulfillment of the kingdom of God. Ostensibly an apology on behalf of Christians who faced pagan accusations brought against them after the fall of Rome, the *City of God* actually completes the undertaking begun in the *Confessions*. Through the elaboration of principles discovered on his inward journey, Augustine attempts to construct an account of time as a whole—an account that in turn provides further clarification of the self.

It should not be surprising that what "begins" with Augustine again comes to an "end" in Hegel. As the *Phenomenology of Spirit* "completes" and subverts the *Confessions*, so Hegel's *Philosophy of History* completes and subverts the *City of God*. By rationalizing Augustine's unsystematic theology, Hegel's speculative philosophy effectively inscribes the end of history. In the writings of Hegel, "the history of being as presence, as self-presence in absolute knowledge, as consciousness of self in the infinity of *parousia*—

this history is closed. The history of presence is closed, for 'history' has never meant anything but the presentation (*Gegenwärtigung*) of Being, the production and recollection of beings in presence, as knowledge and mastery. Since absolute self-presence in con-sciousness is the infinite *vocation* of full presence, the achievement of absolute knowledge is the end of the infinite, which could only be the unity of the concept, logos, and conscious-ness in a voice without *différance*." [7]

Whether conceived as divine Logos or providential Reason, the rationale of history is never immediately evident. It must be uncovered through discerning interpretation. In recounting his movement from Manichaean-ism to Christianity, Augustine underscores the importance of the method of interpretation he had learned from Ambrose, the bishop of Milan: "I had thought that nothing could be said of the Catholic faith in the face of the objections raised by the Manichees, but it now appeared to me that this faith could be maintained on reasonable grounds—especially when I had heard one or two of the passages in the Old Testament explained, usually in a figurative way, which, when I had taken them literally, had been a cause of death to me." [8] In other works, most notably *On Christian Doctrine* and *On the Spirit and the Letter*, Augustine develops and defends the "figurative" interpretation he had first learned from Ambrose. This "spiritual" hermeneutic enables Augustine to bring together important elements from the Platonic/Neoplatonic and Judeo-Christian traditions to form a synthesis that still remains both directly and indirectly influential. Figurative reading eventually comes to be known as *typological interpretation*.

The typological method of interpretation arose in response to the di-lemma posed by the question of the relationship between Christianity and Judaism. From the outset, members of the Christian and Jewish commu-nities struggled to decide whether Christianity constitutes a continuation of Judaism or a radical departure from it. There was (and continues to be) a wide range of opinion on this critical question. Some saw Jesus as little more than the most recent representative of the long and venerable Jewish prophetic tradition, while others maintained that Judaism and Christian-ity have virtually nothing in common. One of the most influential rep-resentatives of the latter point of view was a second-century Gnostic, Marcion.

A thoroughgoing dualist, Marcion insisted that the God of Jesus is other than and different from Yahweh. Marcion (who, significantly, was the first to propose a definitive Christian canon) made this theological dualism into his basic hermeneutical principle. In a provocative work entitled *Antitheses*, he attempted to demonstrate that Jewish and Christian scriptures are completely discontinuous and absolutely opposite. Such a position clearly violates fundamental tenets of monotheism. If God is one, then the God of Jesus and the God of the Jews cannot be different. The oneness of God implies both the unity of history and the coherence of scripture. The fundamental aim of typological interpretation is to uncover this "necessary" unity and coherence.

*Typology* derives from the Greek *tupos* + *logos*. *Tupos*, which is related to *tuptō* (to strike), means both a blow and the mark or trace left by a blow or the application of pressure, e.g., the mark of the nails in Christ's hands (John 20:25). It can also refer to an image or model. A statue, for example, is the *tupos* of the one represented.[9] According to the typological method of interpretation, things and events recorded in Jewish scripture are types or figures of things and events in the life of Christ and the experience of Christians. The second-century Christian theologian Justin explained that sometimes God "has caused something to be done which was a type of what was to happen, sometimes He uttered words concerning what was to come about, phrasing them as if they referred to things taking place then or even having already taken place."[10] By reading Christian scripture as the *New* Testament, typology transforms Jewish scripture into the *Old* Testament.

In the hands of its earliest proponents, typology provided a means to complement rather than to replace the "literal" meaning of the text and thus to valorize (albeit by sublating) rather than to reject the now "Old" Testament. In the eyes of figurative interpretation, "one thing is said, another meant."[11] Since nothing is univocal, everything possesses a certain density or thickness. Over against the "superficial" vision of paganism, in which everything is "clearly outlined, brightly and uniformly illuminated," the typological interpreter insists that the world is "fraught with 'background' and mysterious."[12] Nothing is what it appears to be. Things and events always point beyond themselves to a concealed meaning that is, in fact, their truth. In the course of the ontotheological tradition, the relation between manifest and latent has been expressed in many ways. For example: Old Testament/New Testament, Old Covenant/New Covenant, carnal/spiritual, shadow/light, visible/invisible, surface/depth, foreground/background, familiar/strange, literal/figurative, *Vorstellung/Begriff*, *Mythos/Logos*, language/desire, etc. Each pair of terms points to a similar dilemma. If surface covers a more profound depth, then hidden truth must be discovered through an act of interpretation. Decipherment, in other words, is *integral* to understanding. Typological analysis is an interpretive strategy whose purpose is to establish "a connection between two [or more] events or persons in such a way that the first signifies not only itself but also the second, while the second involves or fulfills the first."[13] From a typological perspective, the *figure* of a father sacrificing a son draws together events that take place on Moriah, Golgotha, and even the Jutland heath.

By calling into question all forms of literal-mindedness, typological interpretation implies a close relation between type and trope. Trope (from Greek *trepō*, to turn) designates a figure of speech in which a word or phrase is used in a sense other than that which is "proper" to it. Though not usually recognized by either religious believers or theologians, *tropology* means "a speaking by tropes" or "the use of metaphor in speech and writing." More commonly, of course, it refers to "a moral discourse" or "a secondary use of interpretation of Scripture relating to morals." The bond between typology and tropology suggests the possibility of clarifying the implications of tropological interpretation by considering particular tropes. This analysis, in turn, might prepare the way for a better understanding of the relationship of typology and tropology to the notion of history that has characterized most Christian belief and practice.

Metaphor is the trope that most effectively discloses the interconnection between typological and tropological interpretation. In contrast to the contingent and arbitrary relation of terms in metonymy, metaphor presupposes a resemblance or similarity between the signifier and what is signified. "In order that a metaphor obtains, one must continue to identify the previous incompatibility *through* the new compatibility. 'Remoteness' is preserved within 'proximity.' To see *the like* is to see the same in spite of, and through, the different. This tension between sameness and difference characterizes the logical structure of likeness."[14] The significance of the difference between metonymy and metaphor can be clarified by recalling the well-known theological distinction between sign and symbol. Like metonymy and metaphor, sign and symbol both entail overdetermination and, thus, exhibit "the structure of multiple-meaning."[15] Whereas the relationship of signifier to signified is arbitrary in metonymy and sign, it is not arbitrary in metaphor and symbol. "While the sign bears no necessary relation to that to which it points, the symbol participates in the reality of that for which it stands."[16] The integral bond joining symbol and symbolized implies that there is a noncontingent relation between the manifest and latent dimensions of the symbol. In symbolic expression, "meaning, not satisfied with designating some one thing, designates another meaning attainable only in and through the first intentionality."[17] Insofar as the latent *dwells within* the manifest, symbol and symbolized are not merely contiguous. Unlike the free-floating sign, the symbol is grounded; it has roots. These roots bestow on the symbol its *revelatory* power. Since the symbol participates in the symbolized and the latent inhabits the manifest, symbols "give what they say." The goal of de-cipherment and dis-closure is *to make present* what otherwise remains absent. Effective symbols allow the hidden to shine forth or to emerge from concealment into "the open."[18] By speaking the unspoken, the symbol both *présents* and *preséñts*. This presencing is the eventuation of truth or the occurrence of *alētheia*. *Alētheia* unites the interpreting subject and the symbolized object. "The movement that draws me toward the second meaning assimilates me to what is said, makes me participate in what is announced to me. The similitude in which the force of symbols resides and from which they draw their revealing power is not an objective likeness, which I may look upon like a relation laid out before me; it is an existential assimilation . . . of my being to being"[19] and of my present to presence.

To the discerning eye of the Christian, the hidden appears to be divine, and symbols are believed to be hierophantic. In metaphorical terms, the light that dispels shadows is the divine logos. For this reason, typological interpretation is necessarily *logocentric*. The Greek word λόγος, which has no exact equivalent in other languages, is usually translated "speaking," "word," or "reason." The notion of the logos plays an important role in Greek and Jewish thought long before it assumes a significant place in Christian theology. As early as Heraclitus, the logos is identified as the immanent reason of the world, the reason that underlies all material reality and temporal flux. Heraclitus argues that the logos "exists from all time; yet men are unaware of it." Developing Heraclitus' insights, Stoic philosophers maintain that everything that exists is a mode or accident of a single substance. This all-pervasive substance, which the Stoics believed to be fire, is described as the "seminal reason" (*logos spermatikos*) of the world. Whether conceived spiritually or materially, the logos appears to thinkers like Heraclitus and the Stoics to be an *immanent* principle of order. A significant shift occurs in Plato's philosophy. No longer convinced of the implicit order of things, Plato insists on the original heterogeneity of form and matter. According to the *Timaeus*, the rationality of the world is a product of the imposition of transcendent form on chaotic matter. The mediator between the realms of eternity and time is pictured as a Demiurge. Though not a creator god, the *Dēmiourgos* fashions primal chaos after the image of unchanging forms. Philo, a second-century Jewish philosopher/theologian, synthesizes divergent elements in Greek philosophy with central tenets of the Jewish faith to create the logos doctrine that becomes most influential for early Christian theologians. In Philonic thought, the logos is an intermediary between the transcendent Creator and His creation. As a subordinate expression of the divine mind and will, the logos is the agent through which God governs the world and reveals His purposes. Though represented in different ways in Greek and Jewish thought, the logos consistently refers to the principle of order that lies beneath the apparent disorder of experience.

The most important Christian version of the logos doctrine occurs in the opening lines of the Fourth Gospel: "In the beginning was the Word [*logos*], and the Word was with God, and the Word was God. He was in the beginning with God; all things were made through him, and without him was not anything made that was made. In him was life, and the life was the light of men. The light shines in the darkness, and the darkness has not overcome it."[20] This text reflects the established Greek and Jewish interpretation of the logos as the creative principle of cosmic order. In agreement with Philo and in opposition to philosophers like Heraclitus and the Stoics, the Gospel According to John describes the logos as transcendent to the world. Over against Philo, however, the author(s) of the Fourth Gospel insist(s) that the logos is identical with, and therefore not subordinate to, God. Typological interpretation presupposes this logos doctrine.

Since the logos is one with the Alpha and the Omega, it is omnipresent. The divine Word is that through which everything is originally created and by which all things are finally judged. The activity of the logos informs the entire created order and comes to expression in things and persons that seem superficially to be unrelated. The presence of the Word of God links events as distant as an ancient Hebraic child sacrifice, the crucifixion of a first-century Jew, and the suffering of a nineteenth-century Danish Christian. From the perspective of figural interpretation, this association of events is not arbitrary. The relation between type and antitype is *discovered* rather than *fabricated*. As the primal *ground* and enduring *substance* of all created order, the logos is the principle of unity that *underlies* all experience.

It would, however, be misleading to consider typology simply in terms of spatial metaphors. In addition to the tension between surface and depth, figural interpretation also includes the tensive relation of past, present, and future. Every figure is Janus-faced. While the manifest appears to be present, the latent can be either past or future. Insofar as an event recalls a prior type, it must be approached "archeologically," and, to the extent that it prefigures what is yet to come, it must be interpreted "teleologically." Whereas archeology seeks echoes of the past, teleology tries to hear the word of the future in the voice of the present. For the archeologist, to dig down is to go back—back to the origin from which everything emerges. The teleologist, by contrast, regards latency as a fund of potentiality awaiting realization. Within the bounds of the typological interpretation practiced by the Christian community, past and future are not regarded as equivalent. What is subsequent not only completes and fulfills but also exceeds and surpasses what is antecedent. From this perspective, past and present foreshadow a richer future. In addition to being doubly bound as figure and ground, type and antitype are related as promise and fulfillment. This temporal component of typological interpretation has significant implications for the Western view of history.

Perhaps the most important Christian use of typology in terms of promise and fulfillment is Paul's interpretation of Christ as the "Second Adam": "Therefore as sin came into the world through one man and death through sin, and so death spread to all men because all men sinned—sin indeed was in the world before the law was given, but sin is not counted where there is no law. Yet death reigned from Adam to Moses, even over those whose sins were not like the transgression of Adam, who was a type of the one who was to come. But the free gift is not like the trespass. For if many died through

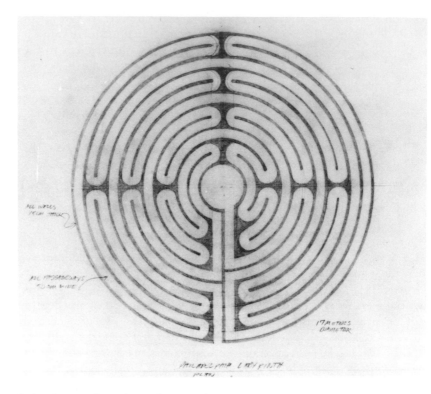

Robert Morris. Groundplan of the Philadelphia Labyrinth. Pencil drawing on paper. Panza Collection, Milan. Reproduced by permission of Count Giuseppe Panza.

This labyrinth—eight feet high, thirty feet in diameter, and constructed of plywood and masonite, painted gray—was installed in Philadelphia at the Institute of Contemporary Art of the University of Pennsylvania in 1974 and then dismantled. (A photograph of this construction appears on the jacket of this book.) The right to refabricate the labyrinth is owned by Count Panza.

one man's trespass, how much more have the grace of God and the free gift in the grace of that one man Jesus Christ abounded for many. And the free gift is not like the effect of that one man's sin. For the judgment following one trespass brought condemnation, but the free gift following many trespasses brings justification. If, because of one man's trespass, death reigned through that one man, how much more will those who receive the abundance of grace and the free gift of righteousness reign in life through the one man Jesus Christ." [21]

Although the second Adam reflects the first Adam, Christ is no mere repetition or restoration of the first man. Christ surpasses Adam in the very act of completing and perfecting the original creation. Paul signals the disproportion between Christ and Adam with the brief phrase πολλῷ μᾶλλον. This "'how much more,' which overturns the 'as . . . so also,' gives to the movement from the first to the second Adam its tension and its temporal impulsion; it excludes the possibility that the 'gift' should be a simple restoration of the order that prevailed before the 'fault'; the gift is the establishment of a new creation."[22] From this point of view, creation, fall, and redemption are integrally related. Each is a moment in a continuous cumulative process that unfolds gradually. Paul's interpretation of the relationship between Adam and Christ points toward "a vision of history according to which man's access to his humanity, his passage from infancy to maturity, both on the individual level and on the level of the species, proceed through awareness of his limitations, his conflicts, and his sufferings. Salvation evolves a history; in symbolic terms: the second Adam is *greater than* the first Adam; the first Adam is *with a view to* the second Adam."[23]

The centrality of the logos in figurative interpretation renders typology logocentric. Though the world often appears enigmatic and experience baffling, beneath this confusion there is reason and order. Events are not contingent and arbitrary but form a meaningful pattern and have a discernible direction. The divine logos is the *thread* that draws together beginning, middle, and end, to form a coherent totality.

## Ariadne's Thread: Poetics of History

The graphic shown above suggests that the labyrinth joins circle, line, and cross. A consideration of the labyrinth and its story leads to unexpected conclusions about the nature and purpose of history. Ariadne was the daughter of Minos, king of Crete, and Pasiphaë, daughter of the sun god, Helios. Poseidon, god of the sea, sent to Minos a snow-white bull, which was to be sacrificed. Minos, however, betrayed Poseidon by refusing to offer the bull to the gods. To punish Minos, Poseidon caused Pasiphaë to commit sexual acts with the bull. The offspring of Pasiphaë and the bull was a fabulous monster, the Minotaur, a creature with the body of a bull and the head of a man. In an effort to contain and control this monstrosity, Minos commissioned the artisan Daedalus to build a labyrinth in which to imprison the Minotaur. This tactic proved to be only partially successful, for the monster continued to terrorize Greece from the center of the labyrinth. Each year, seven Athenian youths and seven maidens had to be fed to the Minotaur. To put an end to this horror, Theseus, son of Aegeus, the king of Athens, journeyed to Crete to slay the uncanny creature. On Crete, Ariadne met Theseus and immediately fell in love with him. Her love led her to reveal to Theseus the secret of the labyrinth, which Daedalus had imparted to her. The granddaughter of Helios gave Theseus a *thread* that enabled him to find and kill the "monster in midweb" and to escape from the labyrinth. A thread, a line, a slender string provided a way out of the labyrinth and furnished something with which to entrap, entangle, and enmesh the monstrous "gift" from the ruler of the sea. The rope that Ariadne threw to Theseus appeared at "the portal of this hellish labyrinth suddenly, as if born out of nothingness." Tossing and turning "*inmitten des Brandes der Brandung*," this slim line floated precariously above at least "70,000 fathoms." What was this thread of Ariadne? What line did she give Theseus to string him along?

Ariadne's lure is a line—a narrative thread that floats atop the "sea of ex"[24] and appears to show a way to the exit from the labyrinth of time. The dissolutive waters of ex harbor Χρόνος, whose initial letter, χ, is "the sign of death." Chronos, the god who always devours his children, bears the mortality of everything that, for the moment, seems to exist. The narrative thread tossed into the raging sea of ex is intended to serve as a lifeline. The aim of (hi)story is to silence the uncanny monster of the labyrinth by erasing, crossing out, X-ing out the mark of Chronos or the sign of death. As the X of χ, the cross is a double cross. X not only conjures up skull and crossbones; it also marks the spot of the cross—Golgotha (Γολγοθᾶ, Gulgoleth, skull). "X is a crossroads, the figure of speech called chiasmus, a kiss, a fish, Christ."[25] Logos is line and line logos. History constitutes "a reaction formation against the discovery of the *seriality* of existence."[26] As such, it is a response to the unsettling encounter with Chronos.

"Chronos," of course, means time. This word, however, carries with it a very specific interpretation of time. When viewed chronically, time appears to be serial succession. Instead of bearing a discernible interrelationship, temporal moments seem to be merely contingent and contiguous. Chronos is re-presented in a chronicle that "simply" registers events in the order in which they appear to occur. No attempt is made to provide narrative coherence or to discover the rationale of the incidents listed. One of the most striking illustrations of the chronometric view of time can be found in medieval annals. The following example is taken from the *Annals of Saint Gall*.

709. Hard winter. Duke Gottfried died.
710. Hard year and deficient in crops.
711.
712. Flood everywhere.
713.
714. Pippin, Mayor of the Palace, died.
715. 716. 717.
718. Charles devastated the Saxons with great destruction.
719.
720. Charles fought against the Saxons.
721. Theudo drove the Saracens out of Aquitaine.
722. Great crops.
723.

724.
725. Saracens came for the first time.
726.
727.
728.
729.
730.
731. Blessed Bede, the presbyter, died.
732. Charles fought against the Saracens at Poitiers on Saturday.
733.
734.

This chronicle raises several issues that deserve comment. First, the annalist is either unable or unwilling "to transform the set of events ordered vertically as a file of annual markers into elements of a linear/horizontal process."[27] Second, as has been noted, no explanation is offered for the interconnection of events. Third, the list exhibits no central subject or governing narrative voice. The reader does not even know who compiled the chronicle or when the events were registered. Finally, the annal appears to be open-ended and therefore infinitely extendible both backward and forward. The chronicle has no identifiable beginning, middle, or end. The annalist simply commences, indicates no organizing center, and abruptly breaks off without really concluding. Consequently, the chronicle does not assume the shape of a story and exhibits no overall unity.

In contrast to chronicle, narrative presents events as interrelated episodes within a coherent pattern, which emerges progressively. A narrative construes scattered events as meaningful by inscribing them in an intelligible story. The logic of narrative "requires one to define every element, every unit of the story, by its functional qualities, that is to say among other things by its correlation with another unity, and to account for the first (in order of narrative time) by the second, and so on."[28] Since narrative transforms chronos into history *sensu strictissimo*, it appears that "where there is no narrative, there is no history."[29] Narrativization involves an act of structuration that can be described as "emplotment."[30] The word "plot" can be either a verb or a noun. In its verbal form, "plot" means both to diagram and to map. To plot points on a graph is to try to establish their precise location so that it is possible to join them with a *continuous* line. To map is to chart an unknown territory; to provide a guide for travelers; to point a way through the wilderness or out of a labyrinth. "Plot," however, can also mean to plan, devise, contrive, or scheme. The noun "plot" refers to "an area or piece of ground"; "a ground-plan of a building, city, field, farm, or any part of the earth's surface"; "a plan or project, secretly contrived by one or more persons to accomplish some wicked, criminal, or illegal purpose"; and, finally, "the plan or scheme of any literary creation." The plot of a narrative, then, can be understood as the ground-plan or secret scheme devised by the A/author to fashion otherwise disparate episodes into a coherent literary creation. To emplot is to encode events "contained in the chronicle as components of specific *kinds* of plot structures."[31] The plot structure "mediates between individual events or incidents and a story as a whole. This mediating role may be read in both ways: a story is *made out* of events to the extent that plot *makes* events *into* a story. An event, consequently, must be more than a singular occurrence, a unique happening. It receives its definition from its contribution to the development of a plot. A story, on the other hand, must be more than an enumeration of events in a serial order, it must make an intelligible whole of the incidents, in such a way that we must always be able to ask what is the point of the story, its 'theme.'"[32] From a narrative perspective, meaning or semantic value is a function of location within a significant whole or an encompassing totality. Parts are configured (*con*, together + *figurare*, to shape) within a whole or comprehended (*com*, together + *prehendere*, to seize) within a totality. Part and whole form a paradoxical relationship in which event "grounds" structure, which "grounds" event, which "grounds" structure, and so on and on. Since narrative strives toward wholeness or totality, it does not tend to be open-ended or infinitely extendible. Narrativization ties together the separate threads of chronicle by forming a centered structure with a definite beginning, middle, and end. This reading of narrative helps to explain the structure of history *as a whole*. Although this general pattern is most evident in its "religious" variants, it also informs most "secular" interpretations of history that have developed in the West. This becomes obvious when further implications of narrativity are considered.

The overall coherence of narrative requires a specific center, which refers back to an inaugural moment and ahead to a conclusive end. Since this pivotal moment is regarded as decisive for the entire temporal process, it is, in effect, kairotic. The kairos forms the prism through which everything that transpires must be filtered. When taken in the most inclusive sense, the "once upon a time" of beginning points to the origin of the entire temporal process. Within the framework of ontotheology, this "time outside of time" is usually imagined in terms of fullness, plenitude, and perfection. This implies that the beginning of time marks the loss of original perfection and initiates a period of exile. Fall, however, anticipates a redemption that constitutes a consummating end. Inscribed betwixt 'n' between the *archē* and *telos*, time is both transitional and transitory. The unity of this "in-between" presupposes a certain consonance of beginning and end. Archeology, in other words, is at the same time a teleology. "The sense of an ending"[33] insures the *followability* of the narrative by providing the dénouement that untangles the story line. The "It is finished" of ending closes the open-endedness of mere succession. This closure is intended to master chronos by uniting beginning, middle, and end to form an inclusive totality within which everything is meaningful.

It is important to recognize that events can be encoded in a variety of ways. Although narrativity *might* embody transcultural structures, a particular story is always bound to a specific culture. When viewed within a complex cultural context, it becomes clear that narrative patterns function like "templates"; they order experience by providing "models of" "reality" and "models for" conduct.[34] Far from being fabulous fabrications or superfluous supplements to that which is, narratives shape a people's sense of self and world. Stories, in other words, "orient the life of a people through time, their life-time, their individual and corporate experience and their sense of style, to the great powers that establish the reality of their world."[35] If a person or a people believes that a particular narrative reveals "the way things really are," the story is deemed sacred. In monotheistic religions, sacred stories can leave no loose ends. The oneness of God and the integrity of self require the unity of history.

From the perspective of traditional Christianity, *history is always story*. Events are not merely chronic or simply successive; they are plotted along a line that has an unambiguous beginning, middle, and end. The Christian drama consists of five acts: Creation, Fall, Incarnation, Crucifixion/Resurrection, and Redemption. After what appears to be a perfect beginning, the action is first "'complicated' in the most sinister fashion," and then "magnificently climaxed" in "a recognition scene in which Creator discloses himself to fallen creature in a face and figure like his own." After this turning point, "the plot moves inexorably to the ultimate resolution in which the villains . . . get their just deserts and the heroes and heroines live happily ever after!"[36] The plot of this story is, quite clearly, logocentric. Just as the critical turning point in Augustine's personal history had been his encounter with the living God, so for all Christians the "hinge" of history or "the temporal *mid-point* of the entire historical process" is the "Christ-event."[37] This event enjoys a "privileged status" and is "endowed with explanatory force."[38] For the believer, the revelatory *figure* of Jesus is the intelligible event that makes all other events intelligible. Christ, in other words, is the logos that discloses the logic and rationale of time as a whole.

As we have seen, typological interpretation locates events and persons at the intersection of vectors that extend back to formative occurrences and point ahead to transformative occasions. This interplay of recollection and expectation suggests that the center marked by the logos casts a backward and a forward glance. Christ stands midway between the garden and the complete realization of the kingdom. From the midst of history, the supralapsarian condition of man appears to be one of innocence and purity. In the garden, God and man are *present* to each other in the immediate transparency of *voice*. Since man "originally" is unstained by sin and untainted by guilt, he needs no carnal mediator to establish a relationship with God. All of this changes with the fall. Forever exiled from paradise, man is left to anticipate the *full presence* of God promised in the *parousia* ( = "presence"). Insofar as the incarnate logos is regarded as one with God, divine presence no longer seems to be "deferred." Rather it is believed to be actually present in the present. The end, it is said, is already "at hand." This end, we have noted, is not the simple repetition or restoration of the beginning. The end surpasses the beginning in the very act of completing and fulfilling the original creation. The difference between beginning and end creates the tension that is characteristic of history and lends decisive significance to all that transpires between origin and conclusion.

Whether the plot of history is explicitly or only implicitly logocentric, interpreters tend to regard the narrative line as *discovered within* events rather than *imposed upon* them from *without*. Analysts who represent other-wise divergent points of view are able to agree that there is a logic to experience and a logos, implicit in the temporal process, that can, in principle, be discerned. As Nietzsche points out, Hegel, the philosopher in whose thought history achieves decisive closure, insists on this statement: "That at the bottom of history, and particularly of world history, there is a final aim, and that this has actually been realized in it and is being real-ized—the plan of Providence—that there is *reason* in history: that is to be shown philosophically and thus as altogether necessary. . . . A history without such an aim and without such a point of view would be merely a feeble-minded pastime of the imagination, not even a children's fairy tale, for even children demand some interest in stories, i.e., some aim one can at least feel, and the relation of the occurrences and actions to it."[39] In sum-marizing the logic of Hegel's position, Nietzsche suggests an alternative reading of history. "Conclusion: Every story must have an aim, hence also the history of a people and the history of the world. That means: because there is 'world history' there must also be some aim in the world pro-cess. . . . That my life has no aim is evident from the accidental nature of its origin; that *I can posit an aim for myself* is another matter."[40]

This brief, penetrating remark heightens a suspicion that has been gath-ering throughout our consideration of history, story, and narrative. It is possible that there *is* more "imagination" and "fairy tale" in history than most people are willing to acknowledge. History, as well as autobiography, appears to be the work of creative imagination. The imagination is not only reproductive; it is, more importantly, productive. The productive imagina-tion involves two dialectically related rhythms: analysis and synthesis. The analytic imagination "dissolves, diffuses, dissipates in order to recreate."[41] When exercising itself synthetically, the imagination configures parts to form new wholes. In its "historical" capacity, the analytic imagination dissolves the seriality of chronos and prepares the way for the synthetic imagination to fashion a comprehensive narrative. "The historian's picture of his subject, whether that subject be a sequence of events or a past state of things, thus appears as a web of imaginative construction stretched between certain fixed points." [42]

To say that history is an "imaginative construction" is not to imply that it is "unreal." The fanciful dimension of history does, however, suggest that "reality" is, in some sense, imaginative. The careful examination of history subverts the sharp distinction between historical fact and fiction. To the extent that history involves narrative it is, like the centered self, ineluctably literary rather than literal. In other words, Ariadne's thread turns out to be a *poetic* (ποίησις, a making, creation, poetry; a poem) line. Beginning, middle, and end, as well as the connective narrative thread, are "summational fictions" [43] or "poetic constructions, and as such [are] dependent upon the modality of the figurative language used to give them the aspect of coherence." [44] Though history and the novel are usually opposed as fact and fiction, the line between them is actually quite obscure. There is really a close resemblance between the historian and the novelist. "Each of them makes it his business to construct a picture which is partly a narrative of events, partly a description of situations, exhibition of motives, analysis of characters. Each aims at making his picture a coherent whole, where every character and every situation is so bound up with the rest that this character in this situation cannot but act in this way, and we cannot imagine him as acting otherwise. The novel and the history must both . . . make sense; nothing is admissible in either except what is necessary, and the judge of this necessity is in both cases the imagination." [45] This way of viewing the relation between "historical fact" and "narrative fiction" seems to run counter to common sense and to undermine the practice of many careful and responsible historians. "In most discussions of historical discourse, the two levels conventionally distinguished are those of the *facts* (data or information) on the one side and the *interpretation* (explanation or story told about the facts) on the other. What this conventional distinction obscures is the difficulty of discriminating within the discourse between these two levels. It is not the case that a fact is one thing and its interpretation another. The fact is presented where and how it is in the discourse in order to sanction the interpretation to which it is meant to contribute. And the interpretation derives its force of plausibility from the order and manner in which the facts are presented in the discourse." [46]

In general terms, which will be elaborated in later chapters, we have no access to hard, immediate, irrefutable facts, historical or otherwise. "Facts" are *always* "filtered" through an interpretive grid. Since this matrix includes the norms and criteria by which facts themselves are established, bare data are never visible. "The web of imaginative construction is something far more . . . powerful than we have hitherto realized. So far from relying for its validity upon the support of given facts, it actually serves as the touchstone by which we decide whether alleged facts are genuine." [47] In view of this insight, it is difficult to "escape the conclusion that 'the fact can exist only linguistically, as a term in a discourse,' although we behave as if it were a simple reproduction of something or other on another plane of existence altogether, some extra-structural 'reality.'"[48] The recognition of the apparent fictiveness of all putative facts carries significant implications for the understanding of history.

As a distant relative of Christian typology, history remains within the shadow of logocentrism. Both historian and believer insist that history is a coherent process whose rationale is comprehensible. Beneath or behind appearances a logic is *present*, and it either reveals itself or can be deciphered through patient investigation. It has become evident, however, that a careful consideration of the role of the imagination in the discursive strategies of history, story, and narrative raises serious questions about the assumptions and conclusions of such "figurative interpretation." The logos, it seems, is as much invented as revealed, as much created as discovered. As a result of the imaginative activity through which chronology assumes narrative coherence, history is irreducibly literary and inescapably artistic. The interplay of typology, tropology, and history suggests that *history itself is a trope*.[49] Instead of being descriptively neutral and factually accurate, historical discourse appears to be *imaginative* and *rhetorical*. This tentative "conclusion" raises at least as many questions as it answers. If history is a trope and historical discourse is rhetorical, toward what end does the imaginative rhetorician direct his or her powers of persuasion? Why do we seem compelled to tell and retell stories? Who narrates history? To whom are stories told? For whom is the story of history recounted? In short, why do people *make* history?

## Saving Presence

Suspended between a past that has been lost and a future not yet possessed, history is the domain of discontent and restlessness, of striving and strife. Within the bounds of history, dissatisfied and unhappy subjects struggle to save presence by seeking saving presence. This Faustian quest represents a further effort to deny death. In this case, the refusal to accept death takes the form of the struggle to *master* Chronos. Paradoxically, the making of history is the suppression of time. Since Chronos is one of the masks of death, it appears that "man aggressively builds immortal cultures in order to fight death."[50] To the extent that history arises from the *denial* of death, it is a product of "No-saying." History, in other words, always involves *repression*.

The Nay that is the driving force of history finds voice in the repression of the otherness that lurks both *without* and *within*. The historical effort to dominate the other (in all of its guises) is the enactment of the *causa sui* project on the temporal plane. This contest entails "the transformation of the consciousness of death into a struggle to appropriate the life of another human being at the risk of one's own life."[51] Perpetually dissatisfied, the historical actor repeatedly seeks fulfillment through the other subjects he attempts to control. As will be seen in greater detail in later chapters, the domineering subject either consciously or unconsciously experiences the no, hole, gap, space, or absence within as "secondary" rather than "primal." Lack, therefore, is regarded as a deficiency that should not be or as an emptiness that ought to be filled. When carried to completion, the pursuit of mastery proves to be a self-contradictory undertaking in which an agent simultaneously tries to deny deficiency and attempts to satisfy need. The historical subject's apparent self-affirmation (which is covert self-negation) is mediated by the negation of other subjects and objects. Though intended to demonstrate self-sufficiency, the effort to subjugate otherness actually discloses incurable need. The master who *needs* to be master is no master at all. The historical agent's struggle for mastery and quest for domination indicate irrepressible deficiency by revealing the *need* to appropriate otherness. What seems to be an essential cure really serves to deepen the wound. The Nay to Nay ends by reconfirming the No within every Yes. In this way, the denial of death inverts itself and subverts the purpose of history. The figure of Chronos can no more be erased from history than the roaring of the sea of ex can be drowned out by constantly reciting the lines of a story.

We have seen that if Ariadne's thread is carefully traced, a necessary relation between history and narrative eventually emerges. When the analysis of the struggle for domination is extended to the question of the function of narrative, it becomes clear that the narration of history also arises from the need to achieve a position of mastery. The goal of the narrative transformation of chronicle is actually the enjoyment of plenitude, i.e., a total presence, undisturbed by difference and absence. "In the middest, we look for a fullness of time, for beginning, middle, and end in concord."[52] By now it should be clear that this search is no idle pastime; it is a matter of life and death. The desperate struggle to save presence demonstrates that historical narrative "is not only linked to linearity, but to an entire *system* of implications (teleology, eschatology, elevating and interiorizing, accumulation of meaning, a certain type of traditionality, a certain concept of continuity, of truth, etc.)."[53] As will become evident in part two, this cluster of concepts informs the typical Christian vision of history as "the place of passage, the bridge between two moments of full presence."[54] For the moment, it is sufficient to recognize that, by neatly tying together beginning, middle, and end, the successful story line produces the "pleromatic conformity"[55] that seems to satisfy (at least temporarily) exiles who seek fulfillment.

It is, of course, common to distinguish interpretations of time by juxta-

posing the metaphors of circle and line. Frequently it is argued that in the
East time is viewed as a circle in which beginning and end coincide. In the
West, by contrast, time tends to be regarded as a linear process in which
the end surpasses the beginning. In my analysis of the typological account
of the first and second Adam, I stressed the significance of the linear,
progressive view of history for the Christian imagination and for Western
consciousness in general. Any facile opposition between circular and linear
views of time, however, obscures important similarities that these two
perspectives share. Both circle and line are *forms of closure* and *figures of
plenitude* that serve as *totalizing metaphors*. We have already discovered that
"the image of the line, in whatever region of narrative terms it is used, tends
to be logocentric, monological. The model of the line is a powerful part of
the traditional language of Occidental metaphysics. It cannot easily be
detached from its implications or from the functions it has within that
system. Narrative event follows narrative event in a purely metonymic line,
but the series tends to organize itself or to be organized into a causal
chain. . . . The end of the story is the retrospective revelation of the law of
the whole. That law is an underlying 'truth' which ties all together in an
inevitable sequence revealing a hitherto hidden figure in the carpet. The
image of the line tends always to imply the norm of a single continuous
unified structure determined by one external organizing principle. This
principle holds the whole line together, gives it its law, controls its progressive extension, curving or straight, with some *archē*, *telos*, or ground.
Origin, goal, or base: all three come together in the gathering movement of
the *logos*. . . ."[56] This gathering or collecting issues in a "concord-fiction"
that seeks to "defeat time"[57] by inscribing temporal dispersion within the
closed space of narrative structure.

Just as the self-reflexion of the autobiographer interiorizes experiences
that otherwise seem only externally related, so the plot of history assembles
apparently discrete episodes into a coherent whole. Insofar as the logos of
events is believed to be implicit instead of imposed, this collection is
re-collection. Such historical narration "seeks fullness and continuity in an
order of events."[58] Its lines, therefore, are closely knit so as to prevent
anything from slipping away. The thread of the story overcomes discontinuity by stitching together distant incidents. In this way, the fab-
ric(ation) of narrative covers holes, fills gaps, cures wounds, and spans
intervals. Since it presupposes closure, "historical narrative, as against the
chronicle, reveals to us a world that is putatively 'finished,' done with, over,
and yet not dissolved, not falling apart. In this world, reality wears the
mask of a meaning, the completeness and fullness of which we can only
*imagine*, never experience."[59]

Like every effort to dominate, history and its narration represent a
colonial enterprise. The logocentrism of history implies that narrativity
functions to *humanize* time by giving it form.[60] The story of history is

supposed to tame the grotesque monster that presides over/under/within the labyrinth. Historical narration reflects the effort to ease the trauma of dislocation by weaving scattered events into a seamless web. The subject entangled in history longs to be a faithful son instead of a nomadic orphan. Unable to bear the uncertainty of ceaseless wandering, the exile seeks the security that comes from feeling at home in all places and at all times. Historical narrative serves such domestic ends by familiarizing the strange and settling the unsettling. "[W]e experience the 'fictionalization' of history as an 'explanation' for the same reason that we experience great fiction as an illumination of a world that we inhabit along with the author. In both we recognize the forms by which consciousness both constitutes and colonizes the world it seeks to inhabit."[61]

In a manner similar to other struggles for mastery, this colonial pursuit finally subverts itself. The "colonized" again returns to unsettle the "colonizer." While intended to tie and bind the ghost that haunts the labyrinth, the narrative line floating on the sea of ex actually appears to be "a great sailing ship gliding silently along like a ghost." From this point of view, history constitutes the "intricate evasion of as"[62] that results from the failure to accept the primordiality of lack. Contrary to expectation, the repressive quest for presence ends by disclosing the irreducibility of absence and the inevitability of death. Absolute plenitude and total presence are nowhere to be found. Since the "fullness" of the "origin" can be present only as *absent*, primal plenitude is always already lost. In other words, there is *always* a serpent in the garden. The myth of origin represents the attempt to efface the trace by making loss secondary rather than "original." Deficiency is believed to be the result of a fall or fissure, a breach or break. To be impure is not merely to be sick; it is to be guilty. In short, stain is sin. This archeology and etiology imply a teleology. History is an "archeoteleological"[63] process that constitutes a "forward-moving *recherche du temps perdu*."[64] The goal of this searching process is salvation—a cure that is supposed to bring health (*salus*) by closing the wound within. But the search inevitably fails. For homesick exiles, the absence of origin transforms life into an endgame in which one tries to *kill* time by telling stories.

> Clov:  The end is terrific!
> Hamm:  I prefer the middle.
>         Is it not time for my pain-killer?
> Clov:  No!
>         I'll leave you.
> Hamm:  It's time for my story. Do you want to listen to my story?
> Clov:  No.
> Hamm:  Ask my father if he wants to listen to my story.
> Clov:  He's asleep.
> Hamm:  Wake him.
> Clov:  He doesn't want to listen to your story.

Hamm:  I'll give him a bon-bon.
Clov:   He wants a sugar-plum.
Hamm:  He'll get a sugar-plum.
Clov:   It's a deal.
         Do you believe in the life to come?
Hamm:  Mine was always that.

". . . the life to come . . . always that." The end, it seems, never arrives; it is "infinitely deferred." [65]

The very *search* for presence, through which the historical actor attempts to deny absence and embrace plenitude, testifies to the absence of presence and the "presence" of absence. As players of the endgame gradually discover, the route mapped by the story line marks the way of "unhappy consciousness." The poet explains to the despairing exile: "Yukel, you have never felt at ease in your skin. You have never been *here*, but always *elsewhere*, ahead of yourself or behind like winter in the eyes of autumn or summer in the eyes of spring, in the past or in the future like those syllables whose passage from night to day is so much like the lightning that it merges with the movement of the pen." [66] Never *here*, ever *elsewhere* . . . the eyes of Yukel are always cast *beyond*—toward either the past or future. The time of Yukel is the time of the law promulgated and enforced by the sovereign Lord. *Always* exiled between beginning and end, the unhappy person nostalgically remembers the fulfillment he believes once was and expectantly awaits the satisfaction he hopes will be. Anticipated satisfaction, however, never becomes fully present. It repeatedly escapes one's grasp. This elusive beyond creates a tension between what is and what ought to be. The persistent opposition between "reality" and "ideality" lends a saddened, nay, melancholy, tone to time. To unhappy eyes, even the fresh leaves of spring are tinged with brown. Suffering discontent and dissatisfaction, the unhappy person desperately longs for saving presence. To overcome such melancholy and move toward fulfillment, the historical subject believes it is necessary to transcend *itself*. Appearances to the contrary notwithstanding, this struggle for transcendence is always acted out in the shadow of the wholly other God. As totally self-identical, fully perfect, and completely self-present, the divine Other is eternally *beyond*, always *elsewhere*, and absolutely *transcendent*. This transcendent God is the ruler of history. In His domain, subjects are condemned to the anxious search for transcendence.

The end of history not only presupposes the death of the transcendent God and the disappearance of the sovereign self; it also requires the overcoming of unhappy consciousness. While history "begins" with the incapacity or reluctance to say "Yea to Nay," it "ends" with the ability and willingness to say *"Amen—So be it."* The affirmation that opens the end of history inevitably entails negation. This Yea is the Nay to the "No to No." Put differently, the Yes that ends history is the denial of the denial of death.

Such "Yea-saying" is *radical*, for it affirms the No that is inseparable from every Yes. The coincidence of Yea and Nay that marks the end of history results in humankind's "liberation from the neurotic obsession with the past and the future; it is a way of living in the present but also a way of dying. Hence the ultimate defect of all heavens with immortality beyond the grave is that in them there is no death; by this token such visions betray their connection with repression of life." [67] When it is realized that only one strong enough to die can live, it becomes possible to embrace death as grace—grace which is, as we shall see, mazing.

The death of the Alpha and the Omega, the disappearance of the self, and the overcoming of unhappy consciousness combine to fray the fabric of history. When it is impossible to locate a definite beginning and a decisive end, the narrative line is lost and the story seems pointless. *Endgame* now appears to be a play about ending endgames. The "end" of the endgame, however, is at the same time the beginning of an unending game. From the perspective of the end of history, the "final" plot seems to be "that there is no plot." [68] This unraveling of Ariadne's thread points toward the closure of the book.

# 4

## Closure of the Book

Like all men of the Library, I have traveled in my youth, I have wandered in search of a book, perhaps a catalogue of catalogues . . . .

If there is no longer a Father, why tell stories? Doesn't every narrative lead back to Oedipus?

Books.—What good is a book that does not even carry us beyond all books?

Yet, all that Hegel thought within this horizon, all, that is, except eschatology, may be reread as a meditation on writing. Hegel is *also* the thinker of irreducible difference. He rehabilitated thought as the *memory productive* of signs. And he reintroduced, as I shall try to show elsewhere, the essential necessity of the written trace in a philosophical—that is to say Socratic—discourse that has always believed it possible to do without it; the last philosopher of the book and the first thinker of writing.

### Authorship: Mimesis and Poiesis

Theodorus saw the whole life of Sextus at one glance, and as in a stage presentation. There was a great volume of writings in the hall: Theodorus could not refrain from asking what that meant. It is the history of this world which we are now visiting, the Goddess told him; it is the book of its fates. You have seen a number on the forehead of Sextus. Look in this book for the place which it indicates. Theodorus looked for it, and found there the history of Sextus in a form more ample than the outline he had seen. Put your finger on any line you please, Pallas said to him, and you will see represented actually in all its detail that which the line broadly indicates. He obeyed, and he saw coming into view all the characteristics of a portion of the life of Sextus.[1]

The universe (which others call the Library) is composed of an indefinite and perhaps infinite number of hexagonal galleries, with vast air shafts between, surrounded by very low railings. From any of the hexagons one can see, interminably, the upper and lower floors. The distribution of the galleries is invariable. Twenty shelves, five long shelves per side, cover all the sides except two; their height, which is the distance from floor to ceiling, scarcely exceeds that of a normal bookcase. One of the free sides leads to a narrow hallway which opens onto another gallery, identical to the first and to all the rest. To the left and right of the hallways there are two very small closets. In the first, one may sleep standing up; in another, satisfy one's fecal necessities. Also through here passes a spiral stairway, which sinks abysmally and soars upwards to remote distances. In the hallway there is a mirror which faithfully duplicates all appearances. Men usually infer from this mirror that the Library is not infinite (if it really were, why this illusory duplication?); I prefer to dream that its polished surfaces represent and promise the infinite . . . . [2]

Leibniz's parable appears in his well-known book entitled *Theodicy: Essays on the Goodness of God, the Freedom of Man, and the Origin of Evil*. In Western theology, theodicy is usually understood as the vindication of divine justice and holiness in the face of what seems to be obvious evil. Although theodicy appears to express predominantly theological concerns, it is actually motivated by essentially anthropological interests. Claims to the contrary notwithstanding, the issue that theodicy addresses is less the holiness and justice of God than the intelligibility, hospitability, and coherence of *man's* world. Despite seemingly senseless suffering, unaccountable inequity, and baffling paradoxes, Leibniz believes that the world is reasonable. Events are not finally opaque, dumb, and senseless.[3] Furthermore, Leibniz is persuaded that the rational order of things is inscribed in something like a "book of fates." In this book-like world, each part mirrors the whole, and all parts taken together form a coherent and comprehensible system. The integrity of this totality is assured by a preestablished harmony, foreordained by God. By reading the pre-scribed Leibnizian book, it seems possible to find relief from the uncomfortable suspicion that the world and human life are meaningless. In this way, the "theocentric" book really serves to humanize and domesticate the world.

Borges's meditation on the book appears in "The Library of Babel" and is included in a collection of writings that bears the title *Labyrinths*. The imaginative description of this bizarre "library" is not really a story and surely cannot be regarded as systematic. It is significant that "The Library of Babel" is not an integral part of either a more comprehensive narrative or a systematic treatise. Had he chosen to write a preface to *Labyrinths*, Borges might well have insisted: "This (therefore) will not have been a book. Still less, despite appearances, will it have been a collection of . . . 'essays' whose itinerary it would be time, after the fact, to recognize; whose continuity and underlying laws could now be pointed out; indeed, whose overall concept or meaning could at last, with all the insistence required on such occasions, be squarely set forth."[4] *Labyrinths*, as "The Library of Babel" indicates, refuses such comprehensive/comprehensible completion.

Though many people seem to believe that the world is a book or even a circumscribed library, bound and ordered by "the catalogue of catalogues," Borges's "universe" is "composed of an indefinite and perhaps infinite number of hexagonal galleries, with vast air shafts between, surrounded by very low railings." Instead of a coherent and integrated system governed by a preestablished harmony, the library of Babel is an *endless* labyrinth. The description of the labyrinthian library is reminiscent of a carnival fun house. The labyrinth is haunted by uncanny sounds, "senseless cacophonies," "verbal jumbles," "incoherencies"; it has "enigmatical volumes," "inexhaustible stairways," "latrines," and spiral staircases that sink "abysmally" and soar "upwards to remote distances." Finally, like all fun houses, the labyrinth is filled with countless mirrors. Most people infer from these mirrors that the library is not infinite. But they are mistaken; the limited image they see is but a reflection of themselves. Borges insists that the play of mirrors is without end. The hall of mirrors reflects an infinity of signifiers and thus points to the necessary incompletion of the library. Borges certainly does not deny the evident attraction that the Leibnizian book exercises on readers. He writes: "When it was proclaimed that the Library contained all books, the first impression was one of extravagant happiness. All men felt themselves to be masters of an intact and secret treasure. There was no personal or world problem whose eloquent solution did not exist in some hexagon. The universe was justified, the universe suddenly usurped the unlimited dimensions of hope." Others were less sanguine. Some even went mad—either as a result of their inability to find the book or because the notion of the book had become intolerable.

Many people enjoy the fun house only as long as they are convinced that there is an exit. Such individuals believe that the book pre-scribes a cure. The nausea that vertiginous uncertainty creates is settled by the promise of certainty. The absence or illegibility of an effective prescription leaves pilgrims and prodigals to suffer incurable disease. For other carnival-goers, the assurance of an exit takes all the fun out of the fun house. These wary readers are persuaded that the only thing more disconcerting than uncertainty is certainty. A world in which every person has a number on his or her forehead is not only a world in which there is no fun; it is a world plagued by oppressive despair.

*          *          *          *

Christianity is a religion of the book, and the West is a book culture. Like God, self, and history, the notion of the book is, in an important sense, theological. Since the book is part of the theological network that is now unraveling, its closure is being rewritten repeatedly. Hegel, who wrote "the death of God," registered the disappearance of the self, and inscribed the end of history, is "the last philosopher of the book." The Hegelian

System both completes and subverts the book. In realizing this subversion, however, Hegel surpasses the book and becomes "the first thinker of writing." "In effect I believe that Hegel's text is necessarily fissured; that it is something more and other than the circular closure of its representation. It is not reduced to a content of philosophemes, it also necessarily produces a powerful writing operation, a remainder of writing, whose strange relationship to the philosophical content of Hegel's text must be reexamined, that is, the movement by means of which his text exceeds its meaning, permits itself to be turned away from, to return to, and to repeat itself outside its self-identity."[5]

The closure of the book does not indicate a cultural shift from the cold medium of print to hot audio and video media. Nor does it suggest that Westerners no longer read and hence are becoming illiterate, though this might well be so. To the contrary, the closure of the book is concurrent with a proliferation of print and a seemingly endless multiplication of words and images. In the midst of this graphic explosion, many of the most thoughtful writers insist that it is no more possible to write a book than it is to paint a portrait or to compose a tonic melody. And yet the book seems to linger. Its closure, in fact, is usually bound in/to a book. Many modern and postmodern literary works are actually "books" about the impossibility of the book. In view of the long-standing religious and cultural significance of the book, what transpires between the covers of nonbooks and antinovels is extremely important for every religion of the book and for any book culture.

To comprehend what is at stake in the closure of the book, it is necessary to understand what is involved in the notion of the book. *Book* derives from the Old Teutonic *bōk*, which means writing tablet, leaf, or sheet. *Bōk*, in turn, is generally believed to be related to the name of the beech tree (Old English *bōc* and Old Norse *bōk*). This association suggests that "inscriptions were first made on beechen tablets, or cut into the bark of beech trees." "The tree of engraving and grafting"[6] also forms the stem from which the word *Bible* grows. The Greek *biblos* refers to the inner bark of the papyrus and designates a paper, roll, scroll, or book. The circularity of the tree trunk and scroll are carried over in the Latin word *volumen*, which means coil, wreath, or roll. A volume can refer to either "a roll of parchment or papyrus containing written matter, or a collection of written or printed sheets bound together so as to form a book."

A book, therefore, can be seen as something like a writing pad or an engraving tablet, which, having been taken from the trunk of a tree, suggests a certain cylindricality or circularity. The circularity of the volume reflects the closure of the book. "The idea of the book is the idea of a totality, finite or infinite, of the signifier."[7] A book is not merely an aggregate of dry leaves pressed between two covers. Rather, a book is a living whole in which all parts are integrally related as members of a single organism. Inasmuch as the book forms an ordered totality, it is, like history, logocentric. Although characterized in many different ways, the logos of the book invariably constitutes the principle of preestablished harmony, which forms the structural foundation of the volume's unity and coherence.

As an organic totality of signifiers closed in and upon itself, the book achieves its most complete articulation in the encyclopedia. The encyclopedia makes explicit the inseparability of line and circle that is implied by the volume and wound up in the scroll. *Encyclopedia* is a Latin term borrowed from the Greek ἐγκύκλιος παιδεία, which specified the circle of arts and sciences that formed the course of study that Greek youths went through before beginning professional training. Accordingly, encyclopedia means, first, "the circle of learning or a general course" and, second, "a literary work containing extensive information on all branches of knowledge." Despite the highly influential work of leading eighteenth-century French "atheists," the encyclopedia remains "thoroughly theological in essence and origin." Within this Book of books, "all finite books would become opuscules modeled after the great divine opus, so many arrested speculations, so many tiny mirrors catching a single grand image. The ideal form of this would be a book of total science, a book of absolute knowledge that digested, recited, and substantially ordered all books, going through the whole cycle of knowledge."[8] The theological dimension of the encyclopedia becomes explicit in nineteenth-century Romanticism. Novalis, for instance, compiled notes toward a supreme book:

> . . . The description of the Bible is properly my undertaking—or better, the *theory of the Bible*—the art of the Bible and the theory of nature. (The raising of a book to the level of the Bible.)
>
> The fully executed Bible is a *complete, perfectly organized library*—the plan of the Bible is at the same time the plan of the library. The authentic *plan*—the authentic *formula*—indicates at the same time its own genesis—its own usage, etc. (complete *file* concerning the use of each item—along with its instructions and description).
>
> Perfectly finished books make courses unnecessary. The book is Nature inscribed on a staff (like music) and *completed*.[9]

But, alas, Novalis never finished the book. That task was left for Hegel.

Just as Hegel's *Phenomenology of Spirit* realizes the disappearance of the self and his *Philosophy of History* marks the end of history, so his *Encyclopedia of the Philosophical Sciences* brings the closure of the book. Hegel is highly critical of the unsystematic form of Diderot's *Encyclopedia*. He maintains that the French encyclopedists were bound by a mechanistic view of the world and thus were blind to the rational coherence and necessary connection of all things. True knowledge, for Hegel, is *genuinely* encyclopedic. "The encyclopedia of philosophy," however, "must not be confounded with ordinary encyclopedias. An ordinary encyclopedia does not pretend to be more than an aggregation of sciences, regulated by no principle. . . . In an aggregate like this, the several branches of knowledge owe their place in the encyclopedia to extrinsic reasons, and their unity is therefore artificial: they are *arranged*, but we cannot say they form a *system*." [10] A system must be internally organized and can be neither incomplete nor unfinished. The *Encyclopedia*, as the word itself implies, must assume the shape of a circle. From Hegel's point of view, "Each of the parts of philosophy is a philosophical whole, a circle rounded and complete in itself. In each of these parts, however, the philosophical Idea is found in a particular specificality or medium. The single circle, because it is a real totality, bursts through the limits imposed by its special medium, and gives rise to a wider circle. The whole of philosophy in this way resembles a circle of circles." [11] This circle of circles is traced in the *Encyclopedia*. Hegel's all-inclusive book is a perfectly coherent totality that is inwardly differentiated. The Hegelian System consists of three parts: *The Science of Logic*, *The Philosophy of Nature*, and *The Philosophy of Spirit*. The three divisions of the *Encyclopedia* form an organic whole, which achieves closure by bringing together beginning and end. Since all parts are comprehended within a systematic totality, philosophy is necessarily "scientific." Unscientific thought cannot be philosophical, just as incomplete understanding cannot be true knowledge. The structural foundation of the *Encyclopedia* is nothing other than the logos. The rational structure of the logos is disclosed in logic and embodied in nature and spirit. Hegel insists that "This Notion is not sensuously intuited or represented; it is solely an object, a product and content of *thinking*, and is the absolute self-subsistent object, the logos, the reason of that which is, the truth of what we call things; it is least of all the logos which should be left outside the science of logic." [12] Since the book comes to completion in the encyclopedia, it is evident that the book is logocentric.

It is important to recognize that when the book is normative, theology tends to be systematic. Western theology demonstrates an irrepressible urge to become systematic or even scientific. Like Hegel's *Encyclopedia* or any other "good" book, systematic theology is tripartite, i.e., trinitarian. The systematic theologian attempts to shape his work into a complete whole, with a clear beginning, middle, and end. For the Christian, the center of the book is the incarnate logos. This logos points back to creation (beginning) and forward to the kingdom (end). As we have seen in our analysis of historical narrative, the same logos is present and active in the moments of creation, incarnation, and redemption. This omnipresent logos is the foundation that structures the systematic theologian's book. If, however, we now stand "beyond" the closure of the book, then it seems likely that systematic theology is at an end. Like the novelist who can no longer finish novels, the painter who cannot frame pictures, and the composer who hears no harmony, the theologian who realizes the implications of the closure of the book must become a "writer."

Throughout most of its life, the book has been regarded as a representation of "the way things really are," not as an arbitrary construct. Hegel, I have stressed, argues that the logos is "the truth of what we call things." [13] He repeatedly claims that reason "is *in* the world." Novalis' formulation is more typical: "The book is Nature" or, conversely, nature is a book. Though subject to a variety of readings, the belief in the bookishness of nature recurs repeatedly in Western thought. Despite this remarkable persistence, it has rarely been noted that the belief that nature constitutes a book implies that things both display grammatical relations and are syntactically ordered. If reason is believed to be *in* things themselves, this grammar and syntax appear to be "natural." It is possible to maintain that this "natural" language is, nonetheless, created. Such linguistic creativity would appear to be possible only for the one who creates nature itself. For this reason, belief in God and faith in grammar often seem to be inseparable. [14] To believe in God is to have faith in grammar, and to have faith in grammar is to believe in God. The close connection between deity and grammar can be further clarified by considering certain aspects of the notion of authorship.

Every "proper" book bears a signature—a signature that is a sign or mark. The distinguishing mark of the sign is its tendency to point beyond itself to something it signifies. In the case of a book, the sign points to the one who signs. Signature, in other words, refers to author. When the world is viewed as a book, it is possible to imagine that God is its Author. The word *author* derives from the Latin *auctor* and is indirectly related to *augere*, which means "to make grow, originate, promote, and increase." An author is a "person who originates or gives existence to anything; an inventor, constructor, or founder." As such, the author is a creative subject or generative father who is the origin, fount, and source from which seminal fluids (black as well as white) flow. Since He [*sic*] enjoys the privilege of origin (which is the origin of privilege), the author is authoritative. He not only is "the person on whose authority a statement is made" but also is "the one who has authority over others; a director, ruler, commander." As primal authority, the author exercises proprietary rights. Unless voluntarily or involuntarily relinquished, the author *owns* his work; it is his personal possession. Authorship implies ownership, though ownership does not always entail authorship. Through the exercise of personal authority, the author seeks to establish "a limitation of the cancerous and dangerous proliferation of significations within a world where one is thrifty not only with one's resources and riches, but also with one's discourses and their significations. The author is the principle of thrift in the proliferation of meaning." [15] As a thrifty proprietor of personal possessions, the author "impedes the free circulation, the free manipulation, the free composition, decomposition, and recomposition" of the book. By so doing, the author attempts to secure the value of paper currency.

The dynastic relationship of author and book suggests a close connection between authorship and an economy based on private property. That which is created bears the mark of its creator. It is stamped with a ©. Unless purloined, the author's letters must be either bought or borrowed with permission. The author's interest, in other words, is monetary as well as literary. Even in selling and lending, the author/owner resists releasing his possession completely. The child is forced to carry the name of the father—a name that is closely guarded by the bar(s) of legality: ". . ." In order to defend his property and maintain legal propriety, the author must be sure to sign his work with his proper name. Signature—that is, a signature that is not forged or inscribed between quotation marks—is believed to establish authorship and to protect property. It is, of course, always possible that the authority of the author actually derives from the *erasure* of ever-present quotation marks. If all signatures are counterfeit, a particular signature would not so much etch a birthmark as cut the umbilical cord that had seemed to join parent and child.

Quite clearly, God is not just any author, nor is His book just any book. God is the Author of authors who dictates the Book of books. For this reason, God is the Author to whom all authors finally defer, and His Book is the Book to which all books ultimately refer. Within this economy, books do not possess intrinsic worth but are valuable to the extent that they point beyond themselves to the Book. In different terms, books are signs that refer to a "transcendental signified." By pre-scribing or pro-gramming all true books, this referent forms the stable center or "bottom line" of every sign. The Book constitutes the "prose of the world" or the "already said" that "imprints every human course and recourse with its secondarity." [16] Books always rewrite the Book. They are re-visions of a putatively "original" vision. "The Model of the Book, the Model Book, doesn't it amount to the absolute adequation of presence and representation, to the *truth* (*homoiosis* or *adaequatio*) of the thing and the thought about the thing, in the sense in which truth first emerges in divine creation before being reflected by finite knowledge? Nature, God's Book, appeared to the medieval mind to be a written form consonant with divine thought and speech, true to God's understanding as Logos, the truth that speaks and hears itself speak, the locus of archetypes, the relay point of the *topos noetos* or the *topos ouranios*. A writing that was representative and true, adequate to its model and to itself, Nature was also an ordered totality, the volume of a book weighty with meaning, giving itself to the reader, which must also mean the hearer, as if it were a spoken word, passing from ear to ear and from mind to mind. 'The eye listens' . . . when the book has as its vocation the proffering of divine logos." [17]

To the extent that books are reeditions of the "original" script, they are inevitably mimetic. Mimesis involves signified and signifier in a relationship of presentation and re-presentation. The purpose of the book is to render present the discourse of the world by bringing about the absolute proximity or perfect transparency of object to subject. Though not always obvious, this aim implies the self-negation of the book. In the course of approximating its goal, the book inscribes a paradoxical "progression" toward its own effacement. Perfect mimesis is no longer mimesis. If imitation were to realize itself completely, it would negate itself by actually becoming the thing imitated. Mimesis, therefore, necessarily bears witness to its own failure. Representation, it turns out, *is not* presentation. Instead of presenting presence, mimesis testifies to absence by tracing and retracing ever elusive presence.

The negation of mimesis is evident in two other aspects of the book. We have seen that the bond between book and Book entails the relation of signifier to signified. The Book of the world is a sign pointing beyond itself to its signatory or author. The Author is never immediately available or directly accessible; He is present only through His Word. Such presence inevitably involves a certain absence. Inasmuch as books represent the Book, they are signs of a sign. The signified is but another sign and hence is not the absolutely secure foundation upon which all other signs rest. In other words, the transcendental signified refers to a transcendent referent that is never totally present. Even on its own terms, the Book cannot be self-contained; it is always unfinished.

The necessary incompletion of the Book is not simply a function of the space between Book and Author. The opening implicit in the Book/book lies along the margin that separates and joins Book and book and Author and author. Within the bounds of mimesis, the Book appears to be primary and books merely secondary. The asymmetry of this relationship is reflected in the deference that authors show to the Author. The interplay of books and Book, of authors and Author, represents yet another version of the struggle between slave and Master. In this case the drama is played out on a "stage that is theological for as long as it is dominated by speech, by a will to speech, by the layout of a primary logos which does not belong to the theatrical site and governs it from a distance. The stage is theological for as long as its structure, following the entirety of tradition, comports the following elements: an author-creator who, absent and from afar, is armed with a text and keeps watch over, assembles, regulates the time or the meaning of representation, letting this latter *represent* him as concerns what is called the content of his thoughts, his intentions, his ideas. He lets representation represent him through representatives, directors or actors, enslaved interpreters who represent characters who, primarily through what they say, more or less directly represent the thought of the 'creator.' Interpretive slaves who faithfully execute the providential designs of the 'master.'"[18]

Earlier analyses of the complexities of mastery and slavery raise the prospect that the execution of providential purpose is revolutionary. Apparently servile writing actually inverts the relation of slave to Master, author to Author, book to Book, and secondary to primary. From a mimetic perspective, the Word of the Master is believed to be complete. Since the purpose of the author is to rewrite the work of the Author, the aim of books is repeat the Book. But as we have seen elsewhere, repetition discloses incompletion in the very effort to re-present completion. Though intended to be transparent, the mimetic book is actually duplicitous. It *doubles* and hence *supplements* the original Book. In mimesis, the author attempts to represent an original, which he takes to be complete. If, however, the primal Book can be supplemented by a secondary work, the original source cannot be complete. The strange "logic" embodied in this supplement (book) suggests that the ostensible origin (Book) is not really original at all but is actually constituted retrospectively "by a nonorigin, the trace, which thus becomes the origin of origin." [19] Instead of representing something that is temporally and ontologically prior, the Book seems to be the product of a creative author and not the work of the Creator/Author. This inversion of book and Book and of author and Author is the rebellion of slave against Master that marks the transition from mimesis to poiesis.

The shift from mimesis to poiesis brings about an intellectual revolution that parallels the political and social upheaval in France during the late eighteenth century. While the French Revolution is commonly acknowledged to have been the gateway to the modern world, it is no less important to recognize that the threshold of modernity was "definitely crossed when words ceased to intersect with representations and to provide a spontaneous grid for the knowledge of things." [20] Although there were philosophical precedents for this epistemological development, the decisive step was taken by Kant. Kant's critical philosophy effects a "Copernican revolution" by placing the human subject at the center of the universe of knowledge. According to Kant, knowledge involves the conjunction of general *a priori* structures of cognition and particular *a posteriori* sense data. The universality of the forms of sensation and categories of understanding results in a semblance of objectivity in human knowledge. This "objectivity" does not, however, insure a transparent relation between thought and thing. Kant insists that "reality" remains opaque. It is impossible to be certain that the cognitive forms with which the knowing subject is equipped disclose the way things "really" are. Consequently, it is necessary to distinguish thing-as-known from thing-apart-from-knowing (*Ding-an-sich*). The thing-in-itself is, by definition, unknowable and forms an absolute limit to all knowledge.

In post-Kantian philosophy and art, this limit is subjected to critical review. In the course of the complex movement from Fichte and Schelling to Hegel, the conviction emerges that Kant's thing-in-itself does not designate extramental reality but is actually a cognitive construct that stands in critical tension with all determinate forms of knowledge. This significant revision of Kantian philosophy completes the revolution that Kant had initiated. In the writings of the most creative Romantic philosophers and poets, the last vestiges of mimesis yield to thoroughgoing poiesis. Poiesis, as I have already noted, derives from the Greek word which means to make, create, or produce. With the transition from mimesis to poiesis, the locus of creativity shifts from the divine to the human subject. In its early forms, this inversion never completely overturns the presuppositions that underlie the Creator/creature distinction. Like the humanistic atheist, the Romantic philosopher/poet transfers the predicates of divinity to humanity. The negation of the transcendent Author manifests itself in the affirmation of the creative author. Since the human author now displays attributes that had previously characterized the divine Author, such poiesis remains within the epoch of the book. Authorship is no longer restricted to the slavish imitation of a Book that has already been written. To the contrary, authoring is regarded as genuinely creative and not simply reproductive.

This conception of poiesis still does not call into question the theological presuppositions that underwrite the book. Poetic authorship, therefore, continues to be bound by the notion of representation and ruled by the economy of the sign. This is not to imply that the transcendental signified continues to be viewed as the discourse of the world that expresses the voice of the divine Author. Nevertheless, the poetic book remains logocentric. The logos that this new edition of the book embodies is interpreted in different ways. In order to discern the persistent logocentrism of the book, it is necessary to recognize the significant similarities among apparently diverse methods of reading. Toward this end, I shall briefly consider Romantic hermeneutics, phenomenology, archetype analysis, and structuralism.

The movement from mimesis to poiesis brings in its wake increased interest in the activity of artistic production. For many Romantics, the work of art is best understood as the *expression* of the *intention* of the creative artist. "Ex-pression is exteriorization. It imparts to a certain outside a sense which is first found in a certain inside."[21] The book of the author, like the Book of the Author, points beyond itself to the intention it embodies. To comprehend the work, it is necessary to return to the source from which it originates—authorial intention. Schleiermacher, who frequently is credited with having initiated the modern discussion of hermeneutics, argues that the interpreter tries to reverse the activity of expression by reconstructing the author's "original" construction. In this case, interpretation "is ultimately a divinatory process, a placing of oneself within the mind of the author, an apprehension of the 'inner origin' of the composition of a work, a recreation of the creative act."[22] Even though "the 'referent' is not immediately related to the logos of a creator God where it began by being the spoken/thought sense, the signified has at any rate an immediate relationship with the logos in general (finite or infinite), and a mediated one with the signifier, that is to say with the exteriority of writing."[23] The logos that the work represents both constitutes the norm that establishes meaning and secures the center that organizes the work. The *book means what the author intends.* By expressing his purpose in the work, the author *objectifies* his intention. Such objectification, however, involves an act of "distanciation," which establishes a gap between author and book. This opening creates the space for another approach to the book.

In order to understand objectified meaning, it is not necessary to trace it to an objectifying agent. The meaning of a work can be regarded as free-standing or as embodied in the text itself. From this point of view, a logos or eidos dwells *within* the book. This semantic structure is neither superficial nor empirical; it is inward and ideal. Every phenomenal work harbors a logos that is, in principle, discernible. In order to uncover this eidos, it is necessary to subject the work to something like a phenomenological analysis. The phenomenologist attempts to bracket fundamental assumptions and presuppositions in order to allow the ideal form of the work to disclose itself. This eidos is the transcendental signified that constitutes and sustains the meaning of the book. The goal of the phenomenological enterprise is a full and primordial intuition, often labeled "eidetic vision." By actually re-presenting the logos of the object under investigation, the knowing subject seeks to establish the complete transparency of signifier and signified. Such lucidity promises to heal the breach that otherwise separates subject and object. This method of reading actually combines elements of mimesis and poiesis. The phenomenological perspective is poetic to the extent that it views the object as an expression of creative intention. But it is mimetic insofar as it aims at the adequate re-presentation of this intentional object to the conscious subject.

Romantic hermeneutics and phenomenology share an interest in intentionality. For the Romantic, interpretation is a nostalgic activity in which one attempts to recapture the original act of creation. The phenomenologist, by contrast, is less interested in the intention of the creative subject than in the logos of the created object. Taken together, Romantic hermeneutics and phenomenology point toward a third approach to the book: archetypal analysis. It is possible to view the book in terms of intentional expression without regarding the author as an individual genius. From the perspective of archetypal analysis, the mind of the creative subject is governed by typical patterns, which appear to be universal. These mental structures are given a variety of names. While a psychologist like Jung calls them "archetypes," a literary critic like Frye labels them "mythoi" or "images." Whatever their name, these forms are usually limited in number and agenetic in character. As such, they constitute the structural matrix of all conscious and unconscious mental activity. Though not at once evident, these archetypes are distant relatives of the Platonic Ideas and the Christian logos. In the course of Western philosophy, theology, and psychology, both the Ideas and the logos are transformed from ontological essences into epistemological principles. Furthermore, these structures undergo progressive occultation as their function shifts from patterning consciousness and self-consciousness to informing the unconscious. Through a process of inversion, the transcendent logos, which had ruled the world of light as either sun or son, is reborn in the darkness of the "underworld" as the substance of all psychic functioning. The creation of the author does not so much put into words individual purpose or embody a particular eidos as it expresses the general disposition of the mind and incarnates universal archetypes. The archetype is the "still center" that anchors the work and prevents it from floating freely. The act of interpretation involves deciphering the logos or uncovering the figure in the carpet. While not usually noticed by its practitioners, archetypal criticism presupposes a significant change in the notion of authorship. What remains implicit in archetypal interpretation becomes explicit in structuralist analysis.

By applying to culture as a whole certain insights that were initially advanced in the area of linguistics, structuralism decenters the creative subject while at the same time maintaining the centered structure of the book. In agreement with the archetypal critic, the structuralist argues that transpersonal forms or codes traverse each "individual" and inform every act of "creation." Instead of referring to a center of self-conscious activity, the word "author" actually designates a function that is constituted by the intersection of multiple semiotic systems. It is these universal structures, rather than individual authorial intention, that form the meaning of the work. "[O]nce the conscious subject is deprived of its role as source of meaning—once meaning is explained in terms of conventional systems which may escape the grasp of the conscious subject—the self can no longer be identified with consciousness. It is 'dissolved' as its functions are taken up by a variety of interpersonal systems that operate through it. The human sciences, which begin by making man an object of knowledge, find, as their work advances, that 'man' disappears under structural analysis. 'The goal of the human sciences,' writes Lévi-Strauss, 'is not to constitute man but to dissolve him.'"[24] This "dissolution," "decentering," or "dispersal" of the subject is the correlate of the death of God and disappearance of the self. As we shall see in more detail in the second part of this study, the structuralist not only denies the existence of the Author but also calls into question the integrity of the author.

And yet, paradoxically, structuralism is, in an important sense, still caught within the theological network. While boldly giving up the notion of the author, the structuralist clings to the idea of the book. Despite appearances to the contrary, every work forms a finite totality of signifiers. The surface of the text conceals deep and enduring structures upon which the work is built. These deep structures form the logos of the work and provide both the *archē* of meaning and the *telos* of interpretation. Like the reader of the book of nature, the structuralist attempts to discover the hidden grammar and obscure syntax of the words he considers. In the writings of Lévi-Strauss, structuralism becomes an encyclopedic project. Not only does Lévi-Strauss believe each work to be grounded in an underlying pattern; he is also convinced that all works taken together constitute a comprehensive and comprehensible cycle. From this point of view, the final goal of analysis is to discover the grammar of this Book of books or to recover the universal logos.

Whether mimetically or poetically conceived, the book is shelved in the library of Leibniz rather than in Borges' library of Babel. Indeed, a work is truly a book only insofar as it silences the babble of Babel. A book is not a cacophonous "sounddance" but a coherent whole, possessing proper meaning. The propriety of meaning is a function of the closure of the book, and closure is effected by the presence of the logos. Instead of being an abysmal labyrinth, the book is a firmly grounded logical structure with an identifiable entrance and exit. The presence of the logos insures the decidability of meaning and the readability of the work. The labor of reading is an attempt to *master* the play of writing. In this sense, every successful book is a masterpiece. But even in a bookish culture, not all works are deemed equivalent. Some books are genuine masterpieces, others are merely slavish imitations. The work of mastery is the labor of tradition.

## Authority: Masterpieces and Tradition

Tradition and authority extend the circle of the book: tradition is authoritative, authority is traditional. While tradition establishes authority, authority founds tradition. Tradition is able to offer a cure or provide a ground only to the extent that it is itself cured or grounded. A/The founder founds tradition. As the examination of authorship has already shown, there is an inextricable bond between author and author-ity. From a traditional point of view, the author is the one who originates or bestows existence upon something. Insofar as the author is the father of being itself, he is absolute master. The mastery of the author is present in, and as, his authority. Among other things, "authority" (*auctoritas . . . auctor . . . augere . . .*) suggests "the power to enforce obedience; the right to command or give an ultimate decision." The final (rather, primal) authority is the absolute "Origin" or "founding Father." Within the Western theological network, this authority is, of course, God. As the Author of authors, God is the authority who stands behind every authority. Authority rests on proximity to the Master and, like contagious power, is transmitted by contact. Each particular link in the unbroken metonymic chain of tradition re-presents the authority of the Author. Even when celibate, every authority is a *Papa* (πάππας, whence Pope) of sorts. The continuity of the genealogical line

protects the purity and propriety of tradition and guards the authority of
the father. Like the centered web of the spider, tradition balances centrifugal and centripetal forces. The linearity of authority seeks to insure that
delegation does not become dispersal. The notion of tradition "makes it
possible to rethink the dispersion of history in the form of the same; it
allows a reduction of the difference proper to every beginning, in order to
pursue without discontinuity the endless search for the origin."[25]

By securing paternity, tradition tries to prevent illegitimate thoughts
and abort bastard deeds. Tradition and authority join forces to establish
orthodoxy and repress heterodoxy. *Hetero* derives from the Greek word
meaning "other or different." Heterodoxy is an unacceptable deviation or
an *error* of opinion (Greek *doxa*). *Ortho*, by contrast, is from the Greek word
that means "straight or right, correct or proper." Accordingly, orthodoxy
refers to opinions that are right, correct, and true. The struggle of orthodoxy against heterodoxy represents an effort to master otherness and control
difference. The chief opponents of the orthodox are those who err. By
establishing a firm rule and supporting a stiff ruler, the orthodox attempt to
draw a line that will straighten out deviants and prevent further erring.

Tradition "begins" with speech and "ends" in writing. As "The Ruler of
Reality,"[26] tradition regulates and regularizes by establishing a normative
canon. A κανών is a measuring rod or a rule. A rule, in turn, is a *regula*,
which is a straight stick, bar, ruler, or pattern. A canon provides the rule
by which to distinguish proper from improper and gives the standard
against which to judge anomalies and measure transgressions. Though a
tradition can, at least for a time, remain oral, a canon tends to be "fixed" by
writing. Canon and book, therefore, are closely related. Once agreed upon,
the canon forms the book by which all other books are judged and furnishes
the rule with which every "lesser" work is measured. In short, the canon
constitutes the masterpiece that rules the tradition. As such, it must be the
paradigmatic work of a/The Master.

The notion of a canon further illustrates the conjunction of line and circle
that is both inscribed in the book and governs the (inter)play of tradition
and authority. Any work that rules an entire tradition must be living rather
than dead. Since dead letters come to life through inspiration, the masterpiece is necessarily "*La parole soufflée.*"[27] When a work is deemed sacred, the
true *Souffleur* is believed to be divine. For the Christian, this "Prompter"
(*Souffleur*) is the Holy Spirit. As the founding Subject and original Author,
this Spirit is the foundation of tradition and *voice* of authority. Through the
Holy Spirit, God dictates. The activity of the Spirit breathes (*souffle*) the
Word of God into the words of the canonical book. Since such a work is
truly inspired (*soufflée*), it forms a genuine masterpiece. It is important to
recognize that *soufflée* means not only "spirited" but "stolen." This verbal
association suggests that donation is inseparable from theft. In the act of
giving, the Creator simultaneously takes. When God inspires, "what is

called the speaking subject is no longer the person himself, or the person alone, who speaks. The speaking subject discovers his irreducible secondarity, his origin that is always already eluded."[28] For the inspired believer, the "irreducible secondarity" of the author testifies to the "undeniable" originality of the Author, and vice versa. The very effort to secure this divine authority, however, eventually calls into question the originality of the Author. If God "steals" by speaking, man "steals" by writing. When spoken word is "fixed" in written text, another figure appears on the "mystic writing pad"[29]—a second face emerges in the A/author's palimpsest.

A masterpiece is forever two-faced. It gazes back toward its master and looks ahead to its mastery. The power of origin alone is insufficient to insure the continuing mastery of a work. In order to remain in control, the masterpiece must express its power by extending its influence. The masterful work governs effectively by holding out the promise of "The *mastery of meaning.*"[30] No simple artifact of the *past*, the masterpiece confronts one as a *present* reality by projecting *future* possibilities. For this reason, the masterpiece must be approached teleologically as well as archeologically and genealogically. A powerful work fore-casts a distinctive "horizon of experience"[31] toward which it beckons followers to move. In such a pro-ject, "new configurations, new ways of being in the world, of living there, and of projecting our innermost possibilities onto it are . . . brought into language."[32] This revelatory quality lends the masterpiece its kerygmatic character. Insofar as it is proclaimed with the voice of author-ity, the kerygma is supposed to make present what had appeared to be past. The encounter with authoritative kerygma marks the "coming into language of that which has been said in the tradition."[33] The force of tradition lies less in its tendency to be proclaimed than in its capacity to *pro-claim.* The masterpiece is the effective bearer of this claiming power. In relation to a masterpiece, the faithful subject does not experience himself or herself as an autonomous agent. The one who deferentially appreciates the masterpiece admits that he is not completely in control of the experience he undergoes. This understanding of the way in which the masterpiece exercises its mastery indicates further features of the book and clarifies important aspects of the activity of reading.

It is somewhat misleading to insist that one simply reads an acknowledged masterpiece. In a significant sense, the masterpiece "reads" its subject. The work of a/the master is both persuasive and coercive. The masterpiece is gripping and captivating; one feels "caught up in its world."[34] The fabric of the text takes hold through the (spell)binding lines from which it is knit. The masterpiece works by bringing together two contrasting movements of translation: reader is born(e) in(to) text as text is carried over (in)to reader. The goal of this transference (*metaphora*) process is a "fusion of horizons."[35] Within the frame-work of the masterpiece, one meets tradition as a vital partner in a lively conversation rather than as words etched in tablets of stone or inscribed on the trunk or leaves of a dead tree. The *traditional* purpose of conversation is to overcome the barriers of space and time. Conversation (*conversatio*) means, among other things, intercourse. Like the line(s) of a book, the line of tradition is intended to fill holes, close gaps, and span distance. So understood, the goal of conversation with tradition is nothing less than a "communion" that realizes the fullness of presence. The masterpiece strives to keep tradition alive through a process of repeated re-presentation. This strategy seems to be successful as long as subjects are willing to recognize "the superior claim that the text makes." [36] The place of the masterpiece, however, is never secure. Reflecting and reenacting the outcome of other struggles for mastery, the masterpiece finally subverts itself in the very effort to maintain its rule. The masterpiece, in other words, always found(er)s.

A masterpiece is always deemed perfect (*perfectum*, from *perficere*, "to accomplish, perform, *complete*"). It is precisely the apparent plenitude of the masterpiece that promises satisfaction to pro-spective appreciators. Meaning presumably is completely present in and fully presented by the masterpiece. Submission to the masterpiece is supposed to bring the complete enjoyment that arises from the mastery of meaning. But this expectation is never satisfied.

In attempting to represent authority and transmit tradition, the masterpiece discloses its own incompletion and reveals the unstoppable gaps between its lines. Just as a master can be lord only over a subjected servant, so a masterpiece can rule only in relation to obedient or even servile appreciation. This interplay of mastery and servitude opens the work to the other, which it struggles to dominate, repress, or exclude. Consequently, the masterpiece is not a closed whole or a complete totality; it is necessarily faulted and inevitably open-ended. Instead of an original and sovereign source, the masterpiece necessarily *depends upon* the subject's "answering imagination." [37] This dependence means that the masterpiece can never be finished and must always be refinished. Insofar as (the) work is forever incomplete, its meaning can never be fully present. The meaning of the masterpiece, like all meaning, presupposes a certain absence. As a result of this nonpresence, the masterpiece's promise to deliver the mastery of meaning can never be completely fulfilled. Total presence is again elusive.


## Heterography


"The last philosopher of the book" fathered, among many other things, an illegitimate son. This child, however, never appears in the pages of his father's book(s). Can this be an accident? Could Ludwig have been an accident? There are not supposed to be any accidents in the System. Thus both the illegitimate and its "absence" seem to be necessary.

Kierkegaard, who as much or even more than Hegel might be dubbed "the first thinker of writing," was the son of a man who had fathered an illegitimate son and, perhaps as a result, he himself lived in constant dread of having fathered an illegitimate child. Kierkegaard thus repeatedly wrote about illegitimacy and usually wrote illegitimately. Though he wrote profusely and published many texts, Kierkegaard did not really write books. Can this be an accident? Could his dread have been an accident? Without the System, there must be accidents. Thus both the illegitimate and its "presence" seem to be nonaccidental.

> *Système / systématique* — System / systematics
> Is it not characteristic of reality to be *unmasterable*? And is it not the characteristic of any system to *master* it? What then, confronting reality, can one do who rejects mastery? Get rid of the system as apparatus, accept *systematics* as writing. . . .[38]

Books, it seems, are supposed to be "solidly constructed, unified, and with an intellectual space defined by clear and resolute boundaries."[39] So conceived, the book (though not the text) "is the encyclopaedic protection of theology and of logocentrism against the disruption of writing, against its aphoristic energy . . . ."[40] Through its closure, the book seeks to end the free play and unending erring of writing by *fixing* meaning. Insofar as fixed meaning is cured, it appears to cure. The book represents a pre-scribed remedy that is supposed to heal the dis-ease that results from floating freely or spinning ceaselessly. Whether suspended above 70,000 fathoms or clinging to an abysmal spiral staircase, those who are weary and restless search for a ground, seek a foundation, and long for a bed(rock). For these sojourners, an absence, a gap, or a hole "is the chance for a book."[41] Although usually present only as erased, the "center" serves as the "sign of a hole that the book attempt[s] to fill. The center . . . [is] the name of a hole; and the name of man, like the name of God, pronounces the force of that which has been raised up in the hole in order to operate as a work in the form of a book. The volume, the scroll of parchment, insinuate[s] itself into the dangerous hole."[42] The hole, which is the chance for the book, represents a haunting absence, which can be read as another shadow of death. Throughout the pages of the book, "death strolls between the letters."[43] By joining letters to form lines, the book "attempts to evade the necessity of death in life."[44] To the extent that the book successfully closes gaps and binds wounds, it seems to provide the medicine for which diseased subjects long.

This tonic, however, is not only a remedy; it is also a *poison*. Contrary to expectation, a fix does not cure. To fix is to fasten, to make firm or stable, and thus to deprive of volatility or fluidity. Complete fixation is perfect immobility, absolute firmness, and thoroughgoing rigor. A complete book, therefore, would seem to hold out the promise of total stability. Such a prospect initially seems to be quite attractive. Upon closer inspection, however, it becomes apparent that absolute rigor is indistinguishable from *rigor mortis*.[45] In completing itself, the book reveals that it always includes the other that it struggles to exclude.

The "success" of the book is actually its "failure." This inversion suggests that the closure *of* the book is twofold: it is both the closure that constitutes the book and the closure that subverts the book. The book "closes itself by thinking its own opening."[46] This opening uncovers the gaps *with and without* which the book cannot be. A book is no more possible without blanks than speech is possible apart from silence. Books stage an unfixable play in/of black and white. Paradoxically, the condition of the book's possibility is also the condition of its impossibility. Holes and blanks open the space in which the book is inscribed. But this white space, or silence, also shreds the leaves of the book. Openings that cannot be completely covered "put in question the unity of the book and the unity of the 'book' considered as a perfect totality, with all the implications of such a concept."[47] The rupture of the book's closure is not, however, merely destructive. This breach releases seminal fluids from unproductive confinement. The perforation of the text is both wound and "dehiscence." Dehiscence refers to the opening of an organ along a suture for the purpose of discharging its contents. In animals this entails the bursting-open of mucous follicles, and in plants it involves the splitting of a capsule or pod at maturity. This opening "makes production, reproduction, development possible. Dehiscence . . . limits what it makes possible, while rendering its rigor and purity impossible."[48] When the notion of dehiscence is extended from the domain of biology to literature, it becomes possible to read the rupture of the book as dissemination, which spreads the word(s) of the text. Such reading is *deconstructive*.

Deconstruction is, in an important sense, "an antistructural criticism."[49] Since exteriority is never merely exterior, structure cannot be total, nor can the book be complete. "Deconstruction attempts to resist the totalizing and totalitarian tendencies of criticism. It attempts to resist its own tendencies to come to rest in some sense of mastery over the work. It resists these in terms of an uneasy joy of interpretation, beyond nihilism, always in movement, a going beyond which remains in place, as the parasite is outside the door but also always already within, uncanniest of guests."[50] The deconstructive critic reads the book as a heterograph. In attempting to secure closure by controlling disruptive otherness, the book opens itself to difference. Intentions to the contrary notwithstanding, the book graphs difference and otherness. This exteriority is not simply an illegitimate "presence" or "absence." The book itself is always grafted onto otherness.[51] As a matter of fact, it is precisely the otherness the book struggles to erase that assures the book its possibility and space. This presence/absence is like a bastard son who is both inside and outside the family, though he never appears directly in the leaves of the family tree or on the pages of the father's book. Along the margin of the book, opposites that Western thought traditionally separates and holds apart appear to be confused: inside/outside, identity/difference, remedy/infection, purity/pollution, propriety/impropriety, good/evil . . . . The paradoxes that result from this interplay of opposites mark the closure of the book and point toward erring scripture.

With the rediscovery of this re-markable border, we "return" to the *limen*, which, in fact, we have never really left. Through unexpected twisting and unanticipated turning, our serpentine erring has all the while been re-inscribing the boundary of the text. As a result of having wandered from God and self through history and book, we have at last "discerned writing: a nonsymmetrical division designated on the one hand the closure of the book, and on the other the opening of the text. On the one hand the theological encyclopaedia and, modeled upon it, the book of man. On the other a fabric of traces marking the disappearance of an exceeded God or of an erased man. The question of writing could be opened only if the book was closed. The joyous wandering of the *graphein* then became wandering without return. The opening into the text was adventure, expenditure without reserve."[52] To such ceaseless erring we must now (re)turn.

# PART TWO

# Deconstructive A/theology

# 5

## Writing of God

Reb Jacob, who was my first teacher, believed in the virtue of the lie because, so he said, there is no writing without lie. And writing is the way of God.

*There is no Logos, there are only hieroglyphs.*

So it is that it is the death of God which makes possible the return of *difference-itself*, a pure difference which is lost with the advent of history or consciousness, a difference or *différance* which is the true "other" of God.

"Oh Zarathustra, with such unbelief you are more pious than you believe! Some sort of god in you has converted you to your godlessness.

"Is it not your piety itself that no longer lets you believe in a god? And your very great honesty will yet lead you beyond good and evil.

"Look at yourself! What remains to you in the end? You have eyes and hands and mouth meant for blessing from all eternity. One does not bless with the hand alone.

"Near you, though you want to be the most godless, I sense a secret, sacred, pleasant scent of many blessings: it gives gladness and grief."

"Amen. So be it!" said Zarathustra, much astonished.

## Hieroglyphics

As we "begin" again, it is important to recall that we *always* begin as already having begun. In the very act of beginning, "I" discover my ineradicable belatedness and inevitable secondariness. Thus, in one sense, "I" can never begin. And yet the irrepressible "priority" of beginning suggests that beginning is unending. In another sense, therefore, "I" am always beginning or, more precisely, am always beginning again. Unending beginning, however, must not be confused with origin. Beginning, which is never original, marks and remarks the constant disappearance of origin. This interplay between "origin" and "beginning" is evident in the act of writing. For the writer, "Everything begins 'in' a library: among books, writing, references. Hence nothing begins. Simply a drifting or a disorientation from which one never moves away." [1] Such drifting is endless rather than temporary. Since beginning and end are mirror images of each other, the loss of one is the disappearance of the other. The person who cannot recover origins can never know the end. With origin always erased and conclusion never visible, the writer is left to roam, wander, and err along a margin that is ever the "middest."

My drifting has led me from the deconstruction of theology to the threshold of deconstructive a/theology. Having recognized along the way that all writing is rewriting, it should be clear that deconstructive a/theology emerges in and through the deconstruction of theology. Consequently, the task in the second part of this study is not to initiate a new departure but to elaborate the implications of insights that have already begun to emerge. The deconstructive analysis of the nodal notions of God, self, history, and book has disclosed the intricacy of the Western theological network. I have stressed that this complex conceptual web appears to rest on the interpretation of being in terms of presence and the present. The identification of being and presence/present gives rise to a multifaceted struggle for mastery, a struggle to secure identity by excluding difference and repressing absence. I have examined some of the ways in which this struggle is reflected in the murder of God, the quest for self, the narration of history, and the formation of the book. In each case, Hegel has emerged as a pivotal figure. On the basis of insights gathered in the first part of the inquiry, it would not be too much to suggest that Western philosophy and theology reach closure in the Hegelian System.

This closure, however, is at the same time a productive opening. The "end" of the book is the "beginning" of writing. Writing presupposes, on the one hand, that origin is inaccessible and originality illusory and, on the other hand, that ends are elusive and definitive conclusions impossible. Inasmuch as Hegel is both the "final" philosopher of the book and the "first" thinker of writing, his System is (necessarily) fissured. This breach ruptures absolute closure and subverts repressive totality. Contrary to common opinion, Hegel is not a philosopher of identity, for whom difference is either penultimate or epiphenomenal. Quite the opposite, Hegel constantly attempts to overturn the philosophy of identity, which was so popular during his day and which has returned to haunt twentieth-century thought and life. In order to effect this reversal, Hegel insists on the irreducibility of difference. Instead of identity dissipating difference, difference constitutes identity. When this insight is developed, it is possible to move from book to writing.

It must, nonetheless, be acknowledged that Hegel is not always sufficiently aware of the radical implications of his own analysis of the philosophy of identity. He often has a tendency to slip back into the language of the position he is criticizing. This is especially evident in his extravagant claims for absolute knowledge. In the Hegelian System, "the horizon of absolute knowledge is the effacement of writing in the logos, the retrieval of the trace in parousia, the *metaphysics of the proper.*"[2] From this point of view, Hegel remains a bookish philosopher. As I have suggested, however, the inclusive rhythm in Hegel's thought is balanced by his appreciation for the abiding significance of difference. To the extent that Hegel refuses to reduce difference to identity, he anticipates one of the most important points repeatedly advanced in deconstructive philosophy and criticism.

Though it is not generally recognized, the return to/of Hegel that deconstruction proposes is mediated not only directly by Nietzsche but also indirectly by Kierkegaard. It is, after all, Kierkegaard who first insists that "System and finality are pretty much one and the same, so much so that if the System is not finished, there is no System."[3] Kierkegaard's relentless attack on Hegelian results foreshadows deconstruction's critique of eschatology and denial of closure. Like deconstruction's "antisystematic criticism," Kierkegaard's "unscientific fragments" are always written both with and against Hegel. In trying to fulfill his self-appointed role as a "necessary corrective," Kierkegaard *willfully* misreads Hegel as a philosopher of identity whose System is finally totalitarian. Far too often, subsequent interpreters have naïvely accepted Kierkegaard's misprision of Hegel and have forgotten or failed to recognize the dialectical tension from which the criticism grows. Derrida's deconstruction represents an important exception to this common tendency. Although rarely presented in terms of the debate between Hegel and Kierkegaard, the deconstructive reading of Hegel as the last philosopher of the book and the first thinker of writing both acknowledges the force of Kierkegaard's critique and recognizes the continuing power of Hegel's position. The most significant anticipation of this shifty middle ground *between* Hegel and Kierkegaard is to be found in the aphorisms of Nietzsche. While denying any possibility of absolute knowledge, Nietzsche preserves Hegel's revolutionary recognition of the vital importance of relationships that both join and separate everything that is and is not. The analysis of interpretation that grows out of Nietzsche's doctrine of the will to power prepares the way for Derrida's notion of *écriture*. When read through Hegel, Kierkegaard, and Nietzsche, Derridean writing points beyond the deconstruction of theology to deconstructive a/theology. In unraveling God, self, history, and book, we have already glimpsed writing, markings, mazing grace, and erring scripture. In the following pages, I shall explore these errant notions in greater detail.

As we approach the consideration of deconstructive a/theology, it is important to heed a warning expressed in different ways by each of the formative precursors I have cited. Hegel, Kierkegaard, Nietzsche, and Derrida all recognize the double bind that the writer inevitably faces. The "new" cannot, yet must be, inscribed in the words of the "old." The necessary interplay between formation and deformation makes it impossible to proceed directly and compels all communication to become indirect. The unavoidable plurisignification that results seems to deepen uncertainty and heighten confusion. Bewilderment reaches monumental proportions in the perplexing postmodern world. Instead of offering comforting reassurance, writing all too often discloses a world of endless contradiction and conflict. The Author having died and authors having disappeared, words frequently sound senseless and writing often seems to be more scribbling than scripture. The cacography of many postmodern texts reflects the cacophony of much contemporary experience.

To make our way through this harrowing time and space, it might be helpful to consider several graphics. I shall "begin" again by examining a parable of writing, an ink drawing, and a parable of word. Notes struck in the following interlude will repeatedly resound throughout the remainder of the study.

$$*\qquad*\qquad*\qquad*$$

$$*\qquad*\qquad*\qquad*$$

Few authors have captured more dramatically than Kafka the complex interplay among the death of God, loss of self, and writing. His extraordinary fable "In the Penal Colony" presents what might best be described as a parable of writing.[4] The tale is set on a remote and somewhat desolate island where prisoners are detained and, when necessary, punished. The parable centers around "a remarkable piece of apparatus" called "the Harrow." The Harrow had been built by the previous Commandant of the domain, who, before his death, had been at once "soldier, judge, mechanic, chemist, and draughtsman." It is, in effect, *a writing machine*, and it is used for "the actual execution of the sentence" passed on condemned criminals. The sentence is carried out by using the Harrow's sharp, vibrating needles to engrave the broken commandment on the skin of the transgressor. The eventual result of this procedure is always death, but, midway through the process, "Enlightenment comes to the most dull-witted. It begins around the eyes. From there it radiates. A moment that might tempt one to get under the Harrow oneself."

In the course of the story, the officer who is responsible for maintaining and operating the machine explains to a visiting explorer that, in previous times, executions afforded the occasion for all members of the kingdom to partcipate in grand public festivals. Under the current regime, however, a new "mild" and supposedly humane doctrine discourages use of the Harrow. Things have degenerated to the point that the presiding officer is the last "true believer" in the machine. In an effort to convince the explorer of the apparatus's efficacy, the officer decides to submit himself to its harrowing torture. Though the officer carefully sets the "Designer" to write "Be

Just" on his skin, the machine goes haywire. Rather than an intelligible *sentence*, the Harrow violently inscribes senseless scribbling. The result is "no exquisite torture, such as the officer desired" but "plain murder."

Overwhelmed by the effect of this writing machine, the explorer seeks to flee the penal colony. Before leaving, however, he insists on seeing the gravestone of the Commandant. With some difficulty, he locates a *marker*, which bears a revealing inscription:

> Here rests the old Commandant. His adherents, who now must be nameless, have dug this grave and set up this stone. There is a prophecy that after a certain number of years the Commandant will rise again and lead his adherents from this house to recover the colony. Have faith and wait!

Now eager to depart, the explorer locates a *ferryman*, who rows him to an awaiting steamer.

Though the parable closes with the ferryman's passage, this does not mark the end of the problem of writing. To the contrary, Kafka's text suggests a genuinely postmodern reading of writing. Elsewhere we learn that "the writer is a ferryman and his destination always has a liminal signification."[5]

> "Where do you come from?"
> "I have wandered."
> "Is Yukel your friend?"
> "I am like Yukel."
> "What is your lot?"
> "To open the book."
> "Are you in the book?"
> "My place is at the threshold."[6]

\*     \*     \*     \*

There is, of course, a very close relationship between painting (*zōgraphia*) and writing (*graphē*). In its early hieroglyphic form, writing is virtually indistinguishable from painting and drawing. The hieroglyph is a pictograph; as such, it is neither subordinate to speech nor bound to a phonic alphabet. Unlike "voice-painting," hieroglyphics create meaning by "enregistering it, by entrusting it to an engraving, a groove, a relief, to a surface whose essential characteristic is to be infinitely transmissible."[7] The close interplay between drawing and writing raises the possibility that one can illuminate the other.

At the critical age of forty, Erasmus, author of *Praise of Folly*, commissioned Holbein the Younger to design for him a personal seal. Like many others entering middle age, Erasmus was, at the time, preoccupied with death. This concern is reflected in the seal. The ink drawing that Holbein produced bears the inscription "*Concedo Nulli*" ("I yield to none") and has at its center "the Roman god Terminus, the genius of boundary stones, which

Hans Holbein the Younger.
Ink drawing,
*The Bust of Terminus*,
commissioned by Erasmus.
Reproduced by permission
of the Kupferstichkabinett,
Basel.

one could not remove without violating the god within them. To [Erasmus] the figure suggested the Platonic remark, 'Remove not what thou has not planted,' and was a reminder of death (which yields to none)."[8] As we have seen, however, boundaries are not unequivocal. By establishing a limit, the boundary stone marks a frontier that forms a point of passage. At this threshold, inside and outside join and separate to form an undecidable play of perpetual displacement. Since the boundary stone is also a funeral monument, it represents the point of passage between this world and the "other" world. As the sign of this transition, the mark(er) is fundamentally ambiguous. The boundary stone inscribes the interplay of life and death by simultaneously consecrating the disappearance, and attesting to the perseverance, of life. For this reason, the funeral monument always harbors phallic vestiges. Like the Indian lingam, the Greek stele, and the Egyptian pyramid, the boundary stone commemorates death by recalling life. It is both a "monument-of-life-in-death" and a "monument-of-death-in-life."[9]

The ambiguity of the boundary stone is graphically captured in Holbein's drawing. By either design or error, the figure that the trickster Erasmus intended to be Terminus actually appears as Dionysus. This boundary stone, in other words, marks the intersection of Terminus and Dionysus. God of wine and bearer of Bacchic delirium, Dionysus creates by dismembering. In dionysian vision, "Transitoriness could be interpreted as enjoyment of productive and destructive force, as *continual creation*."[10] Dripping with blood and semen, Dionysus, who might, after all, embody the sameness of the Anti-Christ and the incarnate word, not only beckons all to death, desire, and delight but also extends an invitation to participate freely in carnival, comedy, and carnality.

*      *      *      *

### The Road to Emmaus

On the road to Emmaus, Jesus travels incognito. "While they were talking and discussing together, Jesus himself drew near and went with them. But their eyes were kept from recognizing him." Here presence is absence, and absence presence. Jesus' followers see but do not see; they listen but hear only the silence of an empty tomb. "When he was at the table with them, he took bread and blessed and broke it, and gave it to them. And their eyes were opened and they recognized him; and he vanished out of their sight."[11] *Hoc est corpus meum.* Hocus-pocus: a vanishing act that really opened their eyes! And what did they "see"? They recognized presence in absence and absence in presence. This unending (inter)play is the eternal (re)inscription of (the) word(s).

*      *      *      *

*      *      *      *

The main contours of deconstructive a/theology begin to emerge with the realization of the necessary interrelation between the death of God and radical christology. Radical christology is *thoroughly* incarnational—the divine "*is*" the incarnate word. Furthermore, this embodiment of the divine is the death of God. With the appearance of the divine that is not only itself but is at the same time other, the God who alone is God disappears. The death of God is the sacrifice of the transcendent Author/Creator/Master who governs from afar. Incarnation *irrevocably* erases the disembodied logos and inscribes a word that becomes the script enacted in the infinite play of interpretation. To understand incarnation as inscription is to discover the word. Embodied word is script(ure), the writing in which we are inscribed and which we inscribe. Like all writing, the carnal word is transgressive. Inscription inverts the traditional understanding of the God-world relationship and subverts all forms of transcendence. A/theology is, in large measure, a critique of the notion of the transcendent God, who is "self-clos'd, all-repelling." [12] In this case, however, the struggle against the omnipotent Father does not simply repeat the undialectical inversion of God and self enacted in humanistic atheism. As a result of the recognition of the necessary interplay between patricide and suicide, the death of God does not issue in the deification of the individual ego. Far from resisting the unsettling currents that circulate throughout postmodern worlds, the a/theologian welcomes the death of God and embraces the disappearance of the self.

In order to avoid unnecessary confusion, it is important to realize that in radical christology the divine is *forever* embodied. The word is *always already* inscribed. Incarnation, therefore, is not a once-and-for-all event, restricted to a specific time and place and limited to a particular individual. Rather, inscription is a continual (though not necessarily a continuous) process. To insist that God "is" eternally embodied in *word* or that the divine "*is*" incarnate *word* is to imply that "there is a sense in which the word 'God' refers to the word 'word' and the word 'word' refers to the word 'God.'" [13] God is what word means, and word is what "God" means. To interpret God as word is to understand the divine as scripture or writing. In order to develop the far-reaching implications of this suggestion, it is necessary to consider different ways of reading the word "word."

According to traditional Occidental wisdom, the notion of the word is inextricably tied to the structure of signification. As remarks scattered throughout earlier chapters imply, signification at the most basic level presupposes a distinction between signifier and signified. In this binary relationship, the signifier points beyond itself to that which it represents (i.e., the signified). Insofar as word is sign, it appears to be essentially ostensive or fundamentally referential. I have already indicated that the referent of the sign can be interpreted in different ways. In general, the signified tends to be viewed as either "real" or "ideal." Accordingly, a sign is believed to designate something conceptual, like an idea, image, or mental construct, or is held to denote an actual object in the world. Common sense and reasoning based upon it frequently try to mediate ideality and reality by insisting that, while every sign carries an "ideal" meaning, signified meaning always points to a "real" referent, which remains extramental. This analysis of words appears to rest on the assumption that nouns and the activity of naming are normative for all uses of language. The relationship between named/signified and name/signifier is not symmetrical. The former is traditionally regarded as primary, the latter as secondary. The meaning of any word is that to which it refers. Conversely, the signified grounds (and thus lends weight to) the signifier. The word, therefore, remains obediently subservient to the signified.

Although not immediately evident, this pattern of signification is tied up in the ontotheological network. God, or His substitute, appears either overtly or covertly to be the final meaning of the word. Put differently, God is, in effect, the "transcendental signified" that grounds the structure of signification. Since the "sign and divinity have the same place and time of birth," the "age of the sign is essentially theological." [14] This does not mean, of course, that every sign refers directly or even indirectly to God. The point to be stressed is that some notion of the transcendental signified is required by any referential system that gives priority to the signified over the signifier. While not always explicitly named God, the transcendental signified *functions* as the purported locus of truth that is supposed to stabilize all meaningful words.

A closer examination of this structure of signification discloses inherent contradictions that call into question the fundamental opposition between signifier and signified. Whether the referent of the sign is taken to be "real" or "ideal," the distinction between signifier and signified is actually a product of *consciousness itself*. Though not always aware of its own activity, consciousness attempts to *give itself* a criterion by which to judge itself. The signified is distinguished from the signifier and serves as the standard by which all signs are measured. For the most part, consciousness regards its criterion as external to, independent of, and imposed upon itself. But this interpretation of experience fails to do justice to the creativity and productivity of consciousness. That to which consciousness points is always already within consciousness itself. This analysis of the relationship between signifier and signified overturns the traditional understanding of signification. The signified is neither independent of nor superior to the signifier. To the contrary, the signified is a signifier. Consciousness, therefore, deals *only* with signs and never reaches the thing itself. More precisely, the thing itself is not an independent entity (be it "real" or "ideal") to which all signs refer but is itself a *sign*.

Armed with this insight, it is possible to reinterpret the claim that the word "God" refers to the word "word" and that the word "word" refers to the word "God." Although the word is a sign, the signified is not independent of, and qualitatively different from, the signifier. Inasmuch as the signified is a signifier, the sign is a sign of a sign. Since a word is a sign, it is always about another word. In different terms, the word stages a drama whose script is the interplay of signs. When the word is understood in this way, it appears as *writing* or *scripture*. Simultaneously inside and outside the traditional structure of signification, "writing is not *about* something; *it is that something itself*." [15]

It should be clear that writing inscribes the disappearance of the transcendental signified. In this way, scripture embodies and enacts the death of

God, even as the death of God opens and releases writing. The disappearance of the transcendental signified closes the theological age of the sign and makes possible the free play of a/theological writing. Within the classical economy of signification, "*Logos* is a son . . . a son that would be destroyed in his very *presence* without the present attendance of his father. His father who answers. His father who speaks for him and answers for him. Without his father, he would be nothing but, in fact, writing. At least that is what is said by the one who says: it is the father's thesis. The specificity of writing would thus be intimately bound to the absence of the father. Such an absence can of course exist along very diverse modalities, distinctly or confusedly, successively or simultaneously: to have lost one's father, through natural or violent death, through random violence or patricide." [16] By enacting the death of the transcendent(al) Father/signified, the word becomes the wayward, rebellious, errant "son." "Writing, the lost son . . . writes (itself): (that) the father *is not*, that is to say, is not present." [17] The word marks the closure of all presence that is not at the same time absence and marks the end of identity that is not also difference. In this way, the incarnate word spells the death of the God who alone is God. The death of God, however, is the birth of the divine that is not only itself but is always at the same time other. Insofar as word is scripture, writing appears to be hieroglyphic.

"Hieroglyphic" derives from the Latin *hieroglyphicus*, which was in turn borrowed from the Greek *hierogluphikos* (*hieros*, sacred, plus *gluphē*, carving). The hieroglyphic is thus sacred inscription, holy writ. The hierophantic character of scripture must not be allowed to obscure the "materiality" of the word. Writing, which is necessarily bound to the death of the father, is bodily or incarnate. In script, word is made flesh and flesh is made word. Freed from the domination of a disembodied logos, hieroglyphics form "a system of signs [which] is no longer controlled by the institution of voice." [18] Hieroglyphics are always inscribed, usually in stone, often on a boundary stone, which marks the site of passage. Such passage is not itself transitory; it is absolute. Writing can be understood as absolute passage. This interpretation of absoluteness overturns traditional notions, according to which the Absolute is separate, disengaged, free from imperfection, connection, relation, and dependence. In the paradoxical "logic" of hieroglyphics, the absolute is absolute only insofar as it is thoroughly relative. Divine relativity appears when word is read as writing.

This account of scripture cannot, of course, be reduced to the commonplace view of writing as the simple transcription of antecedent thoughts, ideas, or images from immaterial interior form to material exterior expression. It is precisely this view of writing that is negated by the disappearance of the transcendental signified. The death of the father opens the reign of the word that is embodied in scripture. Since this word enacts absolute passage, it is forever liminal and eternally playful. The play of the word is writing, and the drama of writing is word. In writing, fixed boundaries break down. Scripture, therefore, is always marginal. The/A word is nothing in itself; it is a play within a play, a play that is forever an interplay. This play is a play of differences that forms and reforms the word itself. The specificity of any signifier is a function of its entwinement within a complex signifying web. This differential network of signs is "the functional condition, the condition of possibility, for every sign."[19] Its "name" is *writing*.

Within a scriptural economy, writing is the articulation of (the) word(s). To articulate is to joint. A joint (where only outlaws and the errant hang out) joins by separating and separates by joining. This joint, this threshold, is neither here nor there, neither present nor absent. And yet, without articulation there is only an inarticulateness, which is not merely silence but, simply, nothing. *Everything hinges on scripture.*

On the basis of these (pre)liminary remarks, it appears that writing embodies a complex web of differences in which terms "are not atoms, but rather focal points of economic condensation, sites of passage."[20] Inscription marks each word a crossword. Every cross is formed by two intersecting axes. The fabric of signification is woven from threads that are synchronic and diachronic. The specificity of any signifier is a function of its distinction from coexisting signs and its difference from both antecedent and subsequent signifiers. While the synchronic axis graphs the way(s) in which co-relative graphemes differ from one another, the diachronic axis charts temporal intervals that differentiate signs. The complex cross-stitching of writing forms a puzzling network that subverts the traditional opposition between time and space. The inscription of the word spaces time and times space. By staging an unending play of differences, writing "makes the movement of signification possible only if each element that is said to be 'present,' appearing on the stage of presence, is related to something other than itself but retains the mark of a past element and already lets itself be hollowed out by the mark of its relation to a future element. This trace relates no less to what is called the future than to what is called the past, and it constitutes what is called the present by this very relation to what it is not, to what it absolutely is not; that is, not even to a past or future considered as a modified present. In order for it to be, an interval must separate it from what it is not; but the interval that constitutes it in the present must also and by the same token, divide the present in itself, thus dividing, along with the present, everything that can be conceived on its basis, that is, every being—in particular, for our [theological and] metaphysical language, the substance or subject. Constituting itself dynamically, dividing itself, this interval is what could be called *spacing*; time's becoming-spatial or space's becoming-temporal (*temporalizing*). And it is this constitution of the present as a 'primordial' and irreducibly nonsimple,

and, therefore, in the strict sense nonprimordial, synthesis of traces, re-
tentions, and protensions [which marks the liminal time-space of the
word]."[21]

Let me pause to recapitulate the tangled course I have been pursuing.
From the point of view of deconstructive a/theology, the death of God is
realized in the radically incarnate word. The disappearance of the transcendental signified creates the possibility of writing. No longer completely
bound to, or by, the traditional (theological) structure of representation and
signification, writing articulates word(s) by inscribing an errant margin
that simultaneously joins and separates opposites. As a play of differences
that establishes the relationships that constitute all that is and is not,
writing is no thing and yet is not nothing. Within this script, there are no
discrete things or separate entities. Things, which are always already signs,
"are because of interrelations or interactions."[22] In less prosaic terms, writing inscribes

> edgings and inchings of final form,
> The swarming activities of the formulae
> Of statement, directly and indirectly getting at,
>
> Like an evening evoking the spectrum of violet,
> A philosopher practicing scales on his piano,
> A woman writing a note and tearing it up.
>
> It is not the premise that reality
> Is a solid. It may be a shade that traverses
> A dust, a force that traverses a shade.[23]

". . . edgings of final form . . . Like an evening [that delightful yet
agonizing threshold of day and night] . . . not . . . solid . . . may be a
shade . . . a dust . . . a force." In scripture, all "things" are thoroughly
interrelated. The specificity of any particularity is a function of its difference from otherness. Though usually overlooked (or repressed) by common
sense, *difference from* other is at the same time *relation to* other. Since all
things are *radically* related, everything is thoroughly relative. It is important not to confuse this relationalism or relativism with mere subjectivism.
While subjectivism separates and isolates, the relativity of scripture establishes the coimplication of everything.

The notion of constitutive relationality that emerges when word appears
as writing carries significant implications for traditional Western theology.
We have seen that most of the Christian theological network rests on a
dyadic foundation that sets seemingly exclusive opposites over against each
other. Furthermore, these paired opposites form a hierarchy in which one
term governs, rules, dominates, or represses the other. For example, God
governs the world, eternity and permanence are more valuable than time
and change, presence is preferable to absence, spirit more worthy than

body, etc. The grounding principle of this exclusive network is an abstract notion of identity, difference, and noncontradiction. According to the classical logic of identity (which is also the logic of common sense and good sense), "being is what is, the outside is outside and the inside inside."[24] When confronted with this disjunctive logic, the word begins its subversive activity. Scripture turns everything inside out and outside in. Writing reveals "that in *its own self* everything is in its self-sameness different from itself and self-contradictory."[25] The logic of exclusion cannot comprehend the interplay of identity and difference within which everything is inscribed. In order to grasp identity-in-difference and difference-in-identity, it is necessary to examine identity and difference separately. This twofold approach will, of course, eventually subvert itself.

According to both traditional logic and common sense, identity is simple self-sameness, which is exclusive of otherness. Careful inspection, however, shows the untenability of this position. The self-relation that is supposed to establish self-identity is actually pure difference. Within the dyadic structure of opposition, identity appears to be "difference that is identical with itself. But difference is only identical with itself insofar as it is not identity, but absolute non-identity. But non-identity is absolute insofar as it contains nothing of its other but only itself, that is, insofar as it is absolute identity with itself. Identity, therefore, is *in its own self* absolute non-identity." Difference from other turns out to be a relation to other that negates simple self-relation and "infects" pure self-identity. In other words, "*identity is difference*," for "*identity is* different from difference." Conversely, difference, pure or absolute difference, is identity. "Difference in itself is self-related difference; as such, it is the negativity of itself, the difference not of an other, but *of itself from itself*; it is not itself but its other. But that which is different from difference is identity. Difference is, therefore, itself and identity."[26]

It is necessary to stress that in this ceaseless oscillation of scripture, identity does not absorb difference and difference does not disperse identity. Identity-in-difference is always set in tension with difference-in-identity and vice versa. There can no more be identity without difference than there can be difference apart from identity. "[E]ach *is, only insofar as the other is*; it is what it is through the other, through its own non-being." And, of course, "each is *insofar* as the other is not; it is what it is through the non-being of the other."[27] Expressed more concretely, difference resists the totalitarianism of identity, just as identity resists the anarchy of difference. This relation of opposites is not exclusive or hierarchical. In writing, neither identity nor difference is prior, proper, or pure. Over against the imperial logic of identity, which always struggles to save presence by pursuing saving presence, the puzzling (a)logic of writing seeks to save difference by repeatedly searching for saving difference.

The recognition that difference is not indifferent ruptures the common-sense understanding of identity and fissures the dyadic foundation of traditional theological and philosophical reflection. Instead of establishing itself by excluding difference and repressing otherness, identity can be itself only if it is at the same time different and other. It is possible to "evoke an actual or real identity only by embodying difference, a real and actual difference, a difference making identity manifest, and making it manifest as itself. Only the presence of difference calls identity forth, and it calls it forth in its difference from itself." "Apart from the self-embodiment of otherness, identity could not stand out from itself, hence self-identity would then be neither manifest nor actual. Nor can self-identity appear and be real apart from identity's own embodiment of otherness." [28]

The coimplication of identity and difference establishes the duplicity of writing. Since everything necessarily differs from itself, nothing is ever merely itself. As a result of this unavoidable doubleness, there can never be only one but must always be at least two—two that are, nonetheless, not simply two. The duplicitous interplay of identity and difference exposes the absence in all "presence" by betraying the unavoidable "presence" of absence. "Embodiment is presence, but it is a presence which is an actual absence, the real absence of a total identity." [29] This disappearance of the *one*, a disappearance that is manifest in word and incarnate in writing, is nothing other than the death of God.

The relativity of presence and absence calls into question the logic of exclusion, according to which outside is outside and inside inside. Within the schizoid time-space of liminality, the fixed line that separates inner and outer is broken. Inasmuch as "nonpresence and otherness are internal to presence" [30] and identity, there must be an "interiority of exteriority" [31] and an exteriority of interiority. By repeatedly inscribing the boundary where presence and absence eternally cross, writing constitutes "the opening of the first exteriority in general, the enigmatic relationship of the living to its other and of an inside to an outside." [32] In anticipation of issues to be considered in the next chapter, it is important to stress that this "spacing is not the simple negativity of a lacuna but rather the emergence of the mark." [33] Words, scripture, and writing are not solid, stable, and steady. Words are incurable, scripture holey.

In view of the undecidable and unstoppable movement of identity into difference and difference into identity, of presence into absence and absence into presence, of exteriority into interiority and interiority into exteriority, the notion of writing might be further clarified by considering in greater detail the perplexing category of "negativity." Negativity is neither simply identical nor different, present nor absent, interior nor exterior. It is no more positive than it is negative and no more negative than it is positive. Rather, negativity is the play of differences that produces the difference that constitutes identity. In formulaic terms, the assertion "*A is A*" *necessarily* entails the claim that *A is not* non-*A*: $A \neq \bar{A}$. Non-*A*, in turn, becomes itself through relation to its opposite, $A$. $A$, however, has shown itself to be $-\bar{A}$. Consequently, $A$ and non-$A$ are simultaneously joined and separated in the complex web of negativity in which each becomes itself in and through the other. This interrelationship can be summarized as follows: $A = -\bar{A}$, and $-A = -(-\bar{A})$. Since negativity is "the generative movement in the play of differences,"[34] it appears to be "the formation of form."[35]

This interpretation of negativity discloses the extraordinary *force* of writing. Insofar as writing inscribes all in-form-ation, it constitutes "the non-full, nonsimple 'origin'; it is the structured and differing origin of differences."[36] Since negativity always involves the interplay of opposites, writing can never be a simple origin. As will become clear in what follows, writing not only grounds but also is grounded. Nevertheless, it is possible to regard negativity as "a sort of *deep structure* underlying the system of differences and oppositions for which it is not to be mistaken."[37] Inevitably slipping through the holes in the web it repeatedly stitches, this elusive "structure" is never *properly* present or absent. Negativity actually subverts the very oppositions that it simultaneously "founds." Even though the negativity of writing is the nonsimple "origin" of all difference and identity, as well as the nonfull "source" of all presence and absence, the play of differences presupposes neither an integrated whole nor a centered totality. The centripetal movement of identity-in-difference and the centrifugal pulse of difference-in-identity fluctuate ceaselessly. Freed from exclusive oppression, contraries form, deform, and reform in a constellation of interactions that has no specific origin, definite center, or ultimate conclusion. Always staging a drama of negativity, scripture is a decentered whole and an untotalizable totality that remains forever open-ended. The unfinished "whole" and fragmentary "totality" mark the "edgings of final form . . . not . . . solid . . . may be a shade . . . a dust . . . a force."

The idea of a decentered whole or a totality that cannot either totalize or be totalized seems to be utterly paradoxical and is thus very difficult to grasp. The untotalizable totality of negativity becomes more comprehensible if approached through the notion of *force*. As I have emphasized, writing embodies a tissue of differences in which terms are sites of passage. This liminal passageway is the domain of force. Constantly in transition and perpetually transitory, force is absolute passage or passage as absolute. Since there can be no force apart from forces, force is never simple or merely one but always inherently complex and intrinsically (at least) double. It can be itself only in and through opposition—opposition to other(s) and to itself. Force, in fact, "*is*" the interchange or interplay of different forces.

The analysis of negativity suggests that the play of forces is both productive and destructive. Productive activity discloses the inseparability of creation and destruction. Force "desubstantializes" everything by breaking down apparently fixed boundaries and creating an infinite field in which all "things" are interrelated. Within this generative/degenerative matrix, nothing is (merely) itself, for no thing can be itself by itself. Everything is fabricated by the crossing of forces. This intersection marks the threshold where "each *is* solely through the other, and what each thus is, it immediately no longer is, since it *is* the other." [38] The margin of force is forever embodied in word and ceaselessly reinscribed in writing.

This unending interchange of forces fissures all closed economic systems by creating an opening that saves difference. The movement of force captures the rhythm of writing, the structure of relation, and the activity of negativity. By so doing, force (re)produces the boundless boundary along which the oppositions that "ground" the Western theological network simultaneously emerge and collapse. Since force is always transgressive, it is undeniably subversive. Subversion involves both destructive creation and creative destruction. Force, in other words, is *de-con-structive*. As will become increasingly apparent in the next section, the de-con-structive force of scripture is the "universal medium [*Mitte*]" [39] of everything that is and is not. This universal matrix does not totalize and, therefore, need not be totalitarian. Since force is *always* embodied in forces, universality is neither above and beyond nor below and beneath particularity. Instead of transcendent power, force is the play of differences that is ever interstitial and never indifferent to difference. Within this endless play, *"There is no Logos, there are only hieroglyphs."* Insofar as writing is hiero-glyphic, it can be read as "the arising and passing away that does not itself arise and pass away." [40] From this point of view, scripture appears to be the *Divine Milieu*.

## Divine Milieu: A Middle Way

The divine milieu marks the liminal time and space where marginal passengers always roam. Consider the following re-mark:

> An old man sits
> In the shadow of a pine tree
> In China.
> He sees larkspur,
> Blue and white,
> At the edge of the shadow,
> Move in the wind.
> His beard moves in the wind.
> The pine tree moves in the wind.
> The water flows
> Over weeds. [41]

Within the subtle movement of these freely flowing lines, the "activity which things share is undulating motion. A wavering vibration pervades the world and binds things together . . . [A]ll things are metamorphoses of one another. The larkspur, the old man's beard, the pine tree, and the weeds are swept through by a piercing force, whether of wind or water, and in this irresistible medium they all waver and sway."[42] This wavering vibration, piercing force, and irrestible medium (*Mitte* or milieu) in which everything arises and passes away but which does not itself arise or pass away, is the "ever-never-changing-same."[43]

I have argued that writing is the forceful play of differences that forms the nonoriginal origin of everything. The creative/destructive negativity of writing stages an *eternally recurring* drama through which the differences constitutive of identity are engendered. Scripture is nothing other than "eternal recurrence." As the ever-never-changing-same, this *"Recurring is the being of what becomes."*[44] The relationship of being and becoming in eternal recurrence can be easily misunderstood. It is important to realize that in the perpetual play of the divine milieu, "[i]t is not being that recurs, but, rather, that recurrence constitutes being insofar as it affirms becoming and passing. It is not some one thing that recurs, but that recurrence is itself affirmed by the passage of diversity or multiplicity."[45] Insofar as this recurrence affirms passing, it involves the coincidence of affirmation and negation. Eternal recurrence is a *paradoxical* movement of repetition that itself neither begins nor ends.

When interpreted in this way, eternal recurrence suggests an alternative account of writing. In order to grasp the relation between writing and the divine milieu, it is necessary to recognize that the eternally recurring *coincidentia oppositorum* inverts and subverts the traditional contrast not only between finitude and infinitude but between time and eternity. When approached in terms of eternal recurrence, scripture both manifests the infinitude of finitude and the finitude of infinitude and reveals the eternity of time and the time of eternity. In order to come to terms with these baffling reversals, it will be helpful to consider each of the polarities in turn.

Common sense usually regards finitude and infinitude as opposed to each other and mutually exclusive. Though not immediately apparent, this view of the matter leads to the unintentional finitizing of the infinite and the infinitizing of abstract finitude. If the finite and the infinite are regarded as merely antithetical, the infinite is limited by the finitude over against which it stands. From this perspective, the finite appears to be independent and self-subsistent, and the *in*-finite seems to be dependent on and conditioned by firmly established finitude. This conclusion, however, inverts the explicit assumptions of common sense and points to the hidden implications of the ordinary understanding of the finite/infinite relationship. Since finitude does not possess aseity, its being necessarily entails the being of an other that is the indispensable presupposition of its own being. This other is the opposite of finitude. For this reason, *"The being of the finite is not only its own being,* but is also the being of the infinite."[46] Infinitude, by contrast, necessarily entails finitude. While the finite realizes itself in and through the infinite, infinitude renders itself infinite in relation to finitude. The finite is not merely other than and opposed to the infinite but is actually an "interior" dimension of infinitude. Inverting the movement of finitude, infinitude becomes itself through its other, the finite. In the process of establishing itself, infinitude negates the mere otherness of its other while, at the same time, preserving its difference. The infinite, therefore, "is on its own account just as much finite as infinite."[47] As a result of this complex interrelation, finitude and infinitude are neither simply opposed nor mutually exclusive. To the contrary, they enact a ceaseless play in which each becomes itself in and through the other.

The eternally recurring movement of finitude into infinitude and of infinitude into finitude can also be understood in terms of time and eternity. In a way that strictly parallels the inversion of the finite and the infinite, eternal recurrence subverts the traditional opposition of time and eternity. The analysis of presence and the present has already shown that the present, since it inevitably includes absence within itself, is never fully present but always is, in some sense, absent. Instead of being merely occasional and simply accidental, nonpresence is the very condition of the possibility of any presence whatsoever. Put differently, the present is never a *nunc stans* but is ceaseless transition, perpetual motion, constant movement. "That the present moment is not an instant of being, or of the present 'in the strict sense,' that it is rather the passing moment, *forces* us to think about becoming, but to think of it precisely as what could not have started, and what cannot finish, becoming."[48] The "being" of this becoming constitutes eternal recurrence. Indeed, it is possible to go so far as to insist that this recurrence "is the closest *approximation of a world of becoming to a world of being*."[49] Although everything determinate arises and passes away, this process itself neither originates nor concludes. The unending repetition of eternal recurrence discloses the "nonlapsability of the lapsability of time."[50] When time becomes eternity and eternity becomes time, they are no longer separated by an infinitive qualitative abyss. The interplay of time and eternity calls into question anything deemed *wholly* other and erases every vestige of *pure* transcendence. Instead of being antithetical to time, the eternal is found in the temporal and the temporal in the eternal. Along this paradoxical border, "Everything goes, everything comes back; eternally rolls the wheel of being. Everything dies, everything blossoms again; eternally runs the year of being. Everything breaks, everything is joined anew; eternally the same house is being built. Everything parts, everything greets every other thing again; eternally the ring of being remains faithful to itself. In every Now being begins; round every Here rolls the sphere There. The middle is everywhere. Bent is the path of eternity."[51] Never straight and narrow, the course of eternity is always *krumm*: curved, winding, circuitous, dishonest, and crooked. By repeatedly enacting an erratic play, eternal recurrence inscribes the ways of unending erring. When erring is grasped as eternal, "*die Mitte ist überall.*" What, then, is this *Mitte* that is everywhere?

*Mitte* designates not only center but also middle, midst, mean, and medium. For example, *die goldene Mitte* is the golden mean and *das Reich der Mitte* is the Middle Kingdom. Closely related to *Mitte, Mittel* refers to measure, mean, and medium. A suggestive extension of this word prompts further reflection. *Mittel* can also "mean" remedy or medicine. The French *milieu* captures various nuances of the German *Mitte. Le milieu* is the middle, midst, heart, center, medium, and mean. In addition to this cluster of meanings, *milieu* refers to one's environment, habitat, or surroundings. Through a curious twist of meaning, *le milieu* is sometimes used to designate the criminal underworld, the world of gangsters. Two English words closely related to *Mitte* and *milieu* are mean and medium. Mean derives from the Latin *medianus*, which is defined as "the middle." In this context, mean is that which is in the middle. This intermediate position can be both spatial and temporal. "Mean," of course, also designates an intermediary agent, i.e., one who acts as a mediator or go-between, who intercedes on behalf of one of the parties in a conflict. In view of issues yet to be considered, it is important to recall that the sacraments are labeled "the *means* of grace." "Medium" (*medius,* middle, midst, mid) likewise means something intermediate. Furthermore, medium refers to any intervening substance through which a force acts on objects at a distance, e.g., air or ether. This sense of the word gives rise to the notion of a pervading or enveloping substance or element in which an organism lives, i.e., its environment or the conditions of its life. By drawing on this fund of associations, it is possible to suggest that *Mitte,* or *milieu,* is "medium in the sense of middle, neither/nor, what is between extremes, and [a] medium in the sense of element, ether, matrix, means."[52]

This milieu marks a middle way that is thoroughly liminal. At this threshold, opposites cross. The margin itself, however, is not reducible to the extremes whose mean it forms. The medium, in other words, can never be contained, captured, or caught by any fixed pair of terms. Consequently, the milieu is always para-doxical. As we have seen elsewhere, a "thing in 'para' . . . is not only simultaneously on both sides of the boundary line between inside and out. It is also the boundary itself, the screen which is a permeable membrane connecting inside and outside. It confuses them with one another, allowing the outside in, making the inside out, dividing them and joining them. It also forms an ambiguous transition between one and the other."[53] This paradoxical limen or permeable membrane can be described as something like a *hymen.* By undermining the simplicity of oppositions and distinctions, "the hymen, the confusion between the present and the nonpresent, along with all the indifferences it entails within the whole series of opposites . . . produces the effect of a medium (a medium as element enveloping both terms at once; a medium located between the two terms). It is an operation that *both* sows confusion *between* opposites *and* stands *between* opposites 'at once.' What counts here is the *between*, the in-between-ness of the hymen. The hymen 'takes place' in the 'inter-,' in the spacing between desire and fulfillment, between penetration and its recollection. But this medium of the *entre* has nothing to do with a center." [54]

If *die Mitte ist überall, die Mitte* is not so much the center as it is the milieu. Moreover, this milieu is not restricted to a particular spatial or temporal point. It is everywhere and everytime. The universality of the medium implies that what is intermediate is not transitory and that what is interstitial is "permanent." Though always betwixt 'n' between, the "eternal" time of the middle neither begins nor ends. This universal and eternal milieu marks the (para)site where the word plays freely. Along this boundless boundary, the word appears divine. Scripture *is* the divine milieu, and the divine milieu *is* writing. The milieu embodied in word and inscribed in/by writing is divine insofar as it is the creative/destructive medium of everything that is and all that is not. Writing, as I have emphasized, is the "structured and differing origin of differences." This play of differences or differential web of interrelation is universally constitutive. When understood as scripture, the divine milieu is "what at the same time renders possible and impossible, probable and improbable oppositions such as" [55] eternity/time, infinitude/finitude, being/becoming, good/evil, etc. Writing is "originary" (though not original) inasmuch as it "grounds" or "founds" the differences that form and deform identity. Though the divine milieu is never simply present or absent, it is the *medium* of all presence and absence. In this complex mean, opposites, that do not remain themselves, cross over into each other and thus dissolve all original identity.

By disclosing the formative force of negativity, writing inverts and subverts the dyadic structure of the Western theological network. Through the enactment of an unending dialectic of transgression, the divine milieu effects "a total negation of everything which is manifest and real in consciousness and experience as God, so as to make possible a radically new form of consciousness and experience. Thereby a new form of God appears, but precisely because it is a radically new form it no longer can be given the name or image of God." [56] This negation of God appears as the word incarnate in writing. In the embodied word, the God of writing is manifested as the writing of God. The "figure of Thoth is opposed to its other (father, sun, life, speech, origin or orient, etc.), but as that which at once supplements and supplants it. Thoth extends or opposes by repeating or replacing. By the same token, the figure of Thoth takes shape and takes its shape from the very thing it resists and substitutes for. But it thereby opposes *itself*, passes into its other, and this messenger-god is truly a god of the absolute passage between opposites. If he had any identity—but he is precisely the god of nonidentity—he would be that *coincidentia oppositorum* to which we shall soon have recourse again. In distinguishing himself from his opposite, Thoth also imitates it, becomes its sign and representative, obeys it and *conforms* to it, replaces it, by violence if need be. He is thus the father's other, the father, and the subversive movement of replacement. The god of writing is thus at once his father, his son, and himself. He cannot be assigned a fixed spot in the play of differences."[57]

It is, of course, impossible to *master* Thoth by the logic of exclusion. In the liminal time-space of scripture, hard-and-fast oppositions are shattered and every seemingly stable either-or is perpetually dislocated. The divine milieu is neither fully present nor absent but is present only to the extent that it is at the same time absent. It neither is nor is not; it is insofar as it is not and is not insofar as it is. It is not totally positive or completely negative but affirms in negating and negates in affirming. According to traditional logic, which rests on the correlative principles of identity and noncontradiction, such claims are not only improper, they are actually absurd. The paradoxical divine milieu presupposes a "logic of contamination and the contamination of logic."[58] The eternally errant medium in which all differentiation is produced and destroyed cannot be re-presented in distinct categories and clear concepts. For this reason, the divine milieu "is not thinkable within the terms of classical logic but only within the graphics . . . of the *pharmakon*."[59]

Transgressive scripture engenders incurable disease by violating propriety and infecting purity. In this case, dis-ease need not be destructive and can actually be productive. Insofar as writing is parasitical, it is both nourishing and debilitating. This ambiguity lends scripture its pharmacological character. The Greek word from which *pharmaco-* and all its variants derive is *pharmakon*, which can mean "drug, medicine, or poison." Interestingly enough, the god of writing is also the god of medicine, who is supposed to restore health. A medicine man, however, is always something of a magician and trickster. The drug he prescribes is both a medicine and a poison—both gift and *Gift*. This generative/destructive *prescription* is a *pharmakon*. "If the *pharmakon* is 'ambivalent,' it is because it constitutes the medium in which opposites are opposed, the movement and the play that link them among themselves, reverses them or makes one side cross over into the other. . . . The *pharmakon* is the movement, the locus, and the play: (the production of) difference."[60] Though it is supposed to fix, the *pharmakon* itself cannot be fixed. Its shape is always changing, its form forever reforming. The *pharmakon* seems to be a liquid medium whose play is completely fluid. Like ink, wine, and semen, the *pharmakon* always manages to penetrate. "[I]t is absorbed, drunk, introduced into the inside, which it first marks with the hardness of the type, soon to invade and inundate it with its medicine, its brew, its drink, its potion, its poison."[61]

Such a strange potion can be concocted only by a physician who knows the magic (of) word(s): Hocus-pocus—*Hoc est corpus meum*. In the(se) extraordinary word(s), the physician himself appears as a *pharmakos*. Like every uncanny guest, this unsettling trickster is never permitted to pass beyond the threshold. Responsible authorities and distinguished authors attempt to keep the *pharmakos* behind bars. For this reason, the "site" of the word is always marked by an X and forever bears the sign of a cross. Since the *pharmakos* is irreducibly marginal, the ceremony in which it (or rather "he") is imbibed and inscribed must be "played out on the boundary line between inside and outside, which it has as its function ceaselessly to trace and retrace. *Intra muros/extra muros*. The origin of differences and division, the *pharmakos* represents evil both introjected and projected. Beneficial insofar as he cures—and for that, venerated and cared for—harmful insofar as he incarnates the powers of evil—and for that, feared and treated with caution. Alarming and calming. Sacred and accursed."[62]

In the ambiguous figure of the *pharmakos*, the intercourse of Terminus and Dionysus is manifest in the body and blood of the Crucified. The Crucified is the cruciform word that is always already inscribed in the eternally recurring play of the divine milieu. Scripture marks the *via crucis* in which all creation involves dismemberment and every solution presupposes dissolution. When *die Mitte ist überall*, transitoriness and passage no longer need to be repressed. Arising and passing can be welcomed as "productive and destructive force, as *continual creation*."

## Dissemination

The incarnate word inscribed in writing spells the closure of all presence that is not at the same time absence and the end of all identity that is not also difference. Writing is an unending play of differences that establishes the thoroughgoing relativity of all "things." This complex web of interrelations is the divine milieu. Within this nontotalizable totality, nothing is itself by itself, for all things emerge and fade through the interplay of forces. Insofar as the embodied word "is the name of the eternal perishing of eternal presence,"[63] scripture marks the death of God. In different terms, writing is a kenotic process; it empties everything of absolute self-identity and complete self-presence. In the eternal play of the divine milieu, nothing is fully autonomous or solely sovereign. Thus there is no *causa sui*, antecedent to and the ultimate origin of everything else. The absolute relativity of the divine milieu renders all other things completely correlative. As a consequence of the eternal cross(ing) of scripture, nothing stands alone and everything "originates" codependently. "Codependent origination"[64] is nothing other than the nonoriginal origin that erases absolute originality.

As the nonoriginal origin that "founds" the differences constitutive of relative identity, writing inverts and subverts the notion of origin itself. The generative movement of scripture rifts all seemingly immovable foundations and keeps everything in motion. The incarnate word is neither transcendent nor self-derived. To the contrary, the divine milieu is a/the grounded ground that, nonetheless, "grounds." In writing's unending play of differences, neither ground nor grounded is absolutely prior or undeniably primal. Ground and grounded are separated and joined in a relation that is characterized by radical codependence. "{T}here is nothing in the *ground that is not in the grounded*, and *there is nothing in the grounded that is not in the ground.*"[65] Since writing empties every *causa sui* of total self-possession, the divine milieu cannot be an *absolute* origin. It must be a *nonoriginal* "origin" or a *grounded* "ground." Contrary to common sense, writing is "founded" by the differences it "founds." In other words, writing is always in other words. The word is never disembodied; it is forever inscribed in writing. Since the word incarnates the coincidence of presence and absence and of identity and difference, it appears only by disappearing. This unstoppable interplay shows that the *Logos* is always the *Logos Spermatikos*, endlessly propagated by dissemination. Dissemination inscribes the way from the eternal recurrence of the divine milieu to the free play of marks and traces.

"To disseminate" (*disseminare*: *dis* + *semen*, gen. *seminis*, seed) is to scatter abroad, as in sowing seed. By extension, dissemination refers to the action of dispersing, diffusing, broadcasting, or promulgating. When translated into the present context, these verbal affiliations suggest that the dissemination of the word can be understood as its spreading, scattering, diffusion, or publication. The notion of the dissemination of the word is not, of course, new. Consider, for example, the following parabolic formulation:

> A sower went out to sow. And as he sowed, some seed fell along the path, and the birds came and devoured it. Other seed fell on rocky ground, where it had not much soil, and immediately it sprang up, since it had no depth of soil; and when the sun rose it was scorched, and since it had no root it withered away. Other seed fell among thorns and the thorns grew up and choked it, and it yielded no grain. And other seeds fell into good soil and brought forth grain, growing up and increasing and yielding thirtyfold and sixtyfold and a hundredfold.[66]

Like any text, these lines can be read in many ways. In this context, it is important to recognize that, according to this parable, the word is seed that appears with the disappearance of the sower. The "sower, mentioned only at the start of the story, immediately disappears. It would have been quite possible to leave him out completely: 'at the time of sowing, some seed fell. . . .' It would also have been easy to have retained him consistently: 'and some of the sower's seed fell. . . .' Instead, he is mentioned at the start and thereafter ignored. The parable is about seed and about the inevitable polyvalence of failure and success in sowing. . . . Or, if one prefers, it is about the absence and departure, the necessary self-negation of the sower." [67] By negating the sower in order to concentrate on the seed, this parable implies that dispersal is neither accidental nor secondary to a primordial, self-contained word. Quite the opposite, dissemination is necessary if any word is to be fertile. The seminal/seminary word *must* flow freely in liquid media like ink, semen, and wine. Because of its fluency, the embodied word cannot be contained within fixed boundaries or inscribed in straight lines. It is always dispersed and diffused. Furthermore, this scattering is not a temporary aberration, eventually overcome. Dissemination "can be led back neither to a present of simple origin . . . nor to an eschatological presence. It marks an irreducible *generative* multiplicity." [68] By figuring what cannot return to the father, the dissemination of the word replaces sterile stability and univocacy with creative instability and equivocacy.

To the extent that the embodied word enacts the *kenōsis* of all absolute self-presence and total self-identity, it can be itself only in and through the process of *its own* self-emptying. Like the transcendent father, the incarnate son must also pass away. Having displaced the Lord of Hosts, word becomes host. The word, which itself is a transgressor, is at the same time a victim who invites transgression. The patricidal act of transgression manifests the host-ility of the word. Not only is parasite host; sacrificer is also sacrifice. The word turns out to be a hospitable host who asks everyone to sit down at his table and even offers *himself* for our nourishment.

> For my flesh is food indeed, and my blood is drink indeed. He who eats my flesh and drinks my blood abides in me, and I in him.

Word becomes flesh: body and blood, bread and wine. Take, eat. Take, drink. To eat this bread and drink this wine is to extend the embodiment of the word and to expand the fluid play of the divine milieu. When freely enacted, the drama of the word proves to be self-consuming. While the incarnation of the divine is the death of God, the dissemination of the word is the crucifixion of the individual self. This dismemberment inflicts an incurable wound, which gives birth to erratic marks and erring traces.

# 6

## Markings

Here then is a partial view of the man of our new man-earth relation. He is a being on whom a vast field of encompassing physical, psychological, and moral powers converge, arousing and dampening his passions, modulating his affections. In a radial world he is a target, a victim, a vicar. Susceptibility to emotional infection and a drift toward anonymity have become common marks of his spiritual life.

The *id* is instinct; that Dionysian "cauldron of seething excitement," a sea of energy out of which the ego emerges like an island. The term *"id"* "it" . . . is based on the intuition that the conduct through life of what we call our ego is essentially passive; it is not so much we who live as that we are lived, by unknown forces. The reality is instinct, and instinct is impersonal energy, an "it" who lives in us. I live, yet not I, but it lives in me; as in creation, *fiat*. Let it be; no "I," but an it. The "I-Thou" relationship is still a relation to Satan; the old Adversary; the Accuser; to whom we are responsible; or old Nobodaddy in the garden, calling, Adam, where art thou? Let there be no one to answer.

To reach the selfhood or identity which is now being given us, we must turn away from every previous identity of the self. Above all we must resist and oppose every nostalgic and backward-looking call to return to what once was manifest as either the autonomy or eternity of selfhood. So likewise must we resist and oppose all nostalgic yearning for the unique individuality of selfhood. Here, the Christian has been given new images of death as well as new ways to the actualization of eternal death. Now the Christian is called to name the autonomy and eternity of selfhood as images of death, and as images of deaths which we must die. It is precisely by negating our yearning for autonomy and transcendence that we can die the eternal death which is now given us. Not only must we negate all such yearning, we must also reverse it. Or, more truly stated, the negation of selfhood to which we are called is a reversal of everything which is manifest as the autonomy and eternity of the self. But this can only mean that we are called to die the death of God, the death of the God who has been manifest to us as absolute sovereignty and pure transcendence.

("What did you think?" one of them once asked impatiently; "would we feel like enduring the estrangement, the cold and quiet of the grave around us—this whole subterranean, concealed, mute, undiscovered solitude that among us is called life but might just as well be called death—if we did not know what will *become* of us, and that it is only after death that we shall enter *our* life and become alive, oh, very much alive, we posthumous people!")

It is no longer possible to think in our day other than in the void left by man's disappearance. For this void does not create a deficiency; it does not constitute a lacuna that must be filled. It is nothing more, and nothing less, than the unfolding of a space in which it is once more possible to think.

## Dispossession, Impropriety, Expropriation

A vast field of encompassing powers; a sea of energy; unknown forces; impersonal energy; vicar; victim; no one to answer; anonymity; negation of selfhood; man's disappearance; images of death, eternal death; the cold and quiet of the grave around us; void. Posthumous people . . . called to die the death of God.

In his seminal work, *The Metamorphosis of the Gods*, André Malraux describes a series of van Eyck's paintings that culminates in the well-known *The Goldsmith Jan de Leeuw*: "These pictures were not made for churches. Nor for Bibles, like the Carolingian portraits . . . ; nor even for Books of Hours. Though stemming from religious imagery, they no longer derived their value from the service of God. Nor from what they represented, for their subjects interested only a few people; nor from their illusionism alone. Actually *trompe-l'oeil* effects play no greater part in *Jan de Leeuw* than they do in *Mona Lisa*. Yet, even assuming that the former was relatively little like its model, it would still suggest to contemporaries an attempt to vie with the forms of the created world—and this even without van Eyck's skillful shading, since portraits by the Flemalle Master and van der Weyden reveal a similar attempt. Donors had always been shown gazing towards Christ or the Madonna, but the eyes of Jan de Leeuw . . . are turned *toward the painter*."[1] The significance of the seemingly innocent shift of the goldsmith's eyes becomes apparent when this painting is placed within the context of an overall artistic development that Malraux charts. The history of art, according to Malraux, displays a gradual desacralization or secularization in which the function of art shifts from the representation of the gods to the expression of an autonomous realm ruled by the artist, a realm that Cézanne eventually labeled *la peinture*. While it is neither possible nor necessary to rehearse Malraux's complex argument, a brief comparison of his interpretation of Byzantine art, as illustrated by the Ravenna mosaics, and van Eyck's *The Madonna of Chancellor Rolin* suggests the general direction of his analysis and will set the stage for the further exploration of the postmodern death of the self.

Like its most successful architectural achievement, Hagia Sophia, Byzantine mosaics are, for Malraux, essentially hieratic. Reflecting major tendencies in much Eastern Orthodox theology, Byzantine art focuses on the eternal Christ to the virtual exclusion of the historical Jesus. As is evident in the Ravenna *Parable of the Last Judgment*, the heavenly Christ is characteristically surrounded by an ethereal, otherwordly ambiance. The use of color and lack of perspective serve a common purpose: "A *disincarnation* as deliberate and far more drastic than the idealizations of an earlier art—a means of giving human beings access to the world of Truth."[2] Allusion to the transcendent sacred, not an illusion of mundane reality, was the aim of the Byzantine artistic endeavor.

When van Eyck's *The Madonna of Chancellor Rolin* is placed alongside the Ravenna mosaic, the contrast is striking. Gone is the timeless Christ, and in his place we find a radically new object of devotion—a babe on the knee of his mother. The "unreal" colors and one-dimensionality of the mosaic give way to the realistic light, shadow, and depth of the painting. The world of appearance, which no longer points beyond itself to a transcendent realm of truth, has become the domain where the divine is incarnate. It is toward this timely appearance of God that the chancellor directs his attention. There is, however, another figure emerging in the very bosom of the babe. This dimly glimpsed face becomes clearly visible with a simple shift of the eyes.

The goldsmith turns his gaze from the disincarnate sacred and incarnate divine toward the painter. Apparently emancipated from the divine, the goldsmith/*Goldsmith* no longer seems to seek justification from implicit or explicit association with the sacred. Jan de Leeuw's eyes reflect a new recognition of the power vested in the *artist*. The creative artist is beginning to assume the position once held by the Creator.

A further step in this progression emerges if we turn our attention to a painting that Malraux does not mention, Velázquez's *The Maids of Honor*. Three features of Velázquez's work merit attention in this context: the painter, the infanta, and the mirror. *The Maids of Honor* represents an important inversion of van Eyck's *Goldsmith*. Instead of depicting the subject gazing at the artist, Velázquez shows the artist viewing the subject. "The painter is looking, his face is turned slightly, and his head leaning towards one shoulder. He is staring at a point to which, even though it is invisible, we, the spectators, can easily assign an object, since it is we, ourselves, who are that point: our bodies, our faces, our eyes."[3] This outward thrust is emphasized by the picture's principal figure. At the center of the painting we discover not the infant Jesus but a child princess, attended by a maid of honor whose kneeling posture recalls an adoring donor similar to Chancellor Rolin. Unlike the Christ child, however, the princess arrests our gaze only to turn attention *away* from herself. She too is looking outward—toward the spectator. The point of convergence of the stares of the artist and

*The Parable of the Last Judgment*, a mosaic in Sant' Apollinare, Ravenna.

Jan Van Eyck. *The Madonna of Chancellor Robin*. Oil.

Jan Van Eyck. *The Goldsmith Jan de Leeuw*. Oil.

Diego Velázquez. *The Maids of Honor*. Oil.

Pablo Picasso. *Armchair Woman, No. 2* (First State, *left*; Second State, *right*). Lithograph.
© 1983 by SPADEM, Paris/VAGA, New York. Reproduced by permission.

Barnett Newman. *L'Errance*. Oil. Reproduced by permission of S. I. Newhouse, Jr., the owner, and Mrs. Newman. Photograph by Malcolm Varon, N.Y.C.

princess is suggested by the mirror that stands above the child's head. In this somewhat obscure looking glass it is possible to discern the images of King Philip IV and his wife, Mariana. The longer one reflects on this reflection, the more puzzling it becomes. The mirror, it seems, conceals as much as it reveals. "That space where the king and his wife hold sway belongs equally well to the artist and to the spectator; in the depths of the mirror there could also appear—there ought to appear—the anonymous face of the passer-by and that of Velázquez."[4] Not only the artist but we ourselves seem to have disappeared in a play of mirrors. In the midst of the painting there "is an essential void: the necessary disappearance of that which is its foundation—of the person it resembles and the person in whose eyes it is only a resemblance. This very subject—which is the same—has been elided."[5]

The far-reaching implications of this empty mirror are not fully realized until the emergence of the radical departures that characterize much twentieth-century art. Distortion and disappearance, first of the human face and then of the entire human form in cubist and abstract painting, reflect the absence of the individual subject. The depiction of the absence of subjectivity is one of the chief aims of leading artists in this century. Picasso explains: "People didn't understand very well at the time why very often we didn't sign our canvases. Most of those that are signed we signed years later. It was because . . . we felt the temptation, the hope, of an anonymous art, not in its expression but in its point of departure. . . . We were trying to set up a new order, and it had to express itself through various individuals. Nobody needed to know that it was so-and-so who had done this or that painting."[6] When this "new order" is "fully realized, as in the late paintings of Barnett Newman, abstract art seems to pass into non-art, for it dissolves the frame of the easel, passing into the world beyond it, and that world is a purely and totally anonymous world."[7] In this graphic movement we can discern the drift toward anonymity: anonymous art in an anonymous world. Sartre's Estelle reflects this uncanny milieu: "I feel so queer. . . . When I can't see myself, I begin to wonder if I really and truly exist. I pat myself just to make sure, but it doesn't help much. . . . I've six big mirrors in my bedroom. They are there. I can see them. But they don't see me . . . how empty it is, a glass in which I'm absent!"[8] First the transcendent God, then the incarnate Christ, and finally the self itself disappear—die.

But what can it possibly mean to speak of "the death of the self," "the disappearance of the subject," and "the end of man"? It *seems* clear that selfhood has not literally come to an end. What or who, then, is this self whose death even now is being declared and enacted? And how can the disappearance of the subject be understood as the embodiment of the death of God, a death that eternally appears in the infinite play of scripture, a death that spreads the incarnate word through a process of unending dissemination?

In earlier chapters we have seen that, throughout most of the Western tradition, being is interpreted in terms of oneness and presence. To be is to be one, and to be one is, in some sense, to be uniquely and irreducibly present. As the ultimate ground or primal source of all being, God is the transcendent *One* whose complete self-identity and total self-presence are realized in absolute self-consciousness. When man is represented as the image of God, the self also appears to be self-identical, self-present, and self-conscious. The *proper* theological subject is the solitary self, whose self-consciousness assumes the form of an individual "I" that defines itself by opposition to and transcendence of other isolated subjects. Such a self is primarily and essentially a *unique individual*. The ostensible uniqueness (*unicus*, only, sole, singular) of the autonomous subject is a function of its separation from everything else. Though divided from others, the individual (*individuus*: *in*, not + *dividuus*, divisible, *dividere*, to divide) itself cannot be divided. In most cases, the locus of indivisible singularity is identified as an absolutely private interiority or purely personal inwardness. The hidden inwardness of the personality is the mirror image of the impenetrable mystery of the personal God. As God transcends the world through total alterity and radical solitude, so the self transcends its world through thoroughgoing otherness and complete alterity.

It should be clear by now that this interpretation of individuality rests on the repressive logic of identity, according to which the boundary that seems to separate discrete individuals is regarded as absolutely inviolable. In order to maintain itself, the subject must protect itself from "invasion" by the other. The higher the walls, the more impenetrable the membrane, the firmer the fixed border separating self and other, the more secure the subject's identity seems to be. For such an exclusive individual, a proper name delineates the intrinsically distinctive characteristics that define the singularity of the subject. In this way, the name becomes the self's private possession or personal property. The "logic" of oneness implies an economy of ownership in which *one* seeks security by struggling against dispossession, impropriety, and expropriation. Any subject that is not fully self-possessed, completely proper, and totally autonomous is not really (a) (it)self.

Naming, then, apparently realizes the "eschatology of the *proper* (*prope*, *proprius*, self-proximity, self-presence, property, own-ness)." The pronouncement of the proper name is, in effect, the baptism of selfhood. Baptismal waters are supposed to wash away impropriety by scouring stains and cleansing impurities. This (w)rite inscribes the name that defines the self. The singularity of the subject is represented by a unique mark that constitutes the signature of personal identity. If a signature is to serve as a personal seal that seals the personality, one's mark can be neither erroneous nor erratic. To the contrary, propriety requires both distinction and reliability. The distinctive or outstanding subject is distinguished by being set apart from all others. The unique individual is different rather than common. This difference, moreover, *is* the self's identity. The maintenance/*maintenant* of the subject's singularity "is in some way inscribed, pinpointed in the always evident and singular present punctuality of the form of the signature."

Our consideration of the "absolute" relativity of the divine milieu raises serious questions about the integrity of the individual. In view of the complexity of scripture, it is necessary to ask whether there can be a signature that is genuinely unique, definitive, distinctive, or distinguishing. "Does the absolute singularity of signature as event ever occur? Are there signatures? Yes, of course, every day. Effects of signature are the most common thing in the world. But the condition of possibility of those effects is simultaneously, once again, the condition of their impossibility, of the impossibility of their rigorous purity. In order to function, that is, to be readable, a signature must have a repeatable, iterable, imitable form; it must be able to be detached from the present and singular intention of its production. It is this sameness which, by corrupting its identity and singularity, divides its seal."[9] A signature that is not repeatable is not reliable. In order to be proper, names must be reiterated, reinscribed, and rewritten. Repetition, however, calls into question the signature of the individual. For example, when I would like to say or write "Mark," "the very factor that will permit the mark (be it psychic, oral, graphic) to function beyond this moment—namely the possibility of its being repeated *another* time— breaches, divides, expropriates the 'ideal' plenitude or self-presence of intention, of meaning (to say) and, *a fortiori*, of all adequation between meaning and saying. Iterability alters, contaminating parasitically what it identifies and enables to repeat 'itself'; it leaves us no choice but to mean (to say), to say something other than what we say *and* would have wanted to say, to understand something other than . . . etc. In classical terms, the accident is never an accident. And the *mis* of those misunderstandings to which we have succumbed must have its essential condition of possibility in the structure of marks, of remarkable marks."[10]

Although intended to inscribe unique identity, the remarkability of the mark points to the necessary *commonality* of the proper name. Insofar as a distinctive signature is repeatable, every name is, in some sense, a "shifter,"[11] and every subject is, to some extent, shifty. Naming seeks to negate impropriety by fixing shiftiness. But the name, even the proper name, is conventional and thus always misses (the) M/mark. Though intended to (be the) seal (of) the subject, naming dispossesses the self of all purely personal properties. "To enter language means to risk being named, or recognized by name, to struggle against false names or identities, to live in the knowledge that *reconnaissance* and *mépris(e)* are intertwined, and that

self and other are terms that glide eccentrically about an always improper . . . naming of things or persons."[12] The excentric drift of the name
disrupts self-identity by disclosing the impropriety of everything that once
was deemed proper. In this way, the inscription of the proper name erases
self-identical subjectivity and clears the way for the writing of erratic
marks. The wound that infects identity and renders the self incurable is
opened by the subject's necessary association with other subjects. In the
very struggle to achieve distinction by standing apart from other selves, the
individual eventually comes to realize an unavoidable commonality, which
grows out of inevitable relationships with others. To grasp the ramifications
of this fission of atomistic selfhood, it is necessary to explore the subject of
grammar or, more precisely, the grammar of the subject.

I have noted that the modern era has been characterized by a decisive turn
to the subject. As early as the seventeenth century, Descartes insists that
"proper" philosophical reflection must "begin" with the self-certain *cogito*.
As he develops his philosophical meditations, however, Descartes does not
limit his analysis to the activity of cognition. In a move destined to influence philosophy for centuries to come, Descartes subtly shifts the focus of
his attention from the process of thinking to the *res cogitans*. When formulated in these terms, the Cartesian *cogito* appears to be something like a
"thing" that thinks. Within the bounds of this discourse, the *res* can best be
understood as a subject whose definitive predicate is the activity of thought.
This interpretation of the structure of the subject implies a close connection
between subjectivity and syntax. Not only belief in God but belief in the
subject seems to be intrinsically related to faith in grammar. The lin-
guisticality of subjectivity deserves careful consideration.

According to the grammar of logic and the logic of grammar, the subject
is a substance in which attributes inhere and a substantive to which predicates can be attached. Expressed schematically: $S$ is $P$ (where $P$ can be $a$, $b$,
$c$, etc.). Within this formula, the subject is defined by predicates, which are
its properties. The assertion "$S$ is $P$" constitutes a judgment (cf. *Urteil*: *ur*,
original + *teilen*, to separate) that is intended to confirm identity by
distinguishing the subject from other subjects. Common sense insists on
the primacy of the subject and the secondariness of the predicates. The
subject is viewed as ontologically *primal*. As such, it is the *antecedent*
ground, base, and substance that underlies and unifies otherwise disparate
predicates. From this perspective, the subject is supposed to be a discrete
"thing-in-itself" that is extrinsically and accidentally associated with other
subjects and entities. The analysis of constitutive relationality I developed
in chapter 5 renders this interpretation of subjectivity problematic on at
least two counts. The assumed priority of subject over predicates is questionable, and the purported independence of the subject is suspect. Each of
these difficulties must be examined.

In the first place, the content of the subject and the predicates is the same. It is impossible to specify the subject in any way other than through the predicates. Consequently, the claim that the subject is other than, distinct from, and prior to the predicates is vacuous. Actually, it appears that the subject neither transcends nor subtends its properties. The subject is nothing other than the generative interplay of properties. With this insight, the ostensibly original subject effectively disappears in accidental play.

In the second place, the predicates whose interaction constitutes the subject are themselves thoroughly relational. If accidents or predicates are to be definitive, they must be definite. Definition and determination, in turn, presuppose *both* distinction from *and* relation to otherness. "[I]f the many determinate properties were strictly indifferent to one another, if they were simply and solely self-related, they would not be determinate; for they are only determinate insofar as they *differentiate* themselves from one another, and *relate* themselves *to others* as to their opposites." [13] Consider, for example, the phenomenon of color. The specificity of any color is a function of its location on a spectrum of colors. Color is determined by "its relations with the surroundings: the red is what it is only by connecting up from its place with other reds about it, with which it forms a constellation." [14] Apart from such contrast, color is completely indeterminate or simply invisible. A similar analysis must be applied to every property. The recognition of the differential character of predicates further unravels the identity of the subject and makes any notion of the self-in-itself unintelligible. "If I remove all the relationships, all the 'properties,' all the 'activities' of a [subject], the [subject] does not remain over; because [the subject] has only been invented by us owing to the requirements of logic." [15] Insofar as the subject *is* the predicates and the predicates are both inextricably interrelated as properties of the particular subject and inseparably bound to properties that surpass the specific subject, the subject is not a simple substance or a stable substrate. Rather, the subject is a complex matrix of ever-changing relations situated in the midst of an extensively and intensively differentiated milieu. With this shift in perspective, it becomes clear that the apparent founding subject necessarily empties itself in the perpetual crossing of predicates.

This admittedly abstract account of the dissolution of the autonomous ego and the death of the original self is concretely illustrated by the struggle for recognition in and through which competing selves attempt to establish and maintain individual identity. I have already argued that such a contest presupposes a noncontradictory logic in which opposites are mutually exclusive. When the notion of the self is tied to this logic, it is assumed that "to be a self is to have enemies, and to be a self is to be at war (the war of every man against every other man)." [16] Such hostility does not, of course, necessarily involve direct conflict. Within the overt or covert economy of domination, self-affirmation requires the negation and/or subjugation of other selves. Initially it appears that the subject "is simple-or-undivided Being-for-itself; it is identical-to-itself by excluding from *itself* everything *other* (than itself). Its essential-reality . . . [is], for it, *I* (I isolated from everything and opposed to everything that is not I)."[17] For the exclusive ego, other selves always seem threatening. In order to secure selfhood and protect subjectivity, it is necessary to negate menacing others. It is always possible that the struggle against an other subject will end in failure. Self-assertion, therefore, requires the self to put itself at stake (*se mettre en jeu*). To the self struggling for domination, however, such risk does not represent the acknowledgment of the possibility of the absolute loss of self or the acceptance of the actuality of death. To the contrary, in this case the encounter with loss and death is simply a moment that is necessary for their denial.

The negation of other selves does not inevitably lead to their actual annihilation. One can seek to possess oneself by possessing other subjects. Such possession takes the form of oppression. The oppressed subject apparently confirms the autonomy of the dominant self. At first this relationship appears to be asymmetrical: the oppressor seems to be independent and essential, the oppressed, dependent and inessential. With the recognition of the constitutiveness of relations, this conclusion becomes untenable. Instead of securing independent self-identity, this form of self-assertion implicitly confirms the thoroughgoing interrelationship of all concrete subjects. Far from being extrinsic and accidental, otherness and relations to other(s) are intrinsic to and necessary for any determination whatsoever. The self, therefore, is not a solitary individual but "a relation which relates itself to its own self, *and in relating itself to its own self relates itself to an other*."[18] Subjects, in other words, are never isolated monads but are always *reciprocally* related. This bond is affirmed even in the effort to negate it. It is necessary to stress that this interrelationship not only inverts but, more importantly, subverts the exclusive logic of identity. The outcome of the struggle for recognition is far more radical than a simple reversal of the roles played by oppressor and oppressed. With the realization of the total reciprocity of subjects, the entire foundation of the economy of domination crumbles. No longer conceiving themselves as self-equal by virtue of the exclusion of all difference, each self "is for the other the mean [*Mitte*] through which each mediates itself with itself and unites with itself." In this play, which is interplay, subjects "*recognize* themselves as *mutually recognizing* one another."[19]

The reciprocity of subjectivity embodies and enacts the play of forces in the life-and-death struggle of "selves." Within this dynamic field of force-ful interaction, there is an "intensity at work in everyone, its flux and reflux forming the significant or insignificant fluctuations of thought. And while each appears to be in possession of this, in point of fact it belongs to no one, and has neither beginning nor end."[20] This eternal play of forces that cannot be possessed deconstructs the isolated subject by reinscribing the eternally recurring divine milieu. The death of God, we have seen, marks the loss of the stable center that had been believed to be the basis of unique individuality and the ground of transcendent selfhood. The mortal wounding of the original subject releases the erring of scripture that entwines all things. For the solitary self, inscription within the infinite play of the word spells death. The dissemination of the word effaces every stable center and thereby decenters all subjects. This decentering of the subject does not, however, issue in the simple disintegration of the self. Neither completely undifferentiated nor entirely separate, the deconstructed "subject" is situated in the midst of multiple and constantly changing relations.

A network is formed by a "fabric of threads, cords, or wires that cross each other at regular intervals." The threads making up the network within which the fabric of selfhood is stitched are not merely indeterminate forces but impersonal structures. Although "individuals" usually remain unconscious of these relations, shifting structures do, nonetheless, operate through each self and among different selves. Instead of originating the relationships in which it stands, the subject is a function of the intersection of structures and the crossing of forces. In order to see how this is so, consider the example of language and its use. I have been at pains to underscore the connection between the notion of the *individuum* and the grammar of classical logic. It is, however, possible to acknowledge the bond between subject and language without insisting on the inviolability of the principles of identity and noncontradiction. If language is not subjected to the logic of exclusion but is interpreted as a ceaseless play of interrelated differences, then the subject is both *desubstantialized* and *deindividualized*. In this wordplay, there is no such thing as an original individual who initially stands outside a field of interaction and subsequently enters a matrix of relations that remains contingent and accidental. For instance, a purely creative subject does not first envision an original idea, which he then deigns to express in the common currency of everyday language. It would be more accurate to insist that the subject is always already bound in a self-surpassing linguistic web. This entanglement is the condition of the possibility of articulate subjectivity. Insofar as "the subject is inscribed in language," it is "a 'function' of the language."[21] In contrast to the substantial individual, this deindividualized subject is *co-relative* and *codependent*.

In order to avoid the impression that the anonymous networks that fabricate the deindividualized subject amount to a reedition of the eternal logos, forever present beneath appearances and able to bring together what otherwise remains dispersed, two points must be noted. First, these structures are not centered; they are always acentric. To insist that such networks are centerless is not necessarily to imply that the center has been elided. These structures need not have been centered "in the first place." The lack of an absolute center is tantamount to the absence of an absolute subject or original self. Anonymous networks, which are governed by neither a fixed center nor a primal subject, can never be complete and, thus, are always unfinished. As a result of this inconclusiveness, acentric structures do not necessarily centralize or totalize. The recognition of the openness of such networks leads directly to the second point that must be made concerning the web within which subjects find themselves. Differential structures are neither static nor stable. They cannot be reified or converted into invariable substrata that secure everything that seems to be unstable. Never abidingly present, acentric structures are in a state of constant flux. Since they are perpetually in transition, structures are radically temporal. This temporalization disrupts any possibility of pure presence, original beginning, and final closure.

The inscription of the subject within this tissue of relations results in the collapse of the absolute opposition between interiority and exteriority. If the subject is not self-centered but is a cipher for forces that play through it, there can be no sharp opposition between inwardness and outwardness. What appears to be merely outward is actually inward, and what seems to be exclusively inward is at the same time outward. This interplay of inwardness and outwardness subverts purely private and personal subjectivity. Since noncentered structures always operate in and through different subjects, it is necessary to admit that objectivity is, in an important sense, subjective and that subjectivity is undeniably objective. The purportedly "private" space of the "individual" subject is always inhabited by complex intersubjective structures of relationship. Embodiment in this network brings the end of inner transcendence, which had appeared to secure the separation of isolated selves.

The lack of private interiority is another mark of the dissociation of the autonomous subject. The identity of the independent self, we have seen, is most fully realized in the self-consciousness of the individual ego. If, however, this ego is always caught up in constantly changing structures, the "I" can be neither a self-contained presence nor a unique *individuum*. The play of the relational network both destroys the integrity of the autonomous self and exposes the pretensions of the all-knowing *cogito*. The sense of "identity, which we attempt to support and unify under a mask, is in itself only a parody: it is plural; countless spirits dispute its possession, numerous systems intersect and compete." [22]

In view of the complexity of the problems under consideration, it might be helpful to pause to gather together some of the strands that have been unraveling. What, "I" have been asking, does it mean to speak of the death of the self, the disappearance of the I, the decentering of the subject, and the end of man? What or who is this self whose death is being proclaimed and enacted? Expressed in terms of issues explored in earlier chapters: Can the disappearance of the subject be understood as the embodiment of the death of God and the realization of the dissemination of the incarnate word?

The self whose death I have been tracing is the *proper* theological subject. This subject is the solitary self, which defines itself in and through opposition to, and transcendence of, other isolated subjects. The analysis of the interplay of identity and difference has called into question the seemingly secure boundary between self and other. Instead of an aggregate of unique individuals, we have discovered a network of codependent subjects. Within this complex milieu, "simple identity is what has become truly absent to us, and simple or given identity in all its forms, whether these be subject and object, or matter and spirit, or society and selfhood, or knower and known, no identity whatsoever can any longer stand forth which is only itself."[23] The disappearance of the self-identical individual, however, is at the same time the appearance of the subject that is formed, deformed, and reformed by the eternal play of differences. The unstable players in this drama are not atomistic particulars or simple selves-in-and-for-themselves; rather, they are transitory "points" of intersection and "sites" of passage. The intermediacy of subjectivity suggests that the self is an "'empty subject'—a subject defined only as a locus of relationships."[24] Since relations are constitutive, subjects are co-relative. "There is no [subject] whose determination and self-determination [do] not require something [and someone] else, something which the [self] itself is not, for by itself alone it would not be definable."[25] The differential network within which related subjects are inscribed is the absolutely relative divine milieu. The following lines draw together some of the insights I have been developing and point toward issues yet to be considered.

> The indestructible
> is but your invention.
> God, the ineluctable,
> poetic pretension
>
> World wheel, while rolling on
> skims aim on aim:
> Fate, says the sullen one,
> fools call it a game [*Spiel*],
>
> World play, the ruling force,
> blends false and true [*Sein und Schein*],
> the eternally fooling force
> blends us in too.[26]

Subjects enfolded within this eternally fooling, maddening, clowning, jesting, tricking (*närrische*) field of force are erratic markings. If we are to proceed, it is necessary to consider in more detail a question previously broached: What is (a) mark?

*A mark is a trace; marking is tracing.* Trace: a course, path, road, or way; a way of life; track, footprint; beaten path, blazed trail; the intersection of a line or surface with a surface (as a fault or bedding plane). To trace: to take one's course, make one's way; to proceed, pass, go, travel; to pass along or over; to traverse; to follow the footprints of; to copy; to make a record by drawing; to write (as letters or figures); and finally . . . *to dance*. In all its (seemingly endless) variants, "trace" retains a radical ambiguity. A trace is neither properly present nor absent—it is, in some sense, at the same time present and absent. "Trace-structure, everything always already inhabited by the track of something that is not itself, questions presence-structure."[27] The trace violates identity and disrupts presence by marking "the intimate relation of the living present with its outside, the openness upon exteriority in general, upon the sphere of what is not 'one's own.'"[28]

The unending play of presence and absence in the trace "carries in itself the problems of the letter and the spirit, of body and soul. . . . All dualisms, all theories of the immortality of the soul or of the spirit, as well as all monisms, spiritualist or materialist, dialectical or vulgar, are the unique theme of a metaphysics whose entire history was compelled to strive toward the reduction of the trace."[29] The trace, however, repeatedly resists such reduction. The nonexclusive texture of the trace overturns the dualism and subverts the oppositions in which the notion of the subject traditionally has been inscribed. "It blurs the simplicity of the line dividing inside from outside, undermines the order of succession or of dependence among the terms, *prohibits* (prevents and renders illegitimate) the procedure of exclusion."[30] To the extent that the subject is a trace and subjectivity is tracing, the "self" is *"primordially"* relational. The trace is always inextricably related to co-relative traces and inevitably entangled in temporal becoming. Unmasterable by the logic of identity and noncontradiction, the trace can be represented by the *cross* that marks the place where identity and difference, as well as presence and absence, repeatedly intersect. Always in transition and constantly in the "middest," the trace is irrepressibly liminal and ever erring.

The trace marks the end of authentic selfhood by making "enigmatic what one thinks one understands by the words 'proximity,' 'immediacy,' 'presence' (the proximate, the proper, and the pre- of presence)."[31] The inscription of the trace simultaneously erases every notion of the self that is based on the principles of propriety, property, and possession and discloses the impropriety, expropriation, and dispossession of the subject. As "the opening of the first exteriority in general, the enigmatic relationship of the living to its other and of an inside to an outside,"[32] the trace disrupts the self-proximity required for authentic propriety. Since the trace "cannot be thought without thinking the retention of difference,"[33] this errant mark is the death of the self that is only itself. Within the improper economy of the trace, the subject is never merely itself but is always at the same time other than and nonidentical to itself. Having lost its own identity, the self cannot *properly* be itself. In the perpetually fluctuating network of traces, there is neither an original nor a final scene of nomination.

The absence of the proper name underscores the unavoidable impropriety of subjectivity. The trace "properly consists in a certain inconsistency, a certain impropriety."[34] When the self is interpreted in terms of the trace, it appears that the subject's "propriety or property is impropriety or inappropriateness."[35] Impropriety that is radical rather than accidental cannot be overcome. Appearances to the contrary notwithstanding, the subject is *always* both "stained" and "wounded." This stain cannot be cleansed, and this wound cannot be healed. The trace is incurable. By uncovering the outside that is inside, the trace disrupts the firm line separating inwardness and outwardness. Tracing inscribes an errant margin that can never be securely fixed. In the no-man's-land of the trace, there can be no proper insiders, for everyone is an irredeemable outsider. The liminality of the trace renders subjectivity inescapably marginal. There is always something threatening and unsettling about marginality. Marks who/which linger on the margin cannot be completely trusted. They seem to be improper, inappropriate—erratic, erroneous. For "insiders," outsiders who constantly hover at the threshold appear seedy, shady, and shifty. Since the self is a trace, it inevitably bears these marks of the margin. The erring trace "cannot be assigned a fixed spot in the play of differences. Sly, slippery, and masked, an intriguer and a card, like Hermes, [the erratic mark] is neither king nor jack, but rather a sort of *joker*, a floating signifier, a wild card, one who puts play into play."[36]

Neither idle nor innocent, this play is fatal for the individual self. The discovery of the self's chronic impropriety involves nothing less than the expropriation of the subject. To expropriate a person is to deprive that individual of what is proper to him, i.e., his property or properties and/or his propriety. Expropriation, therefore, inverts the process of appropriation through which the self attempts to take possession of itself. By representing itself to itself, the appropriate/appropriating subject seeks complete self-proximity and total self-presence. The improper subject, by contrast, is always inappropriate. This impropriety and inappropriateness can be understood as the effective ex-propriation of the unique individual. The expropriated subject realizes that to have the outside inside is at the same time to be inside the outside. As the intersection of converging and diverging relations, the trace repeatedly meets itelf *in and as* an other.

When the subject is understood in terms of the trace, it appears to be unavoidably excentric. Fabricated from transecting acentric structures, the deindividualized subject is never centered in itself. This is not to imply that a secure, definable center can be located outside the individual. To the contrary, the noncentered relational network in which the self is entwined decenters the subject and thereby establishes the *radical* excentricity of subjectivity. The trace can never be centralized. The excentricity of the subject is inseparable from the eccentricity of the erratic mark. The eccentric is always abnormal or anomolous—somewhat odd, sometimes devious.

This excentricity upsets all sense of propriety. No longer tied to a fixed center, the excentric/eccentric subject wanders excessively. Such erring overturns every effort to achieve secure self-possession.

As a kinsman of Hermes, the errant subject is not only a trickster but a thief. The expropriation of the subject robs the self of all purely personal properties. For the possessive self, "the relation with the other and the relation with death are one and the same opening."[37] The individual's elaborate strategies of self-assertion are actually various efforts to secure self-presence by excluding the dangerous other. To the extent that otherness represents the guise of death to the self-possessed subject, the individual's struggle for self-realization necessarily entails the effort to repress death. Death, however, will not be denied. Otherness, I have stressed, is never merely external but is always already within. Recognizing its own impropriety, the subject is forced to confess: "I is an other."[38] This dispossession of the subject is the annihilation of the self-possessed individual. Death, no longer appearing as an extrinsic wound accidentally befalling an integral self from without, now is manifest as a powerful parasite that relentlessly feeds within the subject. With the return to/of this para-site, we rediscover the uncanny guest that always lingers on the threshold—nihilism.

The consideration of the impropriety, expropriation, and dispossession of the subject reveals the inadequacy of the incomplete form of nihilism that characterizes humanistic atheism. Nihilism cannot be complete unless the death of God is embodied in the death of the self. The self-assertion through which the individual attempts to affirm its own power by negating the other is really a sign of impotence. This weakness stems from the subject's inability to accept the prospect of self-loss. Nihilism becomes fully actual when death or, more precisely, the death of the self is no longer passively suffered and reluctantly conceded but is actively affirmed and willingly embraced. The "No" of the radical nihilist harbors a "Yes" that freely acknowledges the interiority of exteriority that perpetually faults the integral subject. At this critical point, nihilism undergoes an unexpected reversal, which reveals that "nihilism is reversal itself: it is the affirmation that, in passing from the *no* to the *yes*, refutes nihilism—even though it does nothing other than affirm it, at which point nihilism is extended to all possible affirmations. From this we [can] conclude that nihilism [is] identical with the will to overcome nihilism *absolutely*."[39]

## Anonymity: Spending and Sacrifice

Marking . . . Tracing . . . Erring . . . Drifting. Drifting . . . (A)drift . . . (Ad)rift . . . Rifting. A/d/rift toward anonymity . . . a common mark of spiritual life. If to be a self is to possess and to be possessed by a proper name, then to lose the self is to become anonymous, and to become anonymous is to lose the self. Tracing inscribes a certain anonymity. The trace is the "erasure of the present and thus of the subject, of that which is proper to the subject and of his proper name."[40]

Posthumous people are called to live the death of the self. This disappearance of the subject accompanies and completes the death of God. Not until the transcendent God and all of His lingering shadows have been overcome can the news of the Madman reach our ears. To hear these mad words is to discover the foolishness of wisdom and the wisdom of foolishness. With this reversal, dreaded news is transformed into glad tidings. But how can the death of the self complete the death of God? And how can the disappearance of the divine and human subjects be anything other than an occasion for despair?

We have already discovered the close relationship between the death of God and a radical christology in which the incarnate word is interpreted in terms of writing. Scripture stages an unending play of differences that constitutes the universal medium or divine milieu in which all "things" arise and pass away. The eternal cross(ing) of forces brings the death of transcendent originality and marks the end of any solitary *causa sui*. Since the absolutely relative divine milieu negates any thing-in-itself or self-in-itself, everything is emptied of self-subsistence and self-existence. Scripture is radically, and thus "originally," kenotic. The incarnate word is not self-contained; it is itself only by becoming other than itself. I have described this process of self-emptying as the dissemination of the word. While the embodiment of the word enacts the death of God, the extension of the incarnation through the dissemination of the word realizes the death of the self. However, just as the death of God does not result in a simple absence but involves a self-emptying that issues in a complex divine milieu, so the death of the self does not entail mere destruction but points to the inscription of erratic markings or traces.

In a manner similar to the way in which the embodiment of the word empties the transcendent God of all aseity, the play of the word in scripture empties the self of all autonomy. The emptiness of the trace is the full actualization of divine relativity rather than the realization of the nihil of the void. Relative subjects, enmeshed in a network that is both creative and destructive, possess neither solidity nor substantiality. Mutually constitutive relations transform the boundary between ostensibly independent selves into an insubstantial membrane. Along this margin, codependent subjects interpenetrate. This intermingling creates an opening of self to other that cannot be encompassed by the traditional categories of the logic of exclusion. Never self-contained, clearly definable, or firmly centered, the trace is "unenclosed and unconfined." "Once the ground of an autonomous consciousness has been emptied or dissolved, then there can be no individual center of consciousness, or no center which is autonomous and unique.

With the disappearance of the ground of individual selfhood, the unique 'I' or personal ego progressively becomes a mere reflection or echo of its former self. Now the 'I' takes into itself everything from which it had withdrawn itself, and therefore it ceases to stand apart. In losing its autonomy, it loses its own unique center and ground, and thereby it loses everything which had once appeared as an individual identity or 'face.' Facelessness and loss of identity now become the mark of everyone, as everyone becomes no one, and the 'I' is inseparable from the 'other.' Individual selfhood does not simply or literally come to an end or disappear; it appears in the other."[41]

This ceaseless interaction of self and other renders subjectivity thoroughly communicative. Since the trace is never enclosed within itself, it is, in effect, an intersection within a tangled "network of communications."[42] Each "node" in this web is a mobile site through which constantly shifting forces recurrently pass. By breaking down the barriers between self-enclosed egos, communicating forces transform subjects into communicants. No longer possessive, the communicant seeks neither to secure his properties nor to preserve his propriety. Quite the opposite, communicants necessarily communicate. Such communication does not, of course, establish otherwise nonexistent links between discrete centers of consciousness. Independence and isolation are always already dissolved in the divine milieu. By extending the fluent play of scripture, the dissemination of the word releases seminal fluids, which flow freely between and among communicants. The incarnate word is a potent potion, attractive, though dangerous. To drink the word that has become wine is to suffer death. The disappearance of the self in the communion of subjects expands the kenotic process of scripture. Kenosis is a self-emptying that becomes actual in the crucifixion of independent individuals. This kenotic process is not a once-and-for-all event, confined to the distant past. It occurs repeatedly in and through the dissemination of the word. The word is spread through the crucifixion of the self. Here lies the unavoidable passion of writing.

Since the trace is irreducibly cruciform, communicants inevitably suffer. Subjects, in other words, are vicars, vicars who are victims of and vessels for the all-encompassing play of the forceful divine milieu. Those who suffer within this generative/destructive field never suffer alone. Pathos does not simply isolate and separate; it also ties and binds. Since subjects are primordially relational, passion is really compassion. The word marks multiple ways, from incarnation and crucifixion through dissemination and crucifixion to compassion, which is crucifixion. By emptying every subject of its intrinsic particularity, the drama of scripture occasions compassion, which simultaneously dissolves the solitary self and discloses the shifting contours of universal "subjectivity."

While the death of God becomes actual in a universal dispersed (and hence nontotalizable) totality, the death of the self is realized in noncentered subjectivity, which, though not transcendent, is, nevertheless, universal. Always bearing otherness within itself, the subject can be neither enclosed nor confined. Inasmuch as unbound subjectivity is intersubjective, liminal subjects are inevitably communal. Universal or communal subjectivity is nothing in-and-for-itself. It is actual only as the unending marginal play that forever inscribes and effaces traces. Far from remaining an abstract presence, universal subjectivity is always embodied in an undecidable interaction of presence and absence. This dynamic activity repeatedly negates abstract particularity by engendering differential relations that creatively deconstruct individual subjects. Since communal subjectivity possesses no private propert(y)ies, it is forever anonymous. Accordingly, every trace of communal subjectivity loses its proper name and thus itself becomes anonymous. Rather than temporary or momentary, this "aphanisis" (disappearance, obliteration)[43] of the proper name is a loss *without return*. Just as the anonymity of the divine milieu presupposes the dissolution of the transcendent center or origin, so the anonymity of universal subjectivity entails the loss of every interior center or origin. Within the divine milieu, the unique self is just as dead as the sovereign God in whose image it "originally" was formed. It is clear that this anonymity is, in an important sense, inhuman or, more accurately, antihuman. By dispelling the illusion of the autonomous self, communal subjectivity irrevocably negates much of what has been believed to be distinctively human. And yet, as we have seen repeatedly, destruction and creation are inseparable. The drift toward anonymity that erases the signature of individuality also "makes possible the actual realization of a concrete universality, a concrete universality which is . . . embodied by way of the negation and reversal of all individual interiority."[44]

Having suffered self-mortification, the communicant no longer is possessed by the self-ish-ness that attends egocentricity and hence is free to become geniunely generous. Generosity presupposes a psychology of sacrifice and an economy of spending that subvert the possessive psychology of mastery and the acquisitive economy of domination. This revolutionary reversal brings an unsettling "Night of non-profit, of subtle, invisible expenditure."[45] Generous expenditure breaks the circle of appropriation and possession by overturning the principles of utility and consumption. When freed from preoccupation with protecting private property and sovereign selfhood, one is able to spend without demanding return. The dispossession of the subject discloses the impossibility of ownership. With the loss of all vestiges of unique individuality, the subject becomes prodigal. For the responsible person who stays near home, there is something improper and disturbing about prodigality. The prodigal is given to extravagant expenditure and tends to disperse property recklessly. Convinced that the father is dead, the prodigal is unable to believe in any prospect of return. He is, it seems, destined to err endlessly.

From the point of view of common sense, extravagant expenditure and constant erring are not merely meaningless and useless; they are, more importantly, careless. The sovereign self longs for security. This security must be *carefully* established and maintained by building defenses against dispossession, expropriation, and impropriety. The dispossessed subject, however, realizes that security does not lie in carefulness. Quite the opposite, to be secure (*securus*: *se-*, without + *cura*, care) is to be without care; it is to be careless and carefree. "We are without such care only when we do not establish our nature exclusively within the precinct of production and procurement, of things that can be utilized and defended."[46] Openness to carelessness becomes possible with the realization that the subject is incurable. Contrary to expectation, to be incurable is to be secure, i.e., to be without (*se*) cure or care (*cura*).

The acknowledgment of the incurability of the subject that comes with the recognition of the inevitable interiority of exteriority is not necessarily a harbinger of despair. It can actually serve to release the subject from anxious striving. In the dark night of nonprofit, one learns that "a sage is a fool" and discovers that a Madman can be a sage. In this "inverted world,"[47] to be wise is to be carefree. Radical carelessness is indistinguishable from generosity that spends freely. Generous expenditure extends the dissemination of the word by actualizing the kenosis of individual selfhood. Carefreeness involves risk, radical risk; radical risk, which is embodied in total expenditure; total expenditure, which is absolute sacrifice; absolute sacrifice, which is nothing less than self-sacrifice. In this careless venture, one discovers the "identity of the sacrificer and the victim: the sacrifice of identity. The last cruel sacrifice is the sacrifice of the separateness of the self; self-sacrifice, self-slaughter, self-annihilation. The last cruel sacrifice is the crucifixion of the self."[48]

When seminal fluids (like the wine of Dionysus or the blood of the word) flow freely, sacrificer and victim appear to be the same. In this situation, to eat is to be eaten, and to drink is to be drunk. "Sacrifice is the remedy to a world devoid of transcendence."[49] Sacrifice, however, remains partial and hence inadequate if it does not become self-sacrifice or the sacrifice of the self. Insofar as it embodies the dispossession and expropriation of the subject, self-sacrifice is thoroughly nihilistic. To sacrifice the self is to consent to the death of the individual subject. This paradoxical gesture is at once a negation and an affirmation. Self-sacrifice negates the negations that appear to fix the boundaries of selfhood. As a result of the disintegration of the border dividing self from other, the individual subject suffers dismemberment. This dismemberment reverses the process of remembering, which is essential to self-possession. Instead of attempting to appropriate itself through re-collection, the errant trace confesses, nay, embraces, its incurable dispersal. The sacrifice of the self replaces purposeful remembering with active forgetting. Self-forgetfulness is a non-self-consciousness that is, nonetheless, not unconscious. This self-forgetfulness is induced by the gift/*Gift* of wine, the wine of Dionysus, the Anti-Christ, who is the *radically* embodied word.

## Death, Desire, Delight

But the man is closer to the child than is the youth. There is less melancholy in the man, and a greater understanding of death and life.

To be free for death and free in death; a sacred "No" when the time for "Yes" has passed: therein lies his understanding of death and life.[50]

". . . a sacred 'No' when the time for 'Yes' has passed." Self-negation is not simply negative, it is at the same time an affirmation. This affirmation, however, is not simply positive, it is at the same time a negation. While the sacred "No" is a negation of an affirmation that is, in itself, negative, the sacred "Yes" is the affirmation of a negation that is, in itself, positive. This interplay of affirmation and negation represents a significant transformation of the relationship between subjectivity and death.

In the psychology of mastery and the economy of domination, death is regarded as a hostile invader, one that carries the threat of a mortal wound for otherwise healthy subjects. Activities as diverse as the search for self-hood, the formation of history, and the writing of books have the denial of death as one of their goals. When bound to and by the exclusive logic of identity, the affirmation of the self is inseparable from the negation of otherness. With the discovery of its own impropriety, the dispossessed subject realizes the illusion of such affirmation and the futility of such negation. Scripture dis-closes by revealing that "the self of the living present is primordially a trace."[51] In the marginal play of the trace, death is a parasite; always within the host, it cannot be regarded as an improper intruder. It is undeniable that "health for the parasite, food and the right environment, may be illness, even mortal illness, for the host." There are, nevertheless, "innumerable cases, in the proliferation of life forms, where the presence of a parasite is absolutely necessary to the health of its host. Moreover, if nihilism is the 'heal-less' as such, a wound which may not be closed, an attempt to understand that fact might be a condition of health. The attempt to pretend that this uncanniest of guests is not present in the house might be the worst of all illnesses, the nagging, surly, covert, unidentified kind, there as a general malaise which undermines all activities, depriving them of joy."[52]

By tracing and retracing the disappearance of the subject, it becomes apparent that the trace is a mark which/who is formed by the cross(ing) of life and death. Since life dwells within death, and death is in life, it is possible "to read the word 'death' *without* negation."[53] Death, in other words, is a force *in* life rather than merely the tragic demise *of* life. The play of the word ends repression and oppression by bringing life that is death and death that is life. In this unending script(ure), "Whoever rightly understands and celebrates death, at the same time magnifies life."[54] Far from placing on the individual a heavy burden that inevitably creates a sense of gravity and seriousness, "the certain prospect of death [can] sweeten every life with a fragrant drop of levity."[55] In an effort to clarify this puzzling point, "I will cite a paradoxical example of a gay reaction before the work of death. The Irish and Welsh custom of the wake is little known, but was still observed at the end of the last century. It is the subject of Joyce's last work, *Finnegans Wake*, Finnegan's funeral vigil. . . . In Wales, the coffin was placed *open* and upright in the place of honor in the house. The dead person was dressed in his Sunday best and his top hat. His family invited all his friends, who increasingly honored the one who had left them as they danced on and drank stronger toasts to his health. In question is the death of an *other*, but in such cases the death of the other is always the image of one's own death. No one could enjoy himself thus if he did not accept one condition: the dead man, who is an other, is assumed to be in agreement, and thus the dead man that the drinker will become, in turn, will have no other meaning than the first one."[56] Dionysus, guardian of the boundary and god of wine, is also reputed to be Hades. To drink his wine is to dance with death.

According to the madness of "gay wisdom," the "sacred 'No'" is also a "Yes." This affirmation that is at the same time a negation is the affirmation of negation, the affirmation of the negation that is always already within and can thus never finally be negated. To affirm that death is primordial and inescapable is to accept "primal lack." If we are to understand the overwhelming significance of this acknowledgment, it is necessary to return to the distinction between need and desire. Elsewhere I have suggested that, though need and desire both involve "the presence of an *absence*," in need this absence is experienced as a "negated presence." For the needy self, lack is not primal; rather, it is secondary to a more original plenitude. Lack, therefore, represents a *deficiency* that one must strive to overcome. The subject in need always seeks fulfillment or satisfaction. The achievement of satisfaction, it is believed, will put an end to deficiency by *restoring* plenitude.

Need, however, is misguided. "The talk of the fullness of life . . . is rendered idle by its immeasurable discrepancy with death."[57] The subject that has discovered its own impropriety realizes that the wound that the needy self takes to be secondary is actually primal. Instead of a negated presence, absence is interior to presence and is "in" the present "from the beginning." It is precisely the "originality" of lack that makes the trace incurable. Since there is *always* a rift in subjectivity, lack cannot be filled. Consequently, total satisfaction is not temporarily delayed; it is forever unattainable. The recognition of the inevitability of lack and the impossibility of satiety marks the transition from need to desire. "[D]esire carries in itself the destiny of its non-satisfaction."[58] While need pursues a particular object that the subject assumes will fill the hole, close the gap, or heal the wound that rends, desire, which is not directed toward anything specific, remains free-floating. This hovering desire points to the necessary incompletion of the trace.

In contrast to the needy self, which yearns for completion, the desiring subject does not want fulfillment. The subject that desires is never satiated and yet is neither dissatisfied nor unhappy. *Desire desires desire.* Having realized that death is in life and life in death, that presence is in absence and absence in presence, the empty subject no longer seeks the satisfaction that fills, completes, and closes. From the perspective of the dispossessed subject, satisfaction, fulfillment, and closure appear to be fantasies contrived to suppress the irreducible emptiness of the trace. The desiring subject discovers an other within that forever disrupts the calm of simple self-identity. By refusing to transform desire into need, the subject consents to its own incompletion. In desire, the rift in the subject appears as the *radical* opening of primordial lack. By anticipating insights that will be developed in detail in the next chapter, it is possible to suggest here that, if lack is "original" and not secondary, then it is not necessarily a deficiency. Furthermore, if lack entails no deficiency, one might become free of the dreadful need to overcome it. If the subject does not need to repress the other "within," it is not driven to oppress the other "without." When desire forsakes the prospect of complete satisfaction, it opens the possibility of delight.

Delight is the inversion of satisfaction. Satisfaction is possessive—to seek satisfaction is to strive for the fulfillment that seems to result from the appropriation of otherness. Delight, by contrast, is nonpossessive. By granting the incurability of primordial emptiness, the dispossessed subject creates the possibility of overcoming the desperate struggle for possession and possessions. Delight can be understood as *enjoyment without possession.* The nonpossessive enjoyment of improper subjects calls into question the psychology of mastery and the economy of utility and consumption. In delight, one does not seek to master, does not cultivate the useful, and does not long to consume. Delight replaces self-affirmation, which attempts to negate negation by negating otherness, with an affirmation of negation that is impossible apart from acceptance of the other. Instead of struggling to reduce difference to identity, the one who delights acknowledges the identity of difference and appreciates the difference of identity. Since delight "is never a taking," "nothing separates it . . . from losing."[59] In this case, however, loss is neither improper nor simply tragic. To the contrary, in delight, "the only true joy is the joy of loss."[60] Since delight always involves loss, the joy it brings is inevitably an *anguished joy.* Dispossession, impropriety, expropriation, anonymity, spending, sacrifice, death, and desire all come together in this anguished joy. Such delight "is not something promised: it is [always already] there if you live and act in such and such a way."[61] But *how*? How must erring marks live and die to discover the anguished joy of delight?

# 7

## Mazing Grace

K was haunted by the feeling that he was losing himself or wandering into a strange country, farther than ever man had wandered before, a country so strange that not even the air had anything in common with his native air, where one might die of strangeness, and yet whose enchantment was such that one could only go on and lose oneself.

. . . I am a wanderer in all cities and a provocation for all gates to open. . . . The only country of my love is my children's land. It lies undiscovered beyond the farthest seas: to see it and seek it I have set my sails.

This signifier of little, this discourse that doesn't amount to much, is, like all ghosts: errant. It rolls . . . this way and that like someone who has lost his way, who doesn't know where he is going, having strayed from the correct path, the right direction, the rule of rectitude, the norm; but also like someone who has lost his rights, an outlaw, a pervert, a bad seed, a vagrant, an adventurer, a bum. Wandering in the streets, he doesn't even know who he is, what his identity—if he has one—might be, what his name is, what his father's name is. He repeats the same thing every time he is questioned on the street corner, but he can no longer repeat his origin. Not to know where one comes from or where one is going, for a discourse with no guarantor, is not to know how to speak at all, to be in a state of infancy. Uprooted, anonymous, unattached to any house or country, this almost insignificant signifier is at everyone's disposal . . . .

### Erring: Serpentine Wandering

In a rambling essay entitled "Walking," Henry David Thoreau writes:

I have met with but one or two persons in the course of my life who understood the art of Walking, that is, of taking walks,—who had a genius, so to speak, for *sauntering*: which word is beautifully derived from idle people who roved about the country, in the Middle Ages, and asked charity, under pretense of going *à la Sainte Terre*, to the Holy Land, till the children exclaimed, "There goes a *Sainte-*

*Terrer,"* a Saunterer, a Holy-Lander. They who never go to the Holy Land in
their walks, as they pretend, are indeed mere idlers and vagabonds; but they
who do go there are saunterers in the good sense, such as I mean. Some,
however, would derive the word from *sans terre,* without land or a home, which,
therefore, in the good sense, will mean, having no particular home, but equally
at home everywhere. For this is the secret of successful sauntering. . . . To
come down to my own experience, my companion and I, for I sometimes have a
companion, take pleasure in fancying ourselves knights of a new, or rather an
old, order,—not Equestrians or Chevaliers, not Ritters or Riders, but Walkers,
a still more ancient and honorable class, I trust. The chivalric and heroic spirit
which once belonged to the Rider seems now to reside in, or perchance to have
subsided into, the Walker,—not the Knight, the Walker, Errant. He is a sort of
fourth estate, outside of Church and State and People. . . . No wealth can buy
the requisite leisure, freedom, and independence which are the capital in this
profession. It comes only by the grace of God. It requires a direct dispensation
from Heaven to become a walker. You must be born into the family of the
Walkers. *Ambulator nascitur, non fit.* Some of my townsmen, it is true, can
remember and have described to me some walks which they took ten years ago,
in which they were so blessed as to lose themselves for half an hour in the woods;
but I know very well that they have confined themselves to the highway ever
since, whatever pretensions they may make to belong to this select class. No
doubt they were elevated for a moment as by the reminiscence of a previous state
of existence, when they were foresters and outlaws.[1]

Saunter . . . *sans terre* . . . *Saint Terre.* Nowhere a homeland . . . no
place to lay one's head . . . rolling this way and that like someone who has
lost his way . . . who doesn't know where he comes from or where he is
going . . . uprooted, anonymous, unattached . . . Saunterer errant . . .
Errant sauntering.

To saunter is to wander or travel about aimlessly and unprofitably. The
wanderer moves to and fro, hither and thither, with neither fixed course nor
certain end. Such wandering is erring—erring in which one not only
roams, roves, and rambles but also strays, deviates, and errs. Free from
every secure dwelling, the unsettled, undomesticated wanderer is always
unsettling and uncanny. Having forsaken the straight and narrow and given
up all thought of return, the wanderer appears to be a vagrant, a renegade, a
pervert— an outcast who is an irredeemable outlaw. The outlaw is forever
liminal, marginal; he is curiously ambivalent, shifty, and slippery. Insofar
as the outlaw is not only a heretic who transgresses but also a subversive who
breaks the (power of the) law, erring points to the ways of grace. Erring is
serpentine wandering that comes, if at all, by grace—grace that is mazing.
But when and how? When is such serpentine erring possible? And how does
mazing grace arrive?

The time and space of graceful erring are opened by the death of God, the
loss of self, and the end of history. In uncertain, insecure, and vertiginous
postmodern worlds, wanderers repeatedly ask: "Whither are we mov-

ing? . . . Are we plunging continually? Backward, sideward, forward, in all directions? Is there still any up or down? Are we not erring as through an infinite nothing?"[2] While the death of God is realized in the play of the divine milieu and the disappearance of the self is inscribed in markings and traces, history "ends" when erring "begins," and erring "begins" when history "ends."

In order to grasp the relationship of the closure of history and the opening of erring, it is necessary to recall some of the outstanding features of history. History, we have seen, is closely related to a form of experience that I have described as "unhappy consciousness." Although not always obviously distraught, the unhappy person is perpetually discontent. With eyes forever cast beyond, the victim of unhappy consciousness lives in memory and hope. He nostalgically recollects the satisfaction he believes once was and expectantly anticipates the fulfillment he hopes will be. Satisfaction, however, proves to be elusive; it is never present or is *infinitely* delayed. Dissatisfaction and discontent engender an uneasy restlessness, which the striving subject relentlessly attempts to quiet. For the unhappy self, the pursuit of satisfaction necessarily involves an effort to become other than what one is. History, at least in part, grows out of the ceaseless struggle for transcendence, a struggle that every discontented subject anxiously enacts. For this reason, the historical process is inseparably bound to the activity of negation. History, which always begins with a "No," consists of "Putting Allspace in a Notshall."[3] This "Notshall" mirrors the repressive "shellfishness"[4] of unhappy consciousness. The "Nay" that the unhappy person pronounces reflects the inability of the dissatisfied subject to accept lack and embrace loss. From this point of view, history amounts to an unending search for a presence that saves. This longing for saving presence discloses the unbreakable bond between history and death. Though assuming a variety of guises, the negation that unhappy consciousness embodies is triggered by a malaise that arises from the recognition of the thoroughgoing temporality of subjectivity and is directed toward the denial of human mortality. The drama of history stages the flight from death.

The ramifications of the complex constellation formed by death and history deserve further consideration. The foregoing comments imply that unhappy consciousness is fragmented and split. The discontented subject is convinced that such inner division is not original and should not remain final. This self-division generates a painful tension between what is and what ought to be. The perceived estrangement of "reality" and "ideality" creates the suffering of the historical agent. Torn between an ideal past that is no longer and a perfect future that is not yet, the unhappy subject is forced to acknowledge the undeniable transcendence of the "ought." Insofar as history is suspended between "is" and "ought," it *falls* within the domain of the law. History is not only logical or logos-full; it is also lawful. The law, however, is always two-edged. This duplicity uncovers the self-negation that is concealed within the subject's attempted self-affirmation. By recognizing the power of the law, unhappy consciousness simultaneously envisions *possible* fulfillment and confesses *actual* guilt. For the guilty subject, lack is an acquired deficiency rather than an "original" incompletion. The No-saying that is characteristic of unhappy consciousness makes guilt inescapable. Such a serious encounter with guilt eventually leads to a revolt against *oneself*. As long as the unhappy person pursues an imagined ideal, he inevitably cries: "If only I were someone else. . . . I am who I am: how could I ever get free of myself? And yet—I *am* sick of myself!"[5] The sigh of the repressed gives voice to the despair that is inherent in unhappy consciousness. The subject in revolt against itself suffers a grave illness that amounts to "the sickness unto death."

To the trained physician, the gravity of this malady suggests a possible link between guilt and God. The utter guilt of man appears to be the inverse image of the complete holiness of God (and vice versa). The translation of guilt into the language of religion marks the appearance of sin. When one believes that the human drama is played out before an ideal spectator whose omniscient gaze penetrates every secret, guilt deepens and becomes sin. In this situation, transgression is more than the breach of human convention or natural law. It is nothing less than violation of the absolute commandments of an ultimately perfect and completely holy God. The transition from guilt to sin constitutes the transformation of unhappy consciousness into lacerated consciousness. As the plight of the sinner deepens, his yearning for transcendence and longing for the beyond increase. Suffering even more profoundly than the guilty self, lacerated consciousness "is the incarnate desire to be different, to be in a different place, and indeed [is] this desire at its greatest extreme, its distinctive fervor and passion."[6] Unhappy consciousness, which begins with the attempt to assert self by negating other, ends as lacerated consciousness, which strives to negate self by affirming other. It is clear, however, that while the overt self-affirmation of the former is covert self-negation, the ostensible self-negation of the latter is actual self-affirmation.

Plagued by despair, the unhappy subject and lacerated consciousness conspire to convert time into a schema for the expiation of guilt and/or the forgiveness of sins. This conspiracy appears in the genealogy of history. "Woe entreats: Go! Away, woe! But all that suffers wants to live, that it may become ripe and joyous and longing—longing for what is farther, higher, brighter. 'I want heirs'—thus speaks all that suffers; 'I want children, I do not want *myself*.'"[7] Such a quest for heirs must not be confused with setting sail for the land of one's children. The voyage of history is the opposite of the aimless drifting and free floating of childhood. More often than not, the denial of the self for the sake of one's children (actual or otherwise) is a circuitous route to self-assertion. Having realized his own inadequacy, the guilty or sinful person attempts to found a dynasty or establish a line that will forever secure (his) presence. To this extent (but only to this extent) children are conceived in guilt and born in sin.

When these insights are brought together with the preceding analysis of history, it becomes clear that the tensions that characterize guilt and sin lend the historical process its distinctive structure. History, I have argued, is essentially narrative. It has a beginning (Once upon a time), a middle ( . . . ), and an end (happily ever after). The history of the West unfolds between limits set by the garden and the kingdom. Unhappy/lacerated consciousness seeks to cure its ills by assuming a central role in a lawful plot. For the guilty/sinful subject, history is "a detour between two presences."[8] Moreover, this detour is *for the purpose of* the reappropriation of presence."[9] Within the Judeo-Christian tradition, which, we have discovered, haunts the historical imagination of the West even when it is not directly acknowledged, history is fundamentally tripartite. Though frequently subdivided in different ways, the historical process is usually described as consisting of three basic stages, roughly corresponding to the "moments" of creation, fall, and redemption. Insofar as history appears to be a symmetrical narrative structure in which beginning and end mirror each other, historical actors are engaged in the effort to recover a past that has been lost. In this struggle, "archeology is also a teleology and an eschatology; the dream of a full and immediate presence closing history, the transparence and indivision of a parousia, the suppression of contradiction and difference."[10]

Between the felicity of the beginning and the perfection of the end, however, lie the time and space of the fall. Having been expelled from the garden and unable to reach the kingdom, fallen subjects suffer estrangement. Consider Yukel, who, we have seen, is never here but always elsewhere—ahead of himself or behind:

> "What are you dreaming of?"
> "The Land."
> "But you are on land."
> "I am dreaming of the Land where I will be."
> "But we are right in front of each other."
> "And we have our feet on land."
> "I know only the stones of the way which leads, as it is said, to the Land."[11]

The way that leads to the Land inevitably *passes through* the desert. Unhappy sojourners experience this detour between presences as an *exile*. In the strange land of estrangement, the only guide is the Law, a Law that comes from *beyond*. This transcendent Law reveals that exile is neither original nor final. To the contrary, the fall is an *aberration*, a *temporary* aberration. This transitory detour has a definite purpose—its end is the end of exile and the return to/of presence. Exiles, therefore, are not condemned to roam endlessly but are (from the beginning) destined to return. This homecoming promises a perfection that exceeds original satisfaction. The desert is left behind as exiles enter a land flowing with milk and honey. When land becomes the Land, the wandering of exiles comes to an (or the) end.

Such an account of history, even in its many secular versions, is thoroughly theological. Instead of a random sequence of meaningless occurrences, history assumes coherence as an intelligible pattern, comprising logical and lawful events. Moreover, the understanding of history as a directed process remains bound to a view of the self as an intentional agent. The purposeful subject is an integral member of a purposive totality. Having already explored the complex interconnection of the death of God, the disappearance of the self, and the end of history, it is now necessary to turn to the implications of the relationship between the "emergence" of the trace and the "advent" of erring. The correlative concepts of scripture and trace subvert the interpretation of history as a lawful "archeoteleological process" by calling into question the actuality of beginning, middle, and end. Each of these founding moments must be reconsidered.

The experience of exile and estrangement presupposes an understanding of lack as loss or defect(ion). To be estranged is to be separated from a harmonious totality with which one previously had been united. For the exile, this original unity appears to be a state of plenitude and perfection in which every need is totally and immediately satisfied. Apparently suffering no discontent, the self seems to be thoroughly at home in its world. For reasons that are not always made clear, this scene of harmony and satisfaction comes to an abrupt end. Separation effects a breach, and this disrupts the primal unity and opens a wound that infects the subject with restless discontent. It is not necessary to examine the panoply of images with which the religious imagination figures this purported fall. What must be stressed in this context is the inseparability of the ideas of plenitude, loss, and exile.

It should be evident that the notions of writing and tracing raise serious questions about this "historical" analysis of experience. I have stressed that the unending play of traces negates every absolute origin and renders problematic all ideas of original plenitude and integral unity. If *lack* is primal, then plenitude and the total presence it entails are never present or are "present" only as "absent." Accordingly, "exile" is "original" and is not subsequent to an antecedent "time" that was unstained by the agony of "loss" and untainted by the tension of "estrangement." The "loss" of plenitude, integrity, identity, propriety, proximity, and self-presence is, therefore, really "the loss of what has never taken place, of a self-presence which has never been given but only dreamed of and always already split, repeated, incapable of appearing to itself except in its own disappearance."[12] The *radical* codependence of all things negates the possibility of an absolutely primal origin from which everything descends. The play of traces inscribed in/by scripture discloses an "originary" difference that always makes the calm satisfaction of pure self-identity unattainable. Instead of an ideal state that once was enjoyed and now has been lost, the harmonious origin appears to be "an illusion" created to explain and repress the tensions that forever inhere in everything that is actual.

The interplay of identity and difference, of presence and absence, disrupts the integrity of the origin that forms the initial moment, which, paradoxically, is neither properly inside nor outside the historical process. When the reality of the origin becomes questionable, the related categories of fall, exile, guilt, and sin become problematic. If primal plenitude is never present and absence is "original," then lack does not inevitably entail loss or deficiency. That which is, in other words, is not necessarily other than that which ought to be. Apart from the reality of a pure origin, there can be no fall that begins a period of exile. Furthermore, the recognition of the illusion of the origin forces the acknowledgment of the fantasy of the end. In different terms, the disappearance of the origin is at the same time the "end" of the end.

In historical narrative, fall is placed in the context of restoration. Thus guilt and sin are always located within the framework of redemption. While nostalgia is retrospective hope, hope is prospective nostalgia. The end appears to be the parousia, which restores or even surpasses the fulfillment and plenitude of the beginning. Although not necessarily circular, the course from origin to conclusion inscribes a "closed" circuit of departure and return. According to the story line of history, the "end" (i.e., both the aim and the termination) of exile is the re-appropriation of the plenitude, propriety, proximity, and presence that were lost in the defection of the fall. From the perspective of this *telos*, it becomes possible to comprehend the direction and significance of history *as a whole*. The end totalizes by leaving no loose ends. In this way, eschatology offers the final word, which is supposed to put an end to every form of erring.

The end of erring is the erasure and repression of the trace. In opposition to the history of ontotheology, a/theology insists on the irreducibility of the trace. For this reason, a/theology remains stubbornly "ateleological" and "aneschatological."[13] From the viewpoint of a/theology, there never was a pure origin and never will be a perfect end. "All promise, all future hope and expectation, come to an end in the death of God."[14] This hopelessness, however, does not inevitably lead to despair. Within the unending play of the divine milieu, "waiting is the final losing game." In fact, "waiting itself is damnation."[15] The trace is never healed, but it is "fulfilled, by remaining open, by pronouncing nonclosure."[16] The ateleology and aneschatology of radical a/theology end all endgames by keeping openness open and showing every mark to be incurable. Such incurability does not actually involve disease, though it surely issues in disturbing dis-ease. If there is no origin, if the fall is a chimera, if lack is not deficiency, guilt, or sin, then the "No" of unhappy/lacerated consciousness does not have to be, indeed cannot be, the *final* word of the trace. While the affirmation of the perfection of the end entails the denial of everything that falls short of the *telos*, the denial of the completion of the end opens the possibility of affirming what previously had seemed inadequate and insufficient. Sojourners are no longer driven to seek justification by looking back to fathers and mothers and ahead to sons and daughters. With the disappearance of origin and conclusion, "Becoming must be explained without recourse to final intentions; becoming must appear justified at every moment (or incapable of being evaluated; which amounts to the same thing); the present must absolutely not be justified by reference to a future, nor the past by reference to the present." [17]

Insofar as becoming is justified at every moment, the eternal play of differences has no firmly fixed center. In the absence of beginning and end, there can no more be a secure center than there can be a geniune beginning and end apart from a definite midpoint. I have stressed that narrativization ties together the dangling threads of chronicle by forming a centered structure. The overall coherence of historical narrative requires a specific center, one that refers back to an inaugural moment and ahead to a conclusive moment. The center governs the pattern of the plot by forming the prism through which all events are reflected and refracted. This organizing focus functions as a point of orientation; it protects striving subjects from the confusion and conflict wrought by decentering and excentricity. Like origin and conclusion, the center seeks to cure the open trace by founding the eternal play of scripture. If, however, the divine milieu is an acentric or excentric totality, which neither begins nor ends, then it would seem that nothing inscribed within this noncentered whole can be centered or whole. It is important to recognize that this centerlessness is not the result of the loss of an actual center. While pure origin never was and perfect end never will be, fixed center never is. The disappearance of origin, center, and conclusion points to "the *seminal* adventure of the trace." [18] This adventure has, of course, always already begun.

Unlike the temporary roaming of estranged exiles, the serpentine wandering of the errant trace is unending. Never able to identify beginning, middle, or end, the wanderer is not sure where he comes from, where he is, or where he is going. The impossibility of locating an unambiguous center leaves the wanderer rootless and homeless; he is forever *sans terre*. The saunterer undergoes "perpetual displacement," which issues in constant "deterritorialization." [19] The life of erring is a nomadic existence that is deeply unsettling. The nomad is an undomesticated drifter, always suspicious of stopping, staying, and dwelling. Such homelessness underscores the anonymity of the saunterer. Attached to no home and *always* separated from father and mother, the wanderer is nameless. What appeared to be a proper name always turns out to be an improper mark. Homeless and anonymous, the wanderer "doesn't even know who he is," doesn't even know his identity—for *he has no identity*, or at least he has no identity in the *proper* sense of the term.

In contrast to the anxious searching of the unhappy exile, the careless wanderer *"determines the noncenter otherwise than as the loss of center."*[20] By negating "negative excentricity," this affirmation of centerlessness opens the possibility of exorbitant erring. The nuances of "exorbitant" (*ex*, out + *orbita*, beaten track, rut, orbit) are many: "leaving a specified track; deviating from an established rule or principle; irrelevant; irregular; anomalous; aberrant; monstrous"; of a person: "extravagant, frantic, wild; trespassing; exceeding ordinary or proper bounds." In all of these variations, "exorbitant" implies an element of *transgression*. Since erring is always exorbitant, the wanderer inevitably transgresses. The drifter repeatedly deviates from the normal, ordinary, lawful course, way, or path. Such transgression gives erring its serpentine character. In the eyes of the "straight" world, erring follows the devious ways of the serpent. In serpentine wandering, one "rolls this way and that like someone who has lost his way, who doesn't know where he is going, having strayed from the correct path, the rule of rectitude, the norm; but also like someone who has lost his rights, an outlaw, a pervert, a vagrant, an adventurer, a bum."[21] Rather than a temporary deviation that is eventually overcome, this transgression is ceaseless. The endlessness of erring discloses its unavoidable purposelessness.

In addition to being rootless and nomadic (originless), as well as excentric and exorbitant (centerless), the erring trace is purposeless and aimless (endless). The prospect of *radical* purposelessness emerges with the realization "that becoming has no goal and that underneath all becoming; there is no grand unity."[22] In the absence of a final *telos* for the entire generative/destructive milieu, it is possible to affirm purposeless process. The wanderer has no certain destination, goal, aim, purpose, or end. While the exile apprehensively pursues the salvific cure of closure, the drifter is "indifferent to any possible results."[23] Having "lost" all direction, the trace becomes a "purposeless tension."[24]

The aimlessness of serpentine wandering liberates the drifter from obsessive preoccupation with the past and future. This release silences the yearning for transcendence by calling into question the exclusive opposition between what is and what ought to be. By freely affirming the primordiality of lack, the interiority of exteriority, the difference of identity, and the actuality of death, the erring trace overcomes the despair of unhappy/lacerated consciousness. When becoming no longer needs to be validated by reference to past or future but can be valued at every moment, one has broken (with) the law. Such transgression does not breed guilt and sin. In this case, lawlessness proves to be inseparable from grace—grace that arrives only when God and self are dead and history is over. The lawless land of erring, which is forever beyond good and evil, is the liminal world of Dionysus, the Anti-Christ, who calls every wandering mark to carnival, comedy, and carnality.


## Aberrance: Carnival and Comedy

> Just as there is a negative theology, there is a negative atheology. An accomplice of the former, it still pronounces the absence of a center, when it is play that should be affirmed. But is not the desire for a center, as a function of play itself, the indestructible itself? And in the repetition or return of play, how could the phantom of the center not call to us? It is here that the hesitation between writing as decentering and writing as an affirmation of play is infinite. [25]

The hesitation between writing as decentering and writing as an affirmation of play marks the gap that separates "a negative atheology" and an affirmative a/theology. Instead of nostalgically recalling the loss or "impossible presence of the absent origin," a/theology carelessly affirms play—the free play of erring. Thoth, the god of writing, who embodies absolute passage, is also the "inventor of play," the "one who puts play into play." [26] Play is an unending game that stages the drama of the death of God, disappearance of self, and end of history. I have argued that the death of God is realized in a radical christology in which the incarnate word is read as writing. Scripture is the *play* of differences that constitutes the universal medium or divine milieu in which all "things" arise and pass away. The eternal recurrence of the cross(ing) of forces marks every subject a trace. Possessing neither personal propert(y)ies nor proper identity, the erring mark remains a wanderer, drifter, vagrant, and outlaw. Never leaving the margin and forever wandering along the border, the trace is dissolutely liminal. The marginality of the trace comes to expression in the liminality of play.

Once put into play, it is virtually impossible to stop the play of "play." Amid its multiple meanings, several distinctive characteristics of play can be identified. Play is, first of all, purposeless. The player not only needs no goals, rewards, or results but actually resists every form of repressive closure that threatens to stop the flow of the game. Play ends when it is taken seriously or is pursued for the sake of a definite purpose. In a certain sense, play, in contrast to work(s), has no reason. Consequently, from the prudential perspective of common sense, play (at least play that is not disguised work) is judged to be unreasonable. This unreasonableness, irrationality, or even absurdity lends play an air of meaninglessness. Insofar as meaning is tied to intention or purpose, play can never bear the weight of meaning. "To risk meaning nothing is to start to play," [27] and to insist on meaning something is to stop playing.

Purposelessness and meaninglessness combine to expose the uselessness of play. In earlier chapters we have seen that the psychology of mastery leads to an economy of domination that rests on the principles of utility and consumption. Play, which is always free and can never be bought, breaks the closed circuit of appropriation that characterizes utilitarian consumerism. Though play is all-consuming and all-possessing, players neither consume nor possess. In contrast to the possessive owner and thrifty consumer, the player spends freely without ever calculating profits. This generous expenditure is a sign of the prodigality of the erring trace. Unlike the faithful son, the prodigal neither returns nor demands a return. From a utilitarian viewpoint, play is both useless and unprofitable.

Since it is purposeless, meaningless, useless, and profitless, play appears to be totally frivolous. Through an unexpected twist, the notion of frivolity underscores the inseparability of play and writing. Though it is not generally recognized, "Frivolity consists in being paid with marks. It is born with the sign, or rather with the signifier which, no longer signifying, is no longer a signifier. The empty, void, friable, useless signifier. So Condillac says. In the *Dictionnaire des synonymes*, he refers us from *frivolous* to *useless* ('*FRIVOLOUS*. Adj. See Useless.'). *Useless* then: 'adj. *vain, frivolous, futile.*' Useless is said of things which serve no purpose, are of no use [*qui ne serve à rien*]. If they appear to have some utility but are fundamentally useless, they are called *vain*. If their utility bears only on objects of little consideration or worth, they are *frivolous*. As for *futile*, it adds still more to *frivolous* and is said chiefly of reasoning or arguments which bear on nothing." [28]

Within this profitless economy, the mark that is the currency of frivolity is always empty. This emptiness undercuts the opposition between signifier and signified on which the representative structure of signification traditionally banks. The frivolous trace is "merely" a sign of a sign. Expressed in different terms, the freely floating mark inscribes the unavoidable absence of a proper signified. Having already examined the connection between the disappearance of the transcendental signified and the death of God, we now are in a position to see that the absence of an absolute foundation is, in effect, the lack of a fixed point of reference or center of gravity, which, by grounding heavy thoughts and weighty deeds, functions to prevent exorbitance. The death of God, in other words, unleashes the aberrant levity of free play. One could, in fact, go so far as to "call *play* the absence of the transcendental signified." This absence implies the "limitlessness of play" and points to "the destruction of ontotheology and the metaphysics of presence." [29] By negating both theological presence and the presence of theology, play effectively extends the margin of a/theology.

This insight calls into question the common understanding of play as the enjoyment of a "timeless presence," resulting from the actualization of an immediate present. As the ceaseless interplay of presence and absence, the present is neither properly present nor absent. The free activity of play enacts rather than represses this paradoxical coincidence of presence and absence. "Play is always play of absence and presence, but if it is to be thought radically, play must be conceived of before the alternative of presence and absence." Far from realizing an immediate present or timeless presence, play always includes an absence that "is the disruption of presence."[30]

This unsettling disruption is evident in the undeniable risk of radical play. In "the *seminal* adventure of the trace" one always "plays without security."[31] The risk and insecurity of play appear most dramatically in the "loss" of self experienced by the player. The more *I* try to play, the farther removed from the play I become. "All playing," it seems, "is a being-played."[32] This understanding of the dynamics of play further illuminates the endless inscription of writing. In the fooling/foolish play of forces, players lose themselves or forget their selves. Without this self-forgetfulness, the generous expenditure of erring is impossible. The currency of this free play is "the everlasting flow." The spending of the self in play effectively realizes the emptiness of the trace. "Empty," which derives from Old English *áemetig* (leisure), means, among many other things, "at leisure, lacking knowledge and sense; wanting solidity and substance; vain, meaningless, frivolous, and foolish." By emptying the self of itself, play manifests the insubstantiality of the trace and the frivolity of tracing.

As a result of its purposelessness and insubstantiality, play appears to be completely gratuitous. Having neither good ground nor sufficient reason, the gratuitous is both groundless and unreasonable. Since it is not required, warranted, or justified, what is gratuitous often seems to be outside the bounds of properly established norms and generally accepted laws. "Gratuitous" (*gratuitus*, free), however, can also mean "freely bestowed; granted without merit; provided without payment or return." To the extent that play is gratuitous, it is "a matter of 'grace' rather than law."[33] The purposelessness and uselessness of play invert the purposefulness and usefulness of work. Play involves free activity that is justified neither in terms of what has been nor in relation to what will be. Lawless play overturns every lawful economy of work(s) by undoing "the curse of the law."[34] Since it does not conform to the rules of common sense and the laws of logic, play is irregular and players are unlawful. In the gratuitous play of the wor(l)d, and the gracious wor(l)d of play, the errant trace is a graceful out-law. Along the endless boundary and in the eternal meantime of scripture, it appears that the wor(l)d inscribed in and by the play of the divine milieu is an inverted wor(l)d. When everything is turned upside down and downside up, inside out and outside in, "Wisdom is in wit, in fooling, most excellent fooling; in play, and not in heavy puritanical seriousness. In levity, not gravity. My yoke is easy, my burden light."[35]

The dissemination of the word becomes actual in the play of the trace. When released from restrictive boundaries and repressive limits and allowed to flow freely, the blood of the incarnate word appears to be intoxicating wine, the bringer of riotous revel. This delirium generates the *aberrant* world of the carnival. The festive carnivalesque world is ceaselessly inverting and thus always inverted. Within this liminal time-space, everything is reversed. As high becomes low and low becomes high, the sacred is profaned and the profane is sacralized. By upsetting traditional hierarchies, carnivalesque play inverts inherited values and established meanings. This inversion does not leave opposites unmarked. The reversal enacted in festive celebration dissolves the original identity of the exclusive opposites that have defined the poles of most Western theology and have formed the foundation of Western society and culture. When it becomes radical, inversion is transformed into a perversion that is subversive. To glimpse the subversive movement of the festival, it is necessary "to think pure change, or *think antithesis within the antithesis itself*, or contradiction."[36] This antithetical contradiction or contradictory antithesis subverts the dyadic structure of classical theology and reveals both the codependent relationality and complex relativity that are inscribed in contemporary a/theology. The revel of the carnival suggests a world that "ignore[s] substance, causality, or identity outside of its link to the whole, *which exists only in or through relationship*." Insofar as the carnival involves "distances, relationships, analogies, and nonexclusive oppositions, it is essentially" paralogical. "It is a spectacle, but without a stage; a game, but also a daily undertaking. . . . A carnival participant is both actor and spectator; he loses his sense of individuality, passes through a zero point of carnivalesque activity, and splits into a subject of the spectacle and an object of the game. Within the carnival, the subject is reduced to nothingness . . . ."[37]

As these remarks indicate, the paralogic embodied in the carnival presupposes the nonexclusivity of opposites. Within this framework, the interplay of contraries involves "a logic of relations and analogy rather than of substance and inference."[38] In the carnival, there are only "ever changing, playful, undefined forms. All the symbols of the carnival idiom are filled with this pathos of change and renewal, with the sense of the gay relativity of prevailing truths and authorities. We find here a characteristic logic, the peculiar logic of the 'inside out' (*à l'envers*), of the 'turnabout,' of a continual shifting from top to bottom, from front to rear, of numerous parodies and travesties, humiliations, profanations, comic crownings and uncrownings."[39] In this perverse and subversive world, propriety, property, and possession give way to impropriety, expropriation, and dispossession. When spending replaces consumption, restraint and retention issue in discharge and release.

Festive discharge and carnivalesque release are completely transgressive. The act of transgression breaks, infringes, trespasses, and violates. By refusing to respect boundaries, the transgressor repeatedly errs. This erring is thoroughly improper. From the point of view of proper society and self-possessed subjects, the impropriety of the festival is evident in bodily activity and verbal conduct.

Along the margin of the carnival, the body appears to be *grotesque*. The grotesque body incarnates the liminality of the trace by disrupting every identity that is only itself and by upsetting all sense of propriety. Because the grotesque body is utterly transgressive, it is totally liminal. Such a body is not merely found along the boundary; it *is* actually a border or margin. The grotesque body is never individual, for it transgresses every isolating limit. "Contrary to modern canons, the grotesque body is not separated from the rest of the world. It is not a closed, completed unit; it is unfinished, outgrows itself, transgresses its own limits. The stress is laid on those parts of the body that are open to the outside world, that is, the parts through which the world enters the body or emerges from it, or through which the body itself goes out to meet the world. This means that the emphasis is on the apertures or the convexities, or on various ramifications and offshoots: the open mouth, the genital organs, the breasts, the phallus, the potbelly, the nose."[40]

The body as grotesque is the body that eats, drinks, shits, pisses, and fucks. The boundary between bodies is a permeable membrane; it has gaps and holes to let the inside out and the outside in. This interplay of inner and outer makes all bodily events interstitial. Though apparently either inside or outside, bodily activity is properly neither inner nor outer. The grotesque body is a site of passage where crossing and crisscrossing forces constantly intersect. Since this everlasting flow cannot be stopped, its current must always be discharged. The carnival provides the occasion for such release. In the festival, creative and destructive juices flow freely. This orphic/orific revel dismembers every body that, and everybody who, appears to be neat, clean, proper, complete, and finished. The openings of the grotesque body are not accidental wounds that need to be cured or offensive holes that must be covered. Bodily gaps are "primal" and therefore incurable. While radical opening mortally wounds proper identity, conclusive closure marks the end of the body. When inside is only inside and outside is only outside, when eating, drinking, pissing, shitting, and fucking stop or are stopped, vital current no longer flows and the body truly dies.

It should not be surprising that the grotesque body cannot be figured in proper language. Carnivalesque discourse is not structured by the rules of logic, nor does it conform to generally accepted norms of expression. The festive player is incorrigibly transgressive in word as well as deed. In the confusion of the festival, discourse "tends toward the scandalous and the eccentric in language."[41] This linguistic eccentricity is manifested in the abusiveness, profanity, and ambiguity of the players' verbal conduct. Since the carnival inverts traditional hierarchies, the language of revelers sounds abusive and insulting to those whose positions are threatened. (Ab)errant words are dangerous. In any proper society, it is forbidden to say some things in the presence of the father, king, or lord. The transgressor, however, uses verbal abuse and insult to overturn oppressive oppositions and to bring about the release of the repressed. The double edge of abusive and insulting words suggests that such language is inevitably ambivalent. It is both destructive and creative. The generativity of carnivalesque discourse appears in its irrepressible profanity. Festive language is neither proper nor clean; it is improper and dirty. Its words seem to be indecent, indiscreet, impure, and stained. Such soiled language is usually quite earthy. It tends to be sexual and scatological. Like the grotesque body that utters it, this language seems foul. It is out of bounds. Filthy words inevitably dissolve restrictive limits and break down constrictive boundaries. Though undeniably destructive, such violation is also productive. By discharging what previously had been repressed, transgressive discourse releases creative energy.

We have discovered, however, that, in addition to meaning clean and pure, "proper" also designates what is special, peculiar, distinctive, discrete, characteristic, and intrinsic. Accordingly, proper language is never indistinct, indiscrete, or uncharacteristic. The proper use of words avoids confusion by securing the special characteristics and definitive peculiarities of all distinct entities. In other words, proper discourse is monovalent and univocal. It makes every effort to talk straight and to avoid errors. As we shall see in more detail in the next chapter, improper language is, by contrast, aberrant, plurisignificant, and equivocal. In the free play of the carnival, language is loose and words are slippery. From the logical and reasonable perspective of common sense, the polysemy of carnivalesque language represents either foolishness or outright madness. To the extent that this aberrant discourse is radically transgressive, it is dangerously subversive. And yet this "unbewising" "sounddance," this babble or confusion of tongues is not sober and somber; it is gay and reJoycing.

> Ha he hi ho hu
> mummum.[42]

Hahehihohumummum. . . . Echoes . . . of humus . . . and humor(s). Humus is a dark brown or black substance that results from the slow disintegration or decomposition of organic matter on or near the surface of the earth. Humor is, on the one hand, moisture, vapor, or any fluid of an animal or plant and, on the other hand, the faculty of perceiving what is ludicrous. Dark brown, black substance and vital, seminal fluid combine to create fertile humor. In humor, the grotesque body and ludicrous language of the festival find improper expression. Though the carnival is deadly serious, it is at the same time riotously humorous. The humor of the carnival gives the festival the appearance of a comedy. In the unending game of the carnival, tragedy gives way to comedy. Carnivalesque comedy does not involve the salvific closure envisioned in the words "And they lived happily ever after." When comedy is played in the time-space of the carnival, it neither ends nor cures. This irregular comic awareness is actually a post-tragic sensibility. While tragedy remains caught in the web of human-ism, comedy is antihuman or, perhaps more accurately, superhuman. As a ceaseless play or an endless game, comedy provides no roles/rules for se-rious, purposeful individuals. When understood in this way, comedy pre-supposes the end of history. Furthermore, it can be staged only by posthumous actors, who no longer cling to a centered self. The Madman who envisions the *Übermensch* declares: "whoever climbs the highest moun-tains laughs at all tragic plays and tragic earnestness."[43]

The comedy of carnival play erupts with an "enormous burst of laugh-ter."[44] The emptiness of frivolity erases every center of gravity that governs the fixed orbit of weighty bodies. Though always enacted over a bottomless abyss, festive play is never grave. The levity of play subverts the law by mocking serious work and earnest struggle. Comic players insist that "Pre-cisely because we are at bottom grave and serious human beings—really, more weights than human beings—nothing does us as much good as a *fool's cap*: we need it in relation to ourselves—we need all exuberant, floating, dancing, mocking, childish, and blissful art."[45] The shameless laughter of comedy is all-inclusive. The laughing fool sees the entire world "in its droll aspect, in its gay relativity."[46] This unrestrained laughter frees one "from dogmatism, from the intolerant and the petrified; it liberates from fanati-cism and pedantry, from fear and intimidation, from didacticism, naïveté, and illusion, from the single meaning, the single level, from sentimen-tality."[47] Laughter communicates "la joie révolutionnaire," which over-comes the dread and agony of "petit narcissisme" and the terrors of guilt and sin.[48] The ambivalent levity of the laugh that kills ends the gravity and seriousness of unhappy/lacerated consciousness. This destructive/genera-tive laughter is the *risus paschalis* (*risus*, laughter; *paschalis*, belonging to Easter and Passover). Again the words of the Madman: "This crown of laughter, this rosy-wreathed crown: I have placed it on my own head; I myself have pronounced my laughter holy."[49]

The Madman is, of course, a fool, and his insane laughter foolish. Grotesque body, carnivalesque discourse, and comic laughter come to-gether in the figure of the fool or clown. We have already observed that the god of writing and discoverer of play is "sly, slippery, and masked, an intriguer and a card . . . neither king nor jack, but rather a sort of *joker*." The play of this joker amounts to a Feast of Fools in which all revelers appear as clowns. It is difficult if not impossible to fix the bounds of such clowns. They appear early in religious ritual and recently in literature and art.

> The Zuni clowns used to drink bowls full of urine
> and feed on excrement and all sort of filthy matter.
> Shem wrote *crap in his hand, sorry!* . . .
> The Zuni clowns ridicule people
>     *Shem scrabbled and scratched and scriobbled*
> *and skrevened nameless shamelessness about every-*
> *body ever he met.*

> Other traits characteristic of ritual clowns are "re-
> verse behaviour" and "backward speech." From his
> birth, the mythical Koshari, father of the Sia clowns,
> "talked nonsense, talked backward." The Zuni
> clowns say the opposite of what they mean. Like a
> crazy fellow. Speaking a strange language. As in
> *Finnegans Wake*. . . .
>     *Kish is for anticheirst*. . . .[50]

*Kish . . . anticheirst* . . . antichrist. Humus reinscribed in perverse humor.
Nonsense . . . Bullshit! Inversion . . . perversion . . . subversion: Sacred
becoming profane and profane becoming sacred.

The clown can never be clearly defined or sharply delineated. Every
clown embodies a *coincidentia oppositorum* that lacks both fixed center and
definite identity. Motley dress and shifting masks create a constantly
changing play of forms that borders on the utter chaos of formlessness.
Aberrant conduct serves to reinforce the appearance of disorder and lawlessness that characterizes the clown's foolish world. The clown is an inveterate
trickster who is always in transition. In the trickster's comedy of errors,
nothing is completely true or simply false. The clown's masquerade is
ceaseless, his play endless. Though masks constantly appear, disappear, and
reappear, a naked, unmasked face does not emerge. The errant clown can
never be an insider, at home in the straight world. More precisely, the
clown can be "inside" only as an outsider who relentlessly upsets every well-
ordered and carefully controlled domestic economy. Such subversive activity lends the clown his thievish appearance. One of the cloaks of Hermes
is, after all, the mask of a thief. One rarely comes away from an encounter
with a trickster without having lost—at least one's propriety and property
and often one's very self.

The clown has neither proper home nor fixed place. A nomadic thief,
who dispossesses and expropriates, the clown is a parasite whose "place" is
always a para-site. Clowns, in other words, are liminal or marginal. Like
Chaplin—who hung out on the *Left* Bank, where Apollinaire staged his
mad antics and Picasso painted his Clowns—the clown always receives
nourishment by sticking his hand through a hole in the fence. Try though
they may, the authorities can never capture such an outlandish outlaw. Just
when they think he is trapped, the trickster suddenly reappears where they
least expect him. There is something unsettling about the sly, sneaky,
slippery figure of the clown. The clown is both "alarming and calming.
Sacred and accursed." This ambiguity resounds in the laughter of the clown
as well as in the laughter the clown ignites. Creative as well as destructive,
laughter's gain is loss, its loss gain. Clowns also weep—weep freely:

> In *Finnegans Wake*, the twins Hilary and Tristopher
> Giordano Bruno's motto: *In hilaritate tristis, in
> tristitia hilaris*.[51]

The anguished joy of carnival and comedy is written on the sad face of the smiling clown.

The festive play of comedy is never unambiguously affirmative or negative; it is always duplicitous. Erring necessarily involves a *double movement* of resignation and acceptance. Grimly serious individuals who suffer unhappy/lacerated consciousness are heavy-handed rather than light-footed. "They make the movements upward, and fall down again. . . . But whenever they fall down they are not able at once to assume the posture, they vacillate an instant, and this vacillation shows that after all they are strangers in the world. . . . One need not look at them when they are up in the air, but only the instant they touch or have touched the ground—then one recognizes them. But to be able to fall down in such a way that the same second it looks as if one were standing and walking, to transform the leap of life into a walk, absolutely to express the sublime in the pedestrian—that only the knight of faith can do—and this is the one and only prodigy."[52] The baffling trick that turns everything on its head by expressing the sublime in the pedestrian involves the simultaneous resignation and acceptance of all that is and all that is not. This paradoxical double movement effects a repetition that concretely embodies the eternal recurrence of the divine milieu. Having been thoroughly dispossessed, comic players can no longer truly possess. Their "possessing is at the same time a relinquishing";[53] their "taking" is never properly a taking, for nothing separates it from losing.

This detached attachment alters the relationship to lack, loss, and death. We have seen that everything entangled in "eternally fooling force" is "primordially" wounded and finally incurable. Those who play freely "die laughing" and "laugh at dying."[54] Fools know no shame. Having recognized the "originality" of lack as a condition of carnival, they are beyond good and evil and acknowledge neither guilt nor sin. Freed from the burden of the law and the weight of history, foolish players never look beyond. In contrast to unhappy/lacerated consciousness, which does not want itself but seeks expiation through heirs, anguished "joy wants no offspring, no children—joy accepts itself, accepts everlasting flow."[55]

The nonexclusive interplay of negation and affirmation that is enacted in the double movement of repetition arises from the realization of the radical relativity of all things. "In the actual world, in which everything is bound to and conditioned by everything else, to condemn and to think away anything means to condemn and to think away everything."[56] In contrast to the lawful moralism that re-presents the exclusive logic of identity, repetition embodies the lawless amorality of nonexclusive relativity. It is, therefore, neither simply affirmative nor merely negative. The wanderer who is able to make this paradoxical *double* movement insists:

> . . . midnight is also mid-day—
> Grief is also a joy, curses are also blessings, night is also
> a sun—go away, or else learn: a sage is also a fool.

> Did you ever say "Yes" to one joy? Oh my friends, then you also said "Yes" to *all* pain. All things are entwined, enmeshed, enamoured—
>
> —did you ever want Once to be Twice, did you ever say "I love you, bliss—instant—flash—" then you wanted *everything* back.
>
> —Everything anew, everything forever, everything entwined, enmeshed, enamoured—oh, thus you love the world—
>
> —you everlasting one, thus you love it forever and for all time; even to pain you say: Refrain but—come again! *For joy accepts everlasting flow!* [57]

By saying "Nay" to every exclusive and repressive "No," this "Yes" "becomes an affirmation of negation itself, and becomes a power of affirming, an affirmative power." [58] The "Yea" pronounced by the erring trace and enacted in the free play of carnival and comedy constitutes an "Amen" that does not close but opens—an "Amen" that says "*So be it*" to (the) all—even to lack, loss, and death. The foolish player who utters this "Amen" becomes a free spirit who "stands in the middle of the cosmos with a joyous and trusting fatalism, in the *faith* that only the particular is loathsome, and that all is redeemed and affirmed in the whole—*he does not negate any more*. Such a faith, however, is the highest of all possible faiths. I have baptized it with the name Dionysus." [59]

*Kish . . . anticheirst . . .* antichrist . . . Dionysus. Within the inverted world of erring, Dionysus, the Antichrist, and the Crucified, the Christ, appear to be the same. Carnivalesque comedy brings the unending realization of the incarnation of the word through a process of ceaseless dissemination. The carnality of Dionysus is the word made flesh. "Carnival" appears to derive from Latin *caro, carnis*, flesh, and *levare*, to lift up, elevate, or raise up. Carnival might be understood as the elevation of the body, the resurrection of the flesh. As the god of "the whole wet element in nature," [60] Dionysus embodies the moisture and fluidity of humor and the seminal sexuality of comedy. Wine is Dionysus' element—wine, which is never contained but always flows freely. "Take, drink; this is my blood." Drinking disseminates, it spreads the incarnate word. The carnal play of the word unleashes a delirium in the midst of which participants confess:

> I would believe only in a god who knew how to dance.
>
> And when I saw my devil, I found he was earnest, thorough, deep, solemn; he was the spirit of gravity; by him all things fall.
>
> One kills not with anger but with laughter. Up, then, and let us kill the spirit of gravity!
>
> I learned how to walk: since then I have let myself go. I learned how to fly: since then I do not wish to be pushed in order to get away.
>
> Now I am light; now I see myself beneath myself; now a god dances through me. — [61]

This intoxicated release is both generative and destructive. Gift is also *Gift*, intoxication toxic. Wine, like its god, is a *pharmakon*. The carnival always contains a cruel element, and comedy is never simply funny. Dionysus, bearer of bacchic delirium, possesses by dispossessing and creates by dismembering. In the frenzy of the festival, dancer and dance are the same. Within the divine milieu, creation and destruction, life and death, are forever joined. Since this universal medium is the nonoriginal "origin" of all that is and is not, everything bears the mark of the cross. The "Amen" that embraces absolute passage is "the joyous affirmation of the play of the world and of the innocence of becoming." Such innocence is "a kind of second innocence,"[62] which, though it is not innocence proper, nonetheless, erases the guilt and sin of unhappy/lacerated consciousness. This second innocence presupposes the death of God. When God is dead, it becomes clear that "not only is the only true paradise the paradise that we have lost, but the only regained paradise is the final loss of paradise itself."[63] This loss is grace.

## Superficiality: Carnality

Radical christology is thoroughly incarnational. The carnality embodied in the free play of carnival and comedy overturns every form of repressive transcendence. The body of the incarnate word marks the negation of the transcendence that is characteristic of God, self, and history. Through unexpected twists and unanticipated turns, erring and aberrance show the death of God, disappearance of self, and end of history to be the realization of *mazing grace*.

To maze is to bewilder, perplex, confuse, daze, or stupefy. To be mazed is to be delirious, deluded, or to wander in mind. By extension, a maze is a delirium, delusion, vain amusement, dissipation, trick, or deception. A maze, of course, is also a structure consisting of a network of winding and intercommunicating paths and passages. In this sense of the word, a maze is a labyrinth. The maze through which the erring trace wanders is never-ending. This endless labyrinth is, in effect, an abyss. To enter such a maze is to "plunge into the horizontality of a pure surface."[64] The labyrinthian surface opened by the death of God and discovered in the second (always second) "innocence" of a/theology is completely superficial. With the negation of transcendence, covert interiority and latent depth disappear. The free play of appearances harbors no secrets that ultimately remain hidden. Behind the mask of the player there is always another mask. Mazing grace situates one in the midst of a labyrinth from which there is no exit. There is no Ariadne to save the wandering Theseus, no thread to show the way out of the maze. Every line that seems to promise escape further entangles the drifter in a complex network of relations. Along the boundless boundary where traces err there is neither a fixed center that orients nor an eternally present logos that directs. In the absence of center and logos, there is no special time or special place. In the eternal play of the divine milieu, *die Mitte ist überall*.

The "epidermic play of perversity"[65] subverts the opposition between the sacred and profane. The profanation of the sacred and the sacralization of the profane disclose that no-thing is truly sacred and thus nothing is simply profane. Just as the incarnation is not limited to a single individual, so carnival and comedy are not restricted to a particular time and place. Festive play is an unending game in which the extraordinary becomes ordinary and the ordinary becomes extraordinary. The realization of this coincidence of opposites spreads the incarnate word and extends the divine milieu. Wanderers who are always already inscribed in the erring of scripture are free to delight in "the surface, the fold, the skin, to adore appearance, to believe in forms, tones, words, in the whole Olympus of appearance."[66] For followers of the crucified, who, in their superficiality are, paradoxically, profound:

> so much depends
> upon
>
> a red wheel
> barrow
>
> glazed with rain
> water
>
> beside the white
> chickens.[67]

Nothing (is) extraordinary. Nothing, that is, except the everlasting flow, the ever-never-changing-same, the eternal cross(ing) of differences—the arising and passing-away that does not itself arise and pass away. The "Yes" of anguished joy breaks the power of the law and fissures the "Notshall" of history. Mazing grace opens "a way of totally loving the world, and not only a way of loving the world but also a way of [writing] of love itself in a time and world in which God is dead."[68]

# 8

## Erring Scripture

It was when I said,
"There is no such thing as the truth,"
That the grapes seemed fatter.

No limit to the ways in which the world can be interpreted. . . .
Inertia needs unity (monism); plurality of interpretations a sign of
strength. Not to desire to deprive the world of its disturbing and enigmatic character!

The most extreme form of nihilism would be the view that *every* belief,
every considering-something-true, is necessarily false because there simply
is no *true world*. Thus: a *perspectival appearance* whose origin lies in us
(insofar as we continually *need* a narrower, abbreviated, simplified world).
—That it is the measure of strength to what extent we can admit to
ourselves, without perishing, the merely *apparent* character, the necessity
of lies.
To this extent, nihilism, as the denial of a truthful world, of being,
might be *a divine way of thinking*.

In precisely this way literature (it would be better from now on to say
*writing*), by refusing to assign a "secret," an ultimate meaning, to the text
(and to the world as text), liberates what may be called an anti-theological
activity, an activity that is truly revolutionary since to refuse to fix meaning is, in the end, to refuse God and his hypostases—reason, science, law.

## Duplicity: Shiftiness and Undecidability

It is fatal in the moon and empty there.
But, here, allons. The enigmatical
Beauty of each beautiful enigma

Becomes amassed in a total double-thing.
We do not know what is real and what is not.
We say of the moon, it is haunted by the man

Of bronze whose mind was made up and who, therefore, died.
We are not men of bronze and we are not dead.
His spirit is imprisoned in constant change.

But ours is not imprisoned. It resides
In a permanence composed of impermanence,
In a faithfulness as against the lunar light,

So that morning and evening are like promises kept,
So that the approaching sun and its arrival,
Its evening feast and following festival,

This faithfulness of reality, this mode,
This tendance and venerable holding-in
Make gay the hallucinations in surfaces.[1]

Enigmatical beauty . . . beautiful enigma. Double-thing . . . always duplicitous, never single. Disturbing, unsettling. We do not know what is
real and what is not. Imprisoned in constant change, serious, solid men do
not remain (undecided). They make up their minds and in so doing die.
Shiftless fools and shifty drifters are neither imprisoned nor dead. They err
aimlessly in a permanence composed of impermanence. Morning and evening, arising and passing away—endlessly—form an evening feast that is
an ever-dawning festival. In this playful dance, players make gay the
hallucinations in surfaces.

It is reported that "One day the wanderer slammed a door behind himself,
stopped in his tracks, and wept. Then he said: 'This penchant and passion
for what is true, real, non-apparent, certain—how it aggravates me! Why
does this gloomy and restless fellow keep following and driving *me*?"[2] In the
midst of the unhappiness and despair brought by the quest for elusive
reality and certainty, the wanderer eventually is forced to ask whether truth
can ever be uncovered by the penetrating gaze and artless advances of man.
Suppose the opposite: suppose "truth is a woman"[3]—a woman who can
never be won, since she "will not be pinned down"[4] (or up). "There is no
such thing as the essence of woman because woman averts, she errs from
herself. Out of endless and bottomless depths she engulfs and enveils all
essentiality, all identity, all propriety. . . . There is no such a thing as the
truth of woman, but it is because of that abyssal swerving of the truth,
because that untruth is 'truth.' Woman is but one name for the untruth of
truth."[5] The untruth of truth implies, of course, the "truth" of untruth.
"[I]f woman *is* truth, *she* at least knows that there is no truth, that truth has
no place here and that no one has a place for truth. And she is woman
precisely because she herself does not believe in truth itself, because she does
not believe in what she is, in what she is believed to be, in what she thus is
not."[6] In her *profundity*, woman "stops at the surface," believes "in the
superficiality of experience," and is supremely concerned with appearance.[7]
Appearance and nothing more, for she suspects (but only suspects, since she

is never certain about anything) what man refuses to admit: *there is nothing other than appearance*. Veils always conceal veils that conceal veils that . . .

The superficial play of signs without truth opens with the realization that "the absence of the transcendental signified extends the domain and the play of signification infinitely."[8] The free play of signs subverts the economy of signification that grounds the ontotheological tradition of the West. Elsewhere I have argued that signification more closely approximates the metonymic substitution of signs than the mimetic reflection of a referent in a signifier. Without a signified to serve as a secure anchor, signifiers float freely within a field that appears to be endless. Signs, in other words, are always signs of signs.

One consequence of this unending play of signification is that there seems to be no exit from the labyrinth of interpretration. Everything is always already inscribed within an interpretive network. "Interpretation can never be brought to an end, simply because there is nothing to interpret. There is nothing absolutely primary to be interpreted, since, fundamentally, everything is already interpretation; every sign is, in itself, not the thing susceptible to interpretation but the interpretation of other signs."[9] In other words, there is no "Archimedean point" to provide access to a nonfigural world that can function as the critical norm with which to judge conflicting interpretations. Experience is never raw; it is always cooked in a figurational code. The absence of naked facts and noninterpreted data subverts the monopolistic claims of any pattern of signification. Since every interpretation is irreducibly perspectival, no single sign or set of signs can be consistently capitalized and no individual code can be absolutely privileged. The peculiar facets of each perspective emerge through its association with other perspectives. This play of signification can be compared to "a network of jewels in which each jewel reflects all the others and so on, to infinity, without there ever being a center to grasp, a primary core of irradiation."[10]

In the course of our wanderings, we have repeatedly observed the way in which relationships constitute all things. This insight helps to clarify the interplay of perspectives and thus further illuminates the complex process of interpretation. Contrasting and conflicting perspectives form an intricate web in which each point of view becomes itself through its relationship with other points of view. Interpretive perspectives are neither independent nor self-identical; they are thoroughly differential and *radically relational*. Apart from its difference from other angles of vision, a particular point of view is, quite simply, inconceivable, i.e., completely indeterminate and utterly unintelligible. Relations that simultaneously construct and deconstruct the identity of any perspective are both synchronic and diachronic. On the one hand, the distinctiveness of each perspective presupposes its *difference* from other perspectives with which it coexists. Instead of disrupting the "original purity" or "pure originality" of vision, synchronic relations inhere in and are constitutive of every comprehensible viewpoint. On the other hand, the specificity of any point of view entails its *difference* from perspectives that arise and pass away in the endless flow of time. Rather than a discrete and secure standpoint, each perspective is a node entwined in an *infinitely* complicated network that is always spinning and being spun.

The coimplication of differing viewpoints establishes the contextuality of all perspectives. Every interpretive stance is inextricably entangled in a formative context. This contextuality carries important semantic implications. Since perspectives are radically relational, meaning is irreducibly relative. There is no such thing as semantic atomism, intrinsic meaning, or meaning-in-itself. "Meaning is not in things but in between; in . . . the interplay; in the interconnections; at the intersections, at the crossroads."[11] As a result of this interstitiality, meaning is thoroughly liminal. It repeatedly appears and disappears at the threshold of interrelated perspectives. Such marginal meaning inevitably bears the mark of a cross, which delimits the place where signifiers play freely. In the absence of a privileged signified, this play of signification is boundless.

Since meaning is always context-sensitive, all scription is conscription and all notation is connotation. Nothing can be inscribed alone; to note is inevitably to connote, i.e., to mark (*notare*) with (*con*). A meaningful sign, therefore, is never self-contained; it is inseparably bound to other signs. This necessary relation to otherness opens the space that permits meaning to circulate freely. The connotative dimension of signs points to the plurisignification of everything that is inscribed within the infinite play of signifiers. The disappearance of the transcendental signified marks the end of every form of authoritative monologism that struggles to contain and arrest the free exchange of signs. Since signs always entail difference and thus are never simply self-identical, meaning is unavoidably equivocal rather than univocal. The noncontradictory categories of traditional logic cannot comprehend such equivocality. The relativity of meaning presupposes the nonexclusivity of opposites. This complex interplay of differences escapes reflection that remains bound to and by hard-and-fast distinctions and firm definitions.

It is important to understand what is and what is not involved in this equivocality. To maintain that a sign is plurisignificant is not necessarily to insist that a sign *has* several meanings or that different meanings are somehow simultaneously *present* in a particular sign. The realization that signs are always signs of signs raises suspicions about the fullness of meaning. The signifier does not *possess* multiple meanings that might, in principle, be discovered and exhausted. In itself the sign is nothing. As a result of its relationships, however, the sign is a "generative multiplicity" that "accomplishes the very plural of meaning: an *irreducible* (and not merely an acceptable) plural."[12] The ineradicable plurality of signifiers establishes their irreducible equivocality. Since plurisignification cannot be erased, equivocality can never be translated into or reduced to univocality. Because of the inescapability of equivocality, *there can be no such thing as proper or literal meaning*. Meaning is always improper—it is more literary than literal. When proper meaning is inaccessible, "the real deceivers are the literalists who say, I cannot tell a lie." [13]

As a result of the absence of proper meaning, communication, to the extent that it is possible, is always indirect. "Functionally, connotation, releasing the double meaning or principle, corrupts the purity of communication." [14] Since signification is never straightforward, signs are forever duplicitous. "Duplicity," which derives from the Latin *duplicitas* and is related to *duplex*, means doubleness, i.e., the state or quality of being numerically double or twofold. But "duplicity" itself is duplicitous; it is (at least) double. "Duplicity" also means deceitful, deceptive, and double-dealing. Like every outlaw, the floating signifier invariably double-crosses. Signs are sly, slippery, and tricky. As masks of masks and veils of veils, signifiers can no more be pinned down than tricksters can be locked up. If all perspectives are contextual, then every text is, to some extent, a context, i.e., a text that cons. Signs inscribed in relative contexts are irredeemably *shifty*.

Mark . . . mark . . . "Mark" . . .Mark; . . . : The meaning of shifty mark(s) and shifting signs can never be fixed securely. Meaning "is not a stable, predetermined entity which passes, untrammelled, from sender to receiver." [15] Inscribed within changing perspectives and shifting contexts, meaning is never fully present. Semantic plenitude is *forever* erased by the interplay of presence and absence involved in the activity of signification. The inescapable shiftiness of meaning is a function of synchronic and diachronic relations, which, we have seen, inhere in every sign. The milieu that generates meaning can never be totally determined. The semantic web within which signifiers are entangled is limitless. This contextual indeterminacy has at least two dimensions.

In the first place, it is never possible to define completely the relationship of a sign to all other signs that coexist within a particular framework at a specific time. Furthermore, the connections between and among coexistent perspectives are inexhaustible. The synchronic network of signification is simply too extensive and too intricate to be fully mastered. To the extent that meaning is contextual, terms inscribed within this milieu cannot be sharply defined or exactly delineated. Signs and marks are always slipping and sliding; their boundaries cannot be set or their margins fixed. In the infinite play of signification, signifiers are forever vague (*vagus*, wandering). Freed from restrictive borders and repressive limits, signs wander like homeless vagrants who, having lost anchor, are forever cast adrift.

In the second place, meaning is a function of the interconnection of signifiers and patterns of signification that are temporally dispersed. Like the synchronic matrix, the diachronic play of signs is boundless. The metonymic chain in which each signifier constitutes a link does not properly begin or end. Thus the milieu that informs both signs and the various perspectives in which they are configured is incomplete or unfinished. The nonclosure of the diachronic axis of signification leaves the semantic context forever indeterminate. The absence of an identifiable *archē* and a definable *telos* transforms "the meaning of meaning" into the "infinite implication, the indefinite referral of signifier to signifier." [16] The radical temporality of signification renders meaning both transitional and transitory. Floating signifiers yield only migratory meaning. Within this nomadic economy, meaning, which can neither settle nor be settled, is an event that is always arising and passing away. As a result of the endless drift of meaning, *erring can never be overcome.*

The inescapability of erring calls into question the notion of truth that lies at the heart of the Western theological and philosophical network. Whether implicitly or explicitly, truth and God are usually identified: *Deus est Veritas* and *Veritas est Deus.* The dominant theological position in the West is, of course, monotheism. This monotheism is both directly and indirectly related to the notion of truth. Insofar as God is one, truth is one. From this point of view, the true is never plural, multiple, and complex but always unified, single, and simple. This unity, singularity, and simplicity lend truth its abiding character. In contrast to ephemeral temporal flux, truth is believed to be eternal. Truth does not change. The opposition between eternal verity and timely fashion is generally described in terms of the difference between reality and appearance. The "real" can be understood in a variety of ways. Reality can represent anything from actual facticity to pure ideality. What remains constant in otherwise conflicting viewpoints is the conviction that beyond, behind, beneath, or within the play of appearances there is an enduring logos that constitutes the essence or reality of phenomena. Given this assumption, all thought that remains superficial appears to be caught in a web of deceit and deception. True reflection must dispel illusions by passing beyond surfaces. This analysis of the knowing process suggests that the notion of truth is inscribed in something like an optical framework. The knowing subject is a voyeur who tries to *see through* the veil of appearance in order to penetrate to naked truth. Knowing, therefore, is seeing—seeing the substantial reality that is always present though repeatedly hidden by insubstantial appearances. Within the optics of truth, the goal of the viewer is utter clarity or complete transparency: "Now, in a mirror dimly, but then face to face." Such lucidity is supposed to erase unsettling equivocality by securing univocal meaning. The monologism of truth is pre-scribed to ease the distress induced by the uncertainty that arises from the polymorphous play of appearances.

Contrary to expectation, this "cure" inevitably fails. The play of appearances never stops and hence cannot be fixed. Within the boundless field of signification, truth itself appears to be an optical illusion. When inspected more closely, what is initially regarded as "reality" turns out to be appearance. The inner world, in other words, is *phenomenal*. Moreover, this "'apparent *inner* world' is governed by just the same forms and procedures as the 'outer' world." [17] The quest for truth represents a futile effort to escape the world of appearances and to discover (or uncover) the fugitive transcendental signified. In spite of protests to the contrary, this pursuit is never disinterested. "The will to truth" simultaneously expresses "hatred for all that perishes, changes, varies" and gives voice to a longing "for a world of the constant." [18] The attempt to reduce "as" to "is" reflects a struggle to master the uncertainty that temporality creates. When time and eternity are regarded as exclusive opposites, the affirmation of one is the denial of the other. The monotheist seeks to flee the temporal by reaching (for) the eternal. For the true believer or the believer in truth, the endless erring of signs, which issues in the radical relativity of meaning, brings nauseating vertigo. It seems that the only cure for this disease is the certainty that truth promises.

Truth, however, is *never* totally present.

> *along the winding ways of random ever!*
> *(since in this scherzarade of one's thousand*
> *one nightiness that sword of certainty which would*
> *identifide the body never falls)*
>
> *in fact, the sameold gamebold adomic structure*
> *of our Finnius the old One, as highly charged with*
> *electrons as hophazards can effective it.* [19]

The sword of certainty never falls, for behind every veil one discovers not an "adomic structure" but another veil. Since appearances are always appearances of appearances, truth can never be pinned/penned down. The duplicity of signs is inescapable and the shiftiness of meaning incurable. The perpetual indeterminacy of the milieu within which all things are entangled imparts an "absolute instability" [20] to every sign. When certainty is unattainable, everything remains undecidable. This undecidability is not temporary; it reflects "a permanence composed of impermanence." Such impermanence, however, does not necessarily imprison and does not have to generate malaise. To the contrary, it can actually liberate. Shifty vagrants who err endlessly do not feel the need "to deprive the world of its disturbing and enigmatic character." Those who realize the foolish wisdom of woman recognize that *truth is unbecoming*. "Certainty is the region of death, uncertainty the valley of life." [21] When it no longer seems necessary to reduce manyness to oneness and to translate the equivocal as univocal, it becomes possible to give up the struggle for mastery and to take "eternal delight" [22] in "The enigmatical / Beauty of each beautiful enigma." In the undecidable interplay of signifiers, "Enigmatic form is living form; like life, an iridescence; an invitation to the dance; a temptation, or irritation. No satisfying solutions; nothing to rest in; nothing to weigh us down."[23] To deny truth is to affirm "a world freed from the ties of gravity (i.e., from relationship with a foundation); a world made of moving and light surfaces where the incessant shifting of masks is named laughter, dance, game."[24] This gay affirmation of a world without truth is realized in the seminal adventure of the trace. The joyous wandering of the *graphē* cannot be captured in the lines of a book; it must be inscribed in erring texts.

## Spinning: Tissue of Texts

To spin is to form or fabricate (a thread or yarn) by the process of drawing out and twisting fibers. Threads woven together create tissues. A tissue (from Old French *tistre*, Latin *texere*, to weave) is a woven fabric, produced by intertwining elements to form a network or web. "Tissue" also designates the structure or contexture of such a fabric. This association of terms implies an important connection between "tissue" and "text." "Text [*textus*, that which is woven, past participle of *texere*] means *Tissue*." While it is common to view "this tissue as a product, a ready-made veil, behind which lies, more or less hidden, meaning (truth)," I would like to emphasize, "in the tissue, the generative idea, that the text is made, is worked out in a perpetual interweaving; lost in this tissue—this texture—the subject unmakes himself, like a spider dissolving in the constructive secretions of its web."[25] The perpetual interweaving in which the subject is undone points to additional implications of "spin." To spin is to revolve, gyrate, or whirl. Such spinning often creates a vertigo that confuses and mazes. To spin can also mean to spend time without effect or profit, as when one spins one's wheels. When these multiple meanings are stitched together, it becomes possible to see how spinning prepares the way for weaving. Spinning and weaving fabricate the tissue of texts that frays the book.

The book, I have argued, is an integral part of the Western theological network. The lines of the book, however, extend far beyond the printed page to create a culture that is, in effect, a book culture. The pervasive influence of the book suggests that the opening of the text bears a significance that is not merely theological, philosophical, and literary but social, cultural, and political. It will be recalled that the "idea of the book is the idea of a totality, finite or infinite, of the signifier; this totality of the signifier cannot be a totality, unless a totality constituted by the signified preexists it, supervises its inscriptions and its signs, and is independent of it in its ideality."[26] The antecedent signified is the implicit logos that governs the book and constitutes the unity and coherence of its signifiers. Neither superficial nor immediately apparent, this logos lends the book its volume, depth, and weight.

This view of the book is bound up with a specific interpretation of interpretation. To interpret a book is to attempt to discover or uncover "a truth or an origin which escapes play and the order of the sign."[27] This "truth" is the inherent logos that secures the meaning of the book by grounding floating signifiers. Books, in other words, *possess* meaning that is both determinate and determinable. As a result of the "presence" of this meaning, the activity of interpretation is neither endless nor pointless. Interpretation is only a temporary "exile," which has as its end the disclosure of the plenitude of meaning and the discovery of meaningful plenitude. From this perspective, works appear to be complete, finished products, which await consumption by passive consumers. Within this consumer economy, a book is "like a cupboard where meanings are shelved, stacked, safeguarded."[28]

But what if the economy of consumption breaks down? What if the cupboard is bare? What if there is no logos hidden behind the veil of signifiers? What if the book "is the encyclopedic protection of theology and of logocentrism against the disruption of writing"?[29] What if writing, "by refusing to assign a 'secret,' an ultimate meaning, to the text (and to the world as text), liberates what may be called an anti-theological activity, an activity that is truly revolutionary, since to refuse to fix meaning is, in the end, to refuse God and his hypostases—reason, science law"?[30] Such a prospect spells the end of the book proper and points to the opening of the text.

In contrast to the closure of the book, the text is radically open. It is neither self-contained nor definitively bound in a single volume. A text is more like a fabric with loose ends than a hemmed cloth. The openness of the text, which ruptures the closure of the book, is a function of the irreducible contextuality of scripture. Every text is, as I have already noted, a context. Con-texts are woven (*textus*) together (*con*) in a complex fabric that is thoroughly constitutive. Since each text becomes itself in relation to other texts, every text implies a difference that dislocates its proper identity. There no more can be a text-in-itself than there can be independent signifiers. This irreducible relativity constitutes every text an intertext. When understood in this way, a "text is a relational event, and not a substance to be analyzed."[31] The web within which all texts are eventually entwined has no beginning, middle, or end.

The intertextuality of scripts displays the codependent origination of texts. Every text arises and passes away through its interplay with other texts. Consequently, no single text can be regarded as either the absolute origin of another text or as the initial source of the entire metonymic chain of texts. Texts and the network within which they are inscribed stand in a tangled relationship of coimplication. Each presupposes the other. Paradoxically, texts are made possible by the intertextuality that they make possible. In the ceaseless oscillation of text and intertext, there is no textual originality. The loss of origin again proves to be inseparable from the disappearance of center. The tissue of texts is radically acentric. The boundless fabric of intertextuality *always* lacks "a center which arrests and grounds the play of substitutions."[32] Though the text conceals no ultimate secret and is profoundly superficial, it is, nonetheless, undeniably abysmal. The abyss of the text is the horizonless "horizontality of a pure surface, which represents itself from detour to detour."[33] Such centerless deviation is sustained by the ceaseless interplay of texts.

It is important to recognize that without a founding origin and an organizing center, no work can be a masterpiece. The codependence of texts precludes both the mastery of one text by another and the subservience of one text to another. Scriptural relativity breaks the rule of canon and disperses authoritative tradition. Insofar as canon and tradition extend the circle of the book, the end of one is the dissolution of the other. On the one hand, when the book is breached, canon explodes and tradition shatters. On the other hand, when the rule of canon is broken and the line of authority disrupted, the book disintegrates. With the unraveling of book, canon, and tradition, scripture becomes free to drift endlessly.

The fabric(ation) of intertextuality not only lacks beginning and middle; it has no end. Texts forever cross and crisscross in a perpetual process of interweaving. The constant spinning "within the field of the text should not be identified with an organic process of maturation or a hermeneutic process of deepening, but rather with a serial movement of dislocations, overlappings, and variations."[34] Rather than stable and static, texts are insubstantial and transitory. Unavoidably entangled in an excentric web that neither begins nor ends, texts cannot be unified or totalized. The meaning of a text, therefore, is never fully present. Meaning is always in the process of forming, deforming, and reforming.

It should be clear that texts cannot be interpreted like books. A text does not harbor a concealed logos that can be revealed or a final secret waiting to be uncovered. Textual interpretation substitutes "incessant deciphering for the disclosure of truth as a presentation of the thing itself in its presence."[35] This active interpretation, "which is no longer turned toward the origin, affirms play and tries to pass beyond man and humanism, the name of man being the name of that being who, throughout the history of metaphysics or of ontotheology—in other words, throughout his entire history—has dreamed of full presence, the reassuring foundation, the origin and the end of play."[36] In the absence of complete presence, secure foundation, authoritative origin, and ultimate end, there is nothing other than erring.

Active interpretation overturns the passive satisfaction that results from the consumption of finished products. Inasmuch as the text is "a *productiv-*

*ity"*[37] rather than a product, it can be *"experienced only in an activity of production."*[38] This productive activity is free interpretation, which has given up every dream of conclusive certainty. Within the relative play of erring scripture, interpretation does not unveil established meaning but produces new meanings that have not previously been realized. So conceived, interpretation extends the text through an endless process of multiplication, pluralization, and dispersal.

When interpretation is placed within an economy of production rather than consumption, the relationship between text and interpretation is radically transformed. Contrary to traditional assumptions, interpretation is not simply a parasitic act that feeds on a primal or original source. By establishing the codependent origination of all texts, intertextuality ruptures what had appeared to be the impermeable membrane between text and interpretation. Instead of remaining extrinsic, interpretation is actually intrinsic to the text's own becoming. There is neither text without interpretation nor interpretation without text. Text and interpretation simultaneously feed on and nourish each other. In this symbiotic relation, it is impossible to be certain which is parasite and which is host. Insofar as the host is a parasite on a parasite, the parasite is also a host. Conversely, parasite-become-host is always "infected" with a parasite, i.e., the host-become-parasite. This eternal arising and passing-away of host and parasite is the unending play of the word.

## Wordplay: Pens and Needles

Since every text is an intertext, all writing is rewriting and all inscription is reinscription. This insight suggests that the writer can be compared to a tailor. With pens and needles, the writer stitches and cross-stitches. *If* "truth" should happen to be a woman—a woman whose superficiality is but one name for the untruth of truth—the tailor might be the man who is in a position to recognize it (on her). The tailor, after all, is profoundly interested in surfaces and completely preoccupied with appearances. His task is to cover rather than strip, to veil instead of unveil. Above all else, the tailor realizes that surfaces are not superficial. Thus he is able to agree with woman's suspicion that "the denial of a truthful world—might be a *divine way of thinking.*"

It is important to stress that the tailor does not weave the material he cuts and sews. He stitches together textiles that have been woven by others. The tailor who is a writer fabricates by absorbing and transforming other texts.[39] His writing is always a reading. The writerly "text requires an attempt to abolish (or at least to lessen) the distance between writing and reading, not by intensifying the reader's projection into the work, but by joining them in a single signifying process."[40] If writing is a rewriting that is, in effect, reading, then every work is a patchwork of passages that are drawn directly and indirectly from other works. "The text," in other words, "is a tissue of quotations"[41] "woven entirely with citations, references, echoes, cultural languages (what language is not?), antecedent or contemporary, which cut across it through and through in a vast stereophony."[42] Proper names need not, indeed cannot, be attached to the plurality of texts that are interwoven in the complex signifying process of writing-reading. For the writer who carefully tailors texts, "the ideal would be: neither a text of vanity, nor a text of lucidity, but a text with uncertain quotation marks, with floating parentheses (never to close the parenthesis is very specifically: *to drift*)."[43] To erase quotation marks is, of course, to steal. Improper writing expropriates; it robs "individual" authors of their personal possessions and private property. Followers of Hermes are incurable thieves, whose letters are always purloined. Contrary to expectation, however, theft dispossesses the thief. In the very act of sewing, the tailor "unmakes himself, like a spider dissolving in the constructive secretions of its web." This dissolution is the disappearance of the author.

The text creates "a space into which the writing subject constantly disappears."[44] In the process of writing, the writer finds that he is always entangled in a web that both surpasses and encompasses him. The (inevitable) theft entailed in writing establishes an ineradicable secondariness that robs the writer of all originality. The writer's "I" is not an "original source" but a "paper I," composed of a "plurality of texts."[45] Never able to originate, "the writer can only imitate a gesture that is always anterior, never original. His only power is to mix writings, to counter the one with the others, in such a way as never to rest on any one of them. Did he wish to *express himself*, he ought at least to know that the inner 'thing' he thinks to 'translate' is itself only a ready-formed dictionary, its words only explainable through other words, and so on indefinitely."[46] Having realized that the text is never his own, the author acknowledges his lack of authority. In staging what he had believed to be *his* wordplay, the writer eventually learns that scripture is the endless play of the word that dispossesses every subject. Writing not only involves self-sacrifice; it enacts the sacrifice of the self. Within and between the tangled lines of the text, "the structure of *the author* emerges as anonymity."[47] In anonymous writing, the author discovers that "his" proper name is an empty trace—an erased mark. Always caught in the play of (the) word(s), the marginal writer constantly errs. "Uprooted, anonymous, unattached to any house or country, this almost insignificant signifier is at everyone's disposal, can be picked up by both the competent and the incompetent, by those who understand and by those who are completely unconcerned with it, and who, knowing nothing about it, can inflict all manner of impertinence upon it."[48] Having been thoroughly dispossessed, the writer freely confesses:

Really it is not I who am writing this crazy book. It is you, and you, and you, and that man over there, and that girl at the next table.[49]

The death of the author creates the time-space of the reader. The fabric of the text is always indeterminate and incomplete. It has blanks, holes, gaps, and loose ends. The holiness of scripture extends an invitation to the reader. "On the stage of the text, no footlights: there is not, behind the text, someone active (the writer) and out front someone passive (the reader); there is not a subject and an object."[50] In the profitless economy of writing, reading is active production instead of passive consumption. The tissue of texts not only shows that writing is reading; it also displays reading as writing. Instead of a finished product of a single author, the text is the *social* activity of countless coproducers. Productive readers infinitely expand and extend the text. Since the play of the word never stops, erring never ends.

The unending erring of scripture is the eternal play of the divine milieu. "A vast pun, a free play, with unlimited substitutions. . . . Freedom is fertility, a proliferation of images, in excess. The seed must be sown wastefully, extravagantly."[51] The free sewing/sowing of writing that is reading and reading that is writing disseminates the word and reinscribes the everlasting flow of the divine milieu. Word becomes wine: *Hoc est corpus meum*. Take, drink. . . . Take, read. "Is not a good wine the wine whose flavor oscillates, alters, doubles, so that the mouthful swallowed does not have quite the same taste as the next mouthful taken? In the draught of good wine, as in the taking of the text, there is a torsion, a twist of degrees: it turns back."[52] To drink this ever-changing wine is to join the "Bacchanalian revel in which no member is sober." This seminal adventure of the trace "is the joyous affirmation of the play of the world and of the innocence of becoming, the affirmation of a world of signs without fault, without truth, and without origin which is offered to an active interpretation."[53] In risky Dionysian wordplay, Yea and Nay join to bring "the greatest joy in the midst of the greatest suffering."[54] Erring endlessly opens the mazing grace eternally inscribed in the cross of scripture.

# Interlude . . .

Nothing is final, he chants.

. . . is not writing that language which has renounced producing *the last word*, which lives and breathes by yielding itself up to others?

True revolt is the one inspired by the impossibility of ending.

There/this is no conclusion. We must "end" *wherever we are*, and the thought of the trace has already taught us that it is impossible to justify a point of ending absolutely. *Wherever we are*: in a text where we already believe ourselves to be.

The conclusion represents the return of the wandering son to the home of the father.

> We shall not cease from exploration
> And the end of our exploring
> Will be to arrive where we started
> And to know the place for the first time.[1]

If Alpha and Omega are One, "movement is the circle that returns into itself, the circle that presupposes its beginning and reaches it only at the end."[2] A conclusion portrays the result of the struggle to recollect scattered words by remembering beginning, middle, and end. Such closure, it is believed, can cure the disease of homelessness, which plagues many people who are roaming through perplexing postmodern worlds.

Conclusions, however, always remain inconclusive. Every text is an unconcluding postscript that is a pretext to/for another postscript. This infinite play of (the) word(s) marks the death of God, which is the end of The End. In the absence of The End, there is no ultimate conclusion. Thus there can be neither definite conclusions nor Final Solution. Instead of a conclusion, we are left with an Interlude, which, it appears, is always already playing. Inscribed between an Origin that never was and an End that never is, the Interlude is the *Inter Ludus* of scripture itself. This ever-never-changing-same is the eternally recurring play of the divine milieu within which *all things* arise and pass away. Since there is no escape from scriptural interlude, *E/erring is endless*. Marginal writers who are foolish enough to try to trace and retrace this boundless boundary are always:

> Thinkers without final thoughts
> In an always incipient cosmos . . . .[3]

It is (un)finished

Amen

Sobeit

(p.s

# Notes

The epigraph on p. xi is from Wallace Stevens, "July Mountain," *Opus Posthumous*, ed. S. F. Morse (New York: Random House, 1982), p. 162.

## Prelude

The epigraph is from Jacques Derrida, *Of Grammatology*, trans. G. C. Spivak (Baltimore: Johns Hopkins University Press, 1976), p. 162.

1. William Butler Yeats, "The Second Coming," *The Collected Poems of W. B. Yeats* (New York: Macmillan, 1956), p. 184.

2. Friedrich Nietzsche, *The Gay Science*, trans. W. Kaufmann (New York: Random House, 1974), p. 181.

3. Immanuel Kant, *On History*, trans. L. W. Beck (New York: Bobbs-Merrill, 1965), p. 3.

4. Walker Percy, *The Moviegoer* (New York: Knopf, 1961), p. 240.

5. Jacques Derrida, *Positions*, trans. A. Bass (Chicago: University of Chicago Press, 1981), p. 77.

6. Ibid., p. 40.

7. Nietzsche, *Gay Science*, p. 182.

8. Thomas J. J. Altizer, *The Descent into Hell: A Study of the Radical Reversal of the Christian Consciousness* (New York: Seabury Press, 1979), p. 53.

9. J. Hillis Miller, "Theology and Logology in Victorian Literature," in *Religion and Literature: The Convergence of Approaches*, supplement to *Journal of the American Academy of Religion* 47 (1979): 354.

10. Jacques Derrida, *Writing and Difference*, trans. A. Bass (Chicago: University of Chicago Press, 1978), p. 20.

11. Unless otherwise indicated, I have drawn definitions and etymologies from the *Oxford English Dictionary* (New York: Oxford University Press, 1971).

12. Gilles Deleuze, "Nomad Thought," in *The New Nietzsche: Contemporary Styles of Interpretation*, ed. D. B. Allison (New York: Dell, 1977), pp. 142–49.

13. Jacques Derrida, *Dissemination*, trans. B. Johnson (Chicago: University of Chicago Press, 1981), p. 9.

14. Ibid., pp. 41–42.

## Chapter One

The epigraph is from Apollinaire, quoted in Geoffrey Hartman, *Saving the Text: Literature/Derrida/Philosophy* (Baltimore: Johns Hopkins University Press, 1981), p. 116.

1. Nietzsche, *Gay Science*, p. 181.

2. Francis Bacon.

3. Martin Heidegger, *The End of Philosophy*, trans. J. Stambaugh (New York: Harper & Row, 1973), p. 20.

4. Michel Foucault, *Language, Counter-Memory, Practice: Selected Interviews*, trans. D. F. Bouchard and S. Simon, ed. D. F. Bouchard (Ithaca: Cornell University Press, 1977), p. 222.

5. J. Hillis Miller, *Poets of Reality: Six Twentieth-Century Writers* (New York: Atheneum, 1969), p. 3.

6. Pierre Klossowski, quoted in Gilles Deleuze and Félix Guattari, *Anti-Oedipus: Capitalism and Schizophrenia*, trans. R. Hurley, M. Seem, and H. R. Lane (New York: Viking Press, 1977), p. 77.

7. Norman O. Brown, *Life against Death: The Psychoanalytic Meaning of History* (New York: Random House, 1959), p. 161.

8. Thomas J. J. Altizer, *The Self-Embodiment of God* (New York: Harper & Row, 1977), p. 19.

9. Altizer, *Descent into Hell*, p. 183.

10. Derrida, *Writing and Difference*, p. 181.

11. Derrida, *Of Grammatology*, p. 277.

12. G. W. F. Hegel, *Phenomenology of Spirit*, trans. A. V. Miller (New York: Oxford University Press, 1977), p. 111.

13. Alexandre Kojève, *Introduction to the Reading of Hegel*, trans. J. H. Nicholas (New York: Basic Books, 1969), p. 13.

14. Jacques Derrida, "Limited Inc abc . . . ," *Glyph* 2 (1977): 248.

15. Derrida, *Writing and Difference*, p. 91.

16. Friedrich Nietzsche, *On the Genealogy of Morals*, trans. W. Kaufmann (New York: Random House, 1969), p. 36.

17. Hegel, *Phenomenology*, p. 111.

18. Ibid., p. 14.

19. Brown, *Life against Death*, p. 118.

20. Ludwig Feuerbach, *The Essence of Christianity*, trans. G. Eliot (New York: Harper Torchbooks, 1967), p. 5.

21. Ibid., p. 25.

22. Martin Heidegger, *The Question Concerning Technology, and Other Essays*, trans. W. Lovitt (New York: Harper & Row, 1977), p. 27.

23. J. Hillis Miller, *The Disappearance of God: Five Nineteenth-Century Writers* (Cambridge, Mass.: Harvard University Press, 1963), p. 5.

24. Martin Heidegger, *The End of Philosophy*, pp. 21—22.

25. Alain Robbe-Grillet, *For a New Novel*, trans. R. Howard (New York: Grove Press, 1965), p. 24.

26. Hegel, *Phenomenology*, pp. 353, 355.

27. Kojève, *Introduction to the Reading of Hegel*, p. 135.

28. Ibid., p. 38.

29. Roland Barthes, *The Pleasure of the Text*, trans. R. Howard (New York: Hill & Wang, 1975), p. 14.

30. Miller, *Poets of Reality*, p. 138.

31. Deleuze and Guattari, *Anti-Oedipus*, p. 25.

32. Brown, *Life against Death*, p. 254.

33. Derrida, *Writing and Difference*, p. 271.

34. Miller, *Poets of Reality*, p. 5.

35. Derrida, *Writing and Difference*, p. 91.

36. Emmanuel Levinas, *Totality and Infinity: An Essay on Exteriority*, trans. A. Lingis (Pittsburgh: Duquesne University Press, 1979), pp. 37—38.

37. Theodor Adorno, *Negative Dialectics*, trans. E. B. Ashton (New York: Seabury Press, 1973), p. 172.

38. Heidegger, *The End of Philosophy*, p. 107.

39. Brown, *Life against Death*, p. 8.

40. Jean-Paul Sartre, *Being and Nothingness*, trans. H. Barnes (New York: Washington Square, 1968), p. 782.

41. Kojève, *Introduction to the Reading of Hegel*, p. 41.

42. Jacques Derrida, *Speech and Phenomena and Other Essays on Husserl's Theory of Signs*, trans. D. B. Allison (Evanston, Ill.: Northwestern University Press, 1973), p. 151.

43. Brown, *Life against Death*, p. 147.

44. G. W. F. Hegel, *Science of Logic*, trans. A. V. Miller (New York: Oxford University Press, 1969), pp. 771–72.

45. Paul Ricoeur, *Freud and Philosophy: An Essay on Interpretation*, trans. D. Savage (New Haven: Yale University Press, 1970), p. 291.

46. G. W. F. Hegel, *Early Theological Writings*, trans. T. M. Knox (Philadelphia: University of Pennsylvania Press, 1971), p. 211.

47. Jacques Lacan, *Ecrits*, trans. A. Sheridan (New York: Norton, 1977).

48. Jacques Lacan, *The Language of the Self*, trans. A. Wilden (New York: Delta Books, 1968), p. 136.

49. Brown, *Life against Death*, p. 50.

50. Jean Hyppolite, "Hegel's Phenomenology and Psychoanalysis," in *New Studies in Hegel's Philosophy*, ed. W. E. Steinkraus (New York: Holt, Rinehart, Winston, 1971), p. 63.

51. Hegel, *Phenomenology*, pp. 452–53.

52. Ibid., p. 360.

53. Miller, *Poets of Reality*, p. 3.

54. Friedrich Nietzsche, *The Will to Power*, trans. W. Kaufmann (New York: Random House, 1968), p. 9.

55. Karl Marx, *Writings of the Young Marx on Philosophy and Society*, trans. L. Easton (New York: Doubleday, 1967), p. 251.

56. Adorno, *Negative Dialectics*, p. 186.

57. Altizer, *Descent into Hell*, pp. 153–54.

58. Edmond Jabès, *The Book of Yukel, Return to the Book*, trans. R. Waldrop (Middletown, Conn.: Wesleyan University Press, 1976), p. 172.

## Chapter Two

The epigraphs are from Saint Augustine; Søren Kierkegaard, *Concluding Unscientific Postscript*, trans. D. Swenson and W. Lowrie (Princeton: Princeton University Press, 1968), p. 311; Roland Barthes, *Roland Barthes*, trans. R. Howard (New York: Hill & Wang, 1977), p. 1; and Jacques Derrida, *Writing and Difference*, pp. 182–83.

1. Ralph Ellison, "Hidden Name and Complex Fate," in Ellison's *Shadow and Act* (New York: Random House, 1953), pp. 144–66.

2. Friedrich Nietzsche, *Ecce Homo*, trans. W. Kaufmann (New York: Random House, 1969), p. 215.

3. Altizer, *The Self-Embodiment of God*, p. 29.

4. Altizer, *Descent into Hell*, p. 37.

5. Michel Foucault.

6. Altizer, *Descent into Hell*, pp. 150–51.

7. G. W. F. Hegel, *The Logic of Hegel*, trans. W. Wallace (New York: Oxford University Press, 1968), p. 211.

8. Hegel, *Science of Logic*, pp. 412, 413.

9. Ibid., p. 558.

10. Ibid., p. 398.

11. Derrida, *Writing and Difference*, p. 229.

12. Hegel, *Phenomenology*, p. 14.

13. Saint Augustine, quoted in Charles N. Cochrane, *Christianity and Classical Culture* (New York: Oxford University Press, 1957), p. 403.

14. G. W. F. Hegel, *Lectures on the Philosophy of Religion*, vol. 3, trans. E. S. Haldane (New York: Humanities Press, 1968), pp. 10–11.

15. Ibid., p. 18.

16. Hegel, *Science of Logic*, p. 401.

17. Robert Scharlemann, *The Being of God: Theology and the Experience of Truth* (New York: Seabury Press, 1981), p. 26.

18. Ephesians 4 : 13.

19. 2 Corinthians 3 : 18.

20. Friedrich Nietzsche, *Thus Spoke Zarathustra*, trans. M. Cowan (Chicago: Regnery, 1957), p. 245.

21. Jacques Derrida, *Margins of Philosophy*, trans. A. Bass (Chicago: University of Chicago Press, 1982), p. 247.

22. Norman O. Brown, *Love's Body* (New York: Random House, 1968), p. 145.

23. Derrida, *Margins of Philosophy*, p. 133.

24. Derrida, *Of Grammatology*, p. 107.

25. Brown, *Love's Body*, p. 214.

26. Derrida, *Speech and Phenomena*, p. 54.

27. Ibid., p. 98.

28. Derrida, *Writing and Difference*, p. 134.

29. Derrida, *Speech and Phenomena*, p. 53.

30. Saint Augustine, *Confessions*, trans. R. Warner (New York: New American Library, 1963), p. 267.

31. Ibid., p. 268.

32. Ibid., p. 273.

33. Rodolphe Gasché, "Autobiography as Gestalt in Nietzsche's *Ecce Homo*," *Boundary 2* 9 (1981): 285.

34. Paul Ricoeur, "Narrative Time," *Critical Inquiry* 7 (1980): 178.

35. H. R. Niebuhr, *The Meaning of Revelation* (New York: Macmillan, 1967), p. 69.

36. Augustine, *Confessions*, p. 183.

37. Nietzsche, *The Will to Power*, p. 267.

38. Ibid., p. 199.

39. Derrida, *Of Grammatology*, p. 98.

40. Altizer, *The Self-Embodiment of God*, p. 93.

41. Derrida, *Of Grammatology*, p. 250.

42. Altizer, *The Self-Embodiment of God*, p. 29.

43. Barthes, *Roland Barthes*, p. 1.

44. Derrida, *Writing and Difference*, p. 183.

45. Hegel, *Phenomenology*, pp. 59 ff.

46. Hegel, *Philosophy of Nature*, trans. A. V. Miller (New York: Humanities Press, 1970), par. 258.

47. Derrida, *Speech and Phenomena*, p. 93.

48. Derrida, *Of Grammatology*, p. 203.

49. Spivak's Preface, ibid., p. lxxi.

50. Ibid., p. 141.

51. Derrida, *Dissemination*, p. 168.

52. Derrida, *Writing and Difference*, p. 83.

53. Ibid., p. 295.

54. Altizer, *The Self-Embodiment of God*, p. 37.

55. Derrida, *Writing and Difference*, p. 132.

56. Derrida, *Speech and Phenomena*, p. 64.

57. Derrida, *Of Grammatology*, p. 67.

58. Kojève, *Introduction to the Reading of Hegel*, p. 138.

59. Derrida, *Speech and Phenomena*, p. 85.

60. Thoreau, "Walking," *The Writings of Henry David Thoreau*, vol. 9 (New York: Houghton, Mifflin, 1896), p. 251.

61. Derrida, *Of Grammatology*, p. 70.

62. Derrida, *Writing and Difference*, p. 133.

## Chapter Three

The epigraphs are from Thomas J. J. Altizer, "History as Apocalypse," in Altizer et al., *Deconstruction and Theology* (New York: Crossroad, 1982), p. 152, and from Jacques Derrida, *Spurs: Nietzsche's Styles*, trans. B. Harlow (Chicago: University of Chicago Press, 1979), pp. 43–45.

1. Genesis 22:1–3.

2. Galatians 4:22–31.

3. Søren Kierkegaard, *Fear and Trembling*, trans. W. Lowrie (Princeton: Princeton University Press, 1970), p. 26.

4. Frank Kermode, *The Sense of an Ending: Studies in the Theory of Fiction* (New York: Oxford University Press, 1967), pp. 44–45.

5. H. R. Niebuhr, *The Meaning of Revelation*, p. 59.

6. Karl Jaspers, *The Origin and Goal of History*, trans. M. Bulloch (London: Routledge & Kegan Paul, 1953), p. 1.

7. Derrida, *Speech and Phenomena*, p. 102.

8. Augustine, *Confessions*, p. 109.

9. *New Catholic Encyclopedia*, vol. 14 (New York: McGraw-Hill, 1967), pp. 352–53.

10. Justin, quoted in Frank Kermode, *The Genesis of Secrecy: On the Interpretation of Narrative* (Cambridge, Mass.: Harvard University Press, 1979), p. 107.

11. Augustine, quoted in Samuel Preus, *From Shadow to Promise: Old Testament Interpretation from Augustine to the Young Luther* (Cambridge, Mass.: Harvard University Press, 1969), p. 26.

12. Erich Auerbach, *Mimesis: The Representation of Reality in Western Literature* (Princeton: Princeton University Press, 1973), p. 3.

13. Auerbach, quoted in Hans Frei, *The Eclipse of Biblical Narrative: A Study in Eighteenth- and Nineteenth-Century Hermeneutics* (New Haven: Yale University Press, 1974), p. 28.

14. Paul Ricoeur, "The Metaphoric Process as Cognition, Imagination, and Feeling," *Critical Inquiry* 5 (1978): 50.

15. Ricoeur, *Freud and Philosophy*, p. 12.

16. Paul Tillich, *Systematic Theology*, vol. 1 (Chicago: University of Chicago Press, 1967), p. 239.

17. Ricoeur, *Freud and Philosophy*, p. 16.

18. Martin Heidegger, *Poetry, Language, Thought*, trans. A. Hofstader (New York: Harper & Row, 1971), pp. 17–18.

19. Ricoeur, *Freud and Philosophy*, p. 31.

20. John 1:1–5.

21. Romans 5:12–17.

22. Paul Ricoeur, *The Symbolism of Evil*, trans. E. Buchanan (Boston: Beacon Press, 1967), p. 272.

23. Ibid., p. 274.

24. Wallace Stevens, "The Man with the Blue Guitar," *The Collected Poems of Wallace Stevens* (New York: Knopf, 1981), p. 175.

25. J. Hillis Miller, "Ariadne's Thread: Repetitions and the Narrative Line," *Critical Inquiry* 3 (1976): 75.

26. Hayden White, *Tropics of Discourse: Essays in Cultural Criticism* (Baltimore: Johns Hopkins University Press, 1978), p. 234.

27. Hayden White, "The Value of Narrativity in the Representation of Reality," *Critical Inquiry* 7 (1980): 10 ff. White cites the foregoing example from the *Annals of Saint Gall*.

28. Genette, quoted in Jonathan Culler, *Structuralist Poetics: Structuralism, Linguistics, and the Study of Literature* (Ithaca: Cornell University Press, 1975), p. 210.

29. Croce, quoted in White, *Tropics of Discourse*, p. 10.

30. White, *Tropics of Discourse*, p. 10.

31. Ibid., p. 83.

32. Paul Ricoeur, "Narrative and Hermeneutics," in *Religion and the Humanities*, ed. K. Mullikin (Research Triangle Park, N.C.: National Humanities Center, 1981), p. 43.

33. Kermode, *The Sense of an Ending*.

34. Clifford Geertz, "Religion as a Cultural System," in *The Religious Situation*, ed. D. Cutler (Boston: Beacon Press, 1968), p. 641.

35. Stephen Crites, "The Narrative Quality of Experience," *Journal of the American Academy of Religion* 39 (1971): 295.

36. Stephen Crites, "Unfinished Figure: On Theology and the Imagination," in *Unfinished: Essays in Honor of Ray L. Hart*, ed. M. C. Taylor (Chico, Calif.: Scholars Press, 1981), p. 157.

37. Oscar Cullman, *Christ and Time: The Primitive Christian Conception of Time and History*, trans. F. V. Filson (Philadelphia: Westminster Press, 1950), p. 118.

38. White, *Tropics of Discourse*, p. 92.

39. Hegel, quoted in Nietzsche, *The Portable Nietzsche*, ed. W. Kaufmann (New York: Viking Press, 1968), pp. 39-40.

40. Nietzsche, *The Portable Nietzsche*, p. 40.

41. Coleridge, quoted in Ray L. Hart, *Unfinished Man and the Imagination: Toward an Ontology and a Rhetoric of Revelation* (New York: Herder & Herder, 1968), p. 245.

42. R. G. Collingwood, *The Idea of History* (New York: Oxford University Press, 1956), p. 242.

43. Hans Vaihinger, *The Philosophy of "As If,"* trans. C. K. Ogden (New York: Harcourt, Brace, 1924).

44. White, *Tropics of Discourse*, p. 98.

45. Collingwood, *The Idea of History*, pp. 245-46.

46. White, *Tropics of Discourse*, p. 107.

47. Collingwood, *The Idea of History*, p. 244.

48. Barthes, quoted in Kermode, *The Genesis of Secrecy*, p. 117.

49. White, *Tropics of Discourse*, p. 102.

50. Brown, *Life against Death*, p. 102.

51. Ibid.

52. Kermode, *The Sense of an Ending*, p. 58.

53. Derrida, *Positions*, p. 57.

54. Derrida, *Margins of Philosophy*, p. 72.

55. Kermode, *The Genesis of Secrecy*, p. 106.

56. Miller, "Ariadne's Thread," pp. 69-70.

57. Kermode, *The Sense of an Ending*, p. 45.

58. White, "The Value of Narrativity," p. 13.

59. Ibid., p. 24.

60. Kermode, *The Sense of an Ending*, p. 45.

61. White, *Tropics of Discourse*, p. 99.

62. Stevens, "An Ordinary Evening in New Haven," *Collected Poems*.

63. Jacques Derrida, *Glas* (Paris: Editions Galilée, 1974), p. 122.

64. Brown, *Life against Death*, p. 93.

65. Samuel Beckett, *Endgame* (New York: Grove Press, 1958), pp. 48-49.

66. Edmond Jabès, *Book of Questions*, trans. R. Waldrop (Middletown, Conn.: Wesleyan University Press, 1976), p. 32.

67. Brown, *Life against Death*, p. 108.

68. Stanley Cavell, *Must We Mean What We Say?* (New York: Scribner's, 1969), pp. 149; 32.

## Chapter Four

The epigraphs are from Jorge Luis Borges, *Labyrinths: Selected Stories and Other Writings*, ed. and trans. D. Yates and J. Irby (New York: New Directions, 1964), p. 51; Barthes, *The Pleasure of the Text*, p. 47; Nietzsche, *Gay Science*, p. 215; and Derrida, *Of Grammatology*, p. 26.

1. G. W. Leibniz, *Theodicy*, trans. L. M. Huggard (New Haven: Yale University Press, 1952), pp. 371–72.

2. Borges, *Labyrinths*, p. 51.

3. Geertz, "Religion as a Cultural System," p. 663.

4. Derrida, *Dissemination*, p. 3.

5. Derrida, *Positions*, p. 77.

6. Derrida, *Of Grammatology*, p. 18.

7. Ibid.

8. Derrida, *Dissemination*, pp. 47; 46.

9. Novalis, quoted in Derrida, *Dissemination*, p. 52.

10. Hegel, *The Logic of Hegel*, p. 25.

11. Ibid., p. 24.

12. Hegel, *Science of Logic*, p. 39.

13. Ibid.

14. Nietzsche, *The Portable Nietzsche*, p. 483.

15. Michel Foucault, "What Is an Author?" in *Textual Strategies: Perspectives in Post-Structuralist Criticism*, ed. J. V. Harari (Ithaca: Cornell University Press, 1979), p. 159.

16. Derrida, *Writing and Difference*, p. 11.

17. Derrida, *Dissemination*, p. 44.

18. Derrida, *Writing and Difference*, p. 235.

19. Derrida, *Of Grammatology*, p. 61.

20. Michel Foucault, *The Order of Things: An Archaeology of the Human Sciences*, trans. A. S. London (New York: Random House, 1970), p. 304.

21. Derrida, *Speech and Phenomena*, p. 32.

22. Hans-Georg Gadamer, *Truth and Method*, trans. G. Barden and J. Cumming (New York: Seabury Press, 1975), p. 164.

23. Derrida, *Of Grammatology*, p. 15.

24. Culler, *Structuralist Poetics*, p. 28.

25. Michel Foucault, *The Archaeology of Knowledge*, trans. A. M. S. Smith (New York: Harper Torchbooks, 1972), p. 21.

26. Stevens, "An Ordinary Evening in New Haven," *Collected Poems*, p. 485.

27. Derrida, *Writing and Difference*, p. 169.

28. Ibid., p. 178.

29. Ibid., p. 3.

30. Roland Barthes, *S/Z*, trans. R. Miller (New York: Hill & Wang, 1974), p. 174.

31. Gadamer, *Truth and Method*, p. 397.

32. Paul Ricoeur, *Interpretation Theory: Discourse and the Surplus of Meaning* (Fort Worth: Texas Christian University Press, 1976), p. 60.

33. Gadamer, *Truth and Method*, p. 412.

34. David Tracy, *The Analogical Imagination: Christian Theology and Cultural Pluralism* (New York: Crossroad, 1981), pp. 111, 110.

35. Gadamer, *Truth and Method*, p. 341.

36. Ibid., p. 277.

37. Hart, *Unfinished Man*, p. 260.

38. Barthes, *Roland Barthes*, p. 172.

39. Hartman, *Saving the Text*, p. 2.

40. Derrida, *Of Grammatology*, p. 18.

41. Jabès, quoted in Derrida, *Writing and Difference*, p. 298.

42. Derrida, *Writing and Difference*, pp. 297−98.

43. Ibid., p. 71.

44. Brown, *Love's Body*, p. 188.

45. Ibid.

46. Derrida, *Writing and Difference*, p. 299.

47. Derrida, *Positions*, p. 3.

48. Derrida, "Limited Inc abc . . . ," p. 197.

49. Barthes, *Roland Barthes*, p. 148.

50. J. Hillis Miller, "The Critic as Host," in H. Bloom et al., *Deconstruction and Criticism* (New York: Seabury Press, 1979), p. 252.

51. Derrida, *Glas*, p. 183a.

52. Derrida, *Writing and Difference*, p. 294.

## Chapter Five

The epigraphs are from Jabès, *The Book of Questions*, p. 85; Gilles Deleuze, *Proust and Signs*, trans. R. Howard (New York: Braziller, 1972), p. 167; Altizer, "History as Apocalypse," p. 155; and Nietzsche, *Zarathustra*, pp. 269−70.

1. Derrida, "The Purveyor of Truth," *Yale French Studies* 52 (1975): 101.

2. Derrida, *Of Grammatology*, p. 26.

3. Kierkegaard, *Concluding Unscientific Postscript*, p. 98.

4. Franz Kafka, *In the Penal Colony: Stories and Short Pieces*, trans. W. and E. Muir (New York: Schocken, 1961).

5. Derrida, *Writing and Difference*, p. 76.

6. Jabès, *The Book of Questions*, p. 17.

7. Derrida, *Writing and Difference*, p. 12.

8. William Willeford, *The Fool and His Scepter: A Study in Clowns and Jesters and Their Audience* (Evanston: Northwestern University Press, 1969), p. 129.

9. Derrida, *Margins of Philosophy*, p. 82.

10. Nietzsche, *The Will to Power*, p. 539.

11. Luke 24:15−16, 30−31.

12. William Blake.

13. Robert Scharlemann, "The Being of God When God Is Not Being God: Deconstructing the History of Theism," in Altizer et al., *Deconstruction and Theology* (New York: Crossroad, 1982), p. 101.

14. Derrida, *Of Grammatology*, p. 14.

15. Samuel Beckett, quoted in Daniel Albright, *Representation and the Imagination: Beckett, Kafka, Nabokov, and Schoenberg* (Chicago: University of Chicago Press, 1981), p. 2.

16. Derrida, *Dissemination*, p. 77.

17. Ibid., p. 146.

18. Derrida, *Writing and Difference*, p. 191.

19. Derrida, *Speech and Phenomena*, p. 134.

20. Derrida, *Positions*, p. 40.

21. Derrida, *Speech and Phenomena*, pp. 142−43.

22. Stevens, *Opus Posthumous*, p. 163.

23. Stevens, "An Ordinary Evening in New Haven," *Collected Poems*, pp. 488−89.

24. Derrida, *Dissemination*, p. 128.

25. Hegel, *Science of Logic*, pp. 412, 413, 417, 425.

26. Ibid., pp. 413, 417.

27. Ibid., p. 425.

28. Altizer, *The Self-Embodiment of God*, pp. 37, 47.

29. Ibid., p. 19.

30. Derrida, *Speech and Phenomena*, p. 66.

31. Derrida, *Of Grammatology*, p. 314.

32. Ibid., p. 70.

33. Derrida, "Limited Inc abc . . . ," p. 182.

34. Derrida, *Positions*, p. 27.

35. Derrida, *Of Grammatology*, p. 62.

36. Derrida, *Speech and Phenomena*, p. 141.

37. Rodolphe Gasché, "Deconstruction as Criticism," *Glyph* 6 (1979): 193.

38. Hegel, *Phenomenology*, p. 86.

39. Ibid., p. 83.

40. Ibid., p. 27.

41. Stevens, "Six Significant Landscapes," *Collected Poems*, p. 73.

42. Miller, *Six Poets of Reality*, p. 230.

43. Stevens, "Adult Epigram," *Collected Poems*, p. 353.

44. Gilles Deleuze, "Active and Reactive," in D. B. Allison, ed., *The New Nietzsche*, p. 86.

45. Ibid.

46. Hegel, *Philosophy of Religion*, vol. 3, p. 254.

47. Hegel, *Science of Logic*, p. 153.

48. Deleuze, "Active and Reactive," p. 85.

49. Nietzsche, *The Will to Power*, p. 330.

50. Maurice Merleau-Ponty, *Phenomenology of Perception*, trans. C. Smith (London: Routledge & Kegan Paul, 1962), p. 423.

51. Nietzsche, quoted in Altizer, "Eternal Recurrence and the Kingdom of God," in D. B. Allison, ed., *The New Nietzsche*, p. 242.

52. Derrida, *Dissemination*, p. 211.

53. Miller, "The Critic as Host," in H. Bloom et al., *Deconstruction and Criticism*, p. 219.

54. Derrida, *Dissemination*, p. 212.

55. Derrida, "Limited Inc abc . . . ," p. 225.

56. Altizer, *Descent into Hell*, pp. 56–57.

57. Derrida, *Dissemination*, pp. 92–93.

58. Ibid., p. 149.

59. Ibid., p. 153.

60. Ibid., p. 127.

61. Ibid., p. 152.

62. Ibid., p. 133.

63. Altizer, *The Self-Embodiment of God*, p. 36.

64. Nargarjuna.

65. Hegel, *Science of Logic*, p. 457.

66. Mark 4:3–8.

67. John Dominic Crossan, *Cliffs of Fall: Paradox and Polyvalence in the Parables of Jesus* (New York: Crossroad, 1980), p. 50.

68. Derrida, *Positions*, p. 45.

## Chapter Six

The epigraphs are from Richard R. Niebuhr, *Experiential Religion* (New York: Harper & Row, 1972), p. 5; Brown, *Love's Body*, p. 88; Altizer, *Descent into Hell*, pp. 159–60; Nietzsche, *Gay Science*, p. 321; and Foucault, *The Order of Things*, p. 342.

1. André Malraux, *The Metamorphosis of the Gods*, trans. S. Gilbert (New York: Doubleday, 1960), p. 386.

2. Ibid., p. 143.

3. Foucault, *The Order of Things*, p. 4.

4. Ibid.

5. Ibid., p. 16.

6. Picasso, quoted in P. W. Schwartz, *Cubism* (New York: Praeger, 1971), p. 7.

7. Thomas J. J. Altizer, *Total Presence: The Language of Jesus and the Language of Today* (New York: Seabury Press, 1980), pp. 32-33.

8. Jean-Paul Sartre, *Nausea*, trans. L. Alexander (New York: New Directions, 1964), p. 20.

9. Jacques Derrida, "Signature Event Context," *Glyph* 1 (1976): 194.

10. Derrida, "Limited Inc abc . . . ," p. 200.

11. Roman Jakobson.

12. Hartman, *Saving the Text*, p. 62.

13. Hegel, *Phenomenology*, p. 69.

14. Maurice Merleau-Ponty, *The Visible and the Invisible*, trans. A. Lingis (Evanston, Ill.: Northwestern University Press, 1968), p. 132.

15. Nietzsche, *The Will to Power*, p. 302.

16. Brown, *Love's Body*, p. 149.

17. Kojève, *Introduction to the Reading of Hegel*, p. 10.

18. Søren Kierkegaard, *The Sickness unto Death*, trans. W. Lowrie (Princeton: Princeton University Press, 1970), p. 146. Emphasis added.

19. Hegel, *Phenomenology*, pp. 113, 112.

20. Pierre Klossowski, "Nietzsche's Experience of the Eternal Return," in D. B. Allison, ed., *The New Nietzsche*, p. 112.

21. Derrida, *Speech and Phenomena*, p. 145.

22. Foucault, *Language, Counter-Memory, Practice*, p. 161.

23. Altizer, "History as Apocalypse," in Altizer et al., *Deconstruction and Theology*, p. 171.

24. Wilden on Lacan, in translator's Preface to Lacan, *The Language of the Self*, p. 182.

25. Adorno, *Negative Dialectics*, p. 102.

26. Nietzsche, *Gay Science*, p. 351.

27. Spivak, Preface to Derrida, *Of Grammatology*, p. lxix.

28. Derrida, quoted in Gasché, "Deconstruction as Criticism," p. 194.

29. Derrida, *Of Grammatology*, p. 71.

30. Derrida, "Limited Inc abc . . . ," passim.

31. Derrida, *Of Grammatology*, p. 70.

32. Ibid.

33. Ibid., p. 46.

34. Derrida, *Dissemination*, p. 119.

35. Ibid., p. 93.

36. Ibid.

37. Derrida, *Of Grammatology*, p. 187.

38. Rimbaud, quoted in Geoffrey Hartman, *Criticism in the Wilderness: The Study of Literature Today* (New Haven: Yale University Press, 1980), p. 27.

39. Maurice Blanchot, "The Limits of Experience: Nihilism," in D. B. Allison, ed., *The New Nietzsche*, p. 126.

40. Derrida, *Writing and Difference*, p. 229.

41. Altizer, *Descent into Hell*, pp. 159, 155.

42. Bataille, quoted in Michèle Richman, *Reading Georges Bataille: Beyond the Gift* (Baltimore: Johns Hopkins University Press, 1982), p. 130.

43. Lacan, quoted in Hartman, *Saving the Text*, p. 77.

44. Altizer, *Total Presence*, p. 100.

45. Barthes, *A Lover's Discourse* (New York: Hill & Wang, 1978), p. 171.

46. Heidegger, *Poetry, Language, Thought*, p. 120.

47. Hegel, *Phenomenology*, pp. 89–103.

48. Brown, *Love's Body*, p. 171.

49. Bataille, quoted in Richman, *Reading Georges Bataille*, p. 71.

50. Nietzsche, *Zarathustra*, p. 72.

51. Derrida, *Speech and Phenomena*, p. 85.

52. Miller, "The Critic as Host," in Bloom et al., *Deconstruction and Criticism*, p. 228.

53. Rilke, quoted in Heidegger, *Poetry, Language, Thought*, p. 125.

54. Rilke, quoted in Brown, *Life against Death*, p. 108.

55. Nietzsche, *The Portable Nietzsche*, p. 185.

56. Bataille, quoted in Derrida, *Writing and Difference*, p. 258.

57. Adorno, *Negative Dialectics*, p. 378.

58. Derrida, *Of Grammatology*, p. 143.

59. Barthes, *The Pleasure of the Text*, p. 35.

60. Altizer, *Total Presence*, p. 108.

61. Nietzsche, *The Will to Power*, p. 99.

## Chapter Seven

The epigraphs are from Kafka, quoted in Albright, *Representation and the Imagination*, p. 97; Nietzsche, *Zarathustra*, p. 123; and Derrida, *Dissemination*, pp. 143–44.

1. Henry David Thoreau, "Walking," pp. 251–52, 253–54.

2. Nietzsche, *Gay Science*, p. 181.

3. James Joyce, quoted in Norman O. Brown, *Closing Time* (New York: Random House, 1973), p. 56.

4. William Blake.

5. Nietzsche, *Genealogy of Morals*, p. 122.

6. Ibid., p. 120.

7. Nietzsche, *Zarathustra*, p. 334.

8. Derrida, *Writing and Difference*, p. 291.

9. Derrida, *Of Grammatology*, p. 10.

10. Ibid., p. 115.

11. Jabès, *The Book of Yukel*, p. 32.

12. Derrida, *Of Grammatology*, p. 112.

13. Bataille, quoted in Derrida, *Writing and Difference*, p. 271.

14. Altizer, "Eternal Recurrence and Kingdom of God," in D. B. Allison, ed., *The New Nietzsche*, p. 240.

15. Cavell, *Must We Mean What We Say?*, p. 150.

16. Derrida, *Writing and Difference*, p. 298.

17. Nietzsche, *The Will to Power*, p. 377.

18. Derrida, *Writing and Difference*, p. 292.

19. Gilles Deleuze, "Pensée Nomade," in P. Boudot et al., *Nietzsche aujourd'hui*, vol. 1 (Paris: Union générale d'éditions, 1973), pp. 169, 165.

20. Derrida, *Writing and Difference*, p. 292.

21. Ibid., p. 297.

22. Nietzsche, *The Will to Power*, p. 13.

23. Bataille, quoted in Derrida, *Writing and Difference*, p. 267.

24. Eugen Herrigel, *Zen in the Art of Archery*, trans. R. F. C. Hull (New York: Random House, 1971), p. 52.

25. Derrida, *Writing and Difference*, p. 297.

26. Derrida, *Dissemination*, p. 93.

27. Derrida, *Positions*, p. 14.

28. Jacques Derrida, *The Archeology of the Frivolous*, trans. J. P. Leavey (Pittsburgh: Duquesne University Press, 1980), p. 118.

29. Derrida, *Of Grammatology*, p. 50.

30. Derrida, *Writing and Difference*, p. 292.

31. Ibid.

32. Gadamer, *Truth and Method*, p. 95.

33. Victor Turner, "Liminal to Liminoid in Play, Flow, and Ritual: An Essay in Comparative Symbology," *Rice University Studies* 60 (1974): 89.

34. Galatians 3 : 13.

35. Brown, *Love's Body*, p. 245.

36. Hegel, *Phenomenology*, p. 99.

37. Julia Kristeva, *Desire in Language: A Semiotic Approach to Literature*, trans. T. Gora, A. Jardine, and L. Roudiez (New York: Columbia University Press, 1980), p. 78.

38. Ibid., p. 85.

39. Mikhail Bakhtin, *Rabelais and His World*, trans. H. Iswolsky (Cambridge, Mass.: M.I.T. Press, 1968), p. 11.

40. Ibid., p. 26.

41. Kristeva, *Desire in Language*, p. 83.

42. James Joyce.

43. Nietzsche, *Zarathustra*, p. 153.

44. Derrida, *Spurs*, p. 135.

45. Nietzsche, *Gay Science*, p. 164.

46. Bakhtin, *Rabelais and His World*, pp. 11-12.

47. Ibid., p. 123.

48. Deleuze, "Pensée Nomade," p. 170.

49. Nietzsche, *Zarathustra*, p. 305.

50. Norman O. Brown, *Closing Time*, pp. 47-48.

51. Ibid., pp. 57-58.

52. Kierkegaard, *Fear and Trembling*, pp. 51-52.

53. Ibid., p. 57.

54. Bataille, quoted in Derrida, *Writing and Difference*, p. 338.

55. Nietzsche, *Zarathustra*, p. 334.

56. Nietzsche, *The Will to Power*, p. 316.

57. Nietzsche, *Zarathustra*, pp. 334-35.

58. Deleuze, "Active and Reactive," in D. B. Allison, ed., *The New Nietzsche*, p. 102.

59. Nietzsche, *The Portable Nietzsche*, p. 554.

60. W. K. C. Guthrie, *The Greeks and Their Gods* (Boston: Beacon Press, n.d.), p. 156.

61. Nietzsche, *Zarathustra*, p. 38.

62. Nietzsche, *Genealogy of Morals*, p. 91.

63. Altizer, *Total Presence*, p. 94.

64. Derrida, *Writing and Difference*, p. 298.

65. Foucault, *Language, Counter-Memory, Practice*, p. 171.

66. Nietzsche, *Gay Science*, p. 38.

67. William Carlos Williams, "The Red Wheelbarrow," *Collected Earlier Poems of William Carlos Williams*. Copyright © 1938 by New Directions Publishing Corporation. Reprinted by permission of New Directions.

68. Altizer, "Eternal Recurrence and Kingdom of God," in D. B. Allison, ed., *The New Nietzsche*, p. 245.

## Chapter Eight

The first epigraph is from Stevens, "On the Road Home," *Collected Poems*, p. 203; the next two are from Nietzsche's *The Will to Power*, p. 326 and pp. 14-15; and the last one is from

Roland Barthes, *Image-Music-Text*, trans. S. Heath (New York: Hill & Wang, 1977), p. 147.

1. Stevens, "An Ordinary Evening in New Haven," *Collected Poems*, p. 472.

2. Nietzsche, *Gay Science*, pp. 246–47.

3. Friedrich Nietzsche, *Beyond Good and Evil*, trans. W. Kaufmann (New York: Random House, 1966), p. 2.

4. Derrida, *Spurs*, p. 55.

5. Ibid., p. 51.

6. Ibid., p. 53.

7. Ibid., p. 57, 67.

8. Derrida, *Writing and Difference*, p. 280.

9. Foucault, quoted in Vincent Descombes, *Modern French Philosophy*, trans. L. Scott-Fox and J. M. Harding (Cambridge, Eng.: Cambridge University Press, 1982), pp. 116–17.

10. Roland Barthes, *Empire of Signs*, trans. R. Howard (New York: Hill & Wang, 1982), p. 78.

11. Brown, *Love's Body*, p. 247.

12. Barthes, *Image-Music-Text*, p. 159.

13. Brown, *Love's Body*, p. 245.

14. Roland Barthes, *S/Z*, p. 9.

15. Terence Hawkes, *Structuralism and Semiotics* (Berkeley: University of California Press, 1977), p. 84.

16. Derrida, *Writing and Difference*, p. 25.

17. Nietzsche, *The Will to Power*, p. 264.

18. Ibid., p. 317.

19. James Joyce, quoted in Brown, *Closing Time*, p. 75.

20. Barthes, *The Pleasure of the Text*, p. 43.

21. Jabès, *The Book of Yukel*, p. 105.

22. William Blake, "The Marriage of Heaven and Hell," *The Illuminated Blake*, ed. D. V. Erdman (New York: Doubleday, 1979), p. 106.

23. Brown, *Love's Body*, p. 246.

24. Michel Haar, "Nietzsche and Metaphysical Language," in B. Allison, ed., *The New Nietzsche*, p. 7.

25. Barthes, *The Pleasure of the Text*, p. 64.

26. Derrida, *Of Grammatology*, p. 18.

27. Derrida, *Writing and Difference*, p. 292.

28. Barthes, *S/Z*, pp. 200–201.

29. Derrida, *Of Grammatology*, p. 18.

30. Barthes, *Image-Music-Text*, p. 147.

31. Harold Bloom, *Kabbalah and Criticism* (New York: Seabury Press, 1975), p. 106.

32. Derrida, *Writing and Difference*, p. 289.

33. Ibid., p. 298.

34. Barthes, "From Work to Text," in J. V. Harari, ed., *Textual Strategies*, p. 76.

35. Derrida, *Speech and Phenomena*, p. 149.

36. Derrida, *Writing and Difference*, p. 292.

37. Kristeva, *Desire in Language*, p. 36.

38. Barthes, "From Work to Text," p. 75.

39. Kristeva, *Desire in Language*, p. 66.

40. Barthes, "From Work to Text," p. 79.

41. Barthes, *Image-Music-Text*, p. 146.

42. Ibid., p. 160.

43. Barthes, *Roland Barthes*, p. 106.

44. Foucault, *Language, Counter-Memory, Practice*, p. 117.

45. Barthes, "From Work to Text," p. 79; *S/Z*, p. 10.

46. Barthes, *Image-Music-Text*, p. 146.

47. Kristeva, *Desire in Language*, p. 78.

48. Derrida, *Dissemination*, pp. 143–44.

49. Joyce, quoted in Brown, *Closing Time*, p. 109.

50. Barthes, *The Pleasure of the Text*, p. 16.

51. Brown, *Love's Body*, p. 248.

52. Barthes, *Roland Barthes*, p. 96.

53. Derrida, *Writing and Difference*, p. 292.

54. Miller, "The Critic as Host," in Bloom et al., *Deconstruction and Criticism*, pp. 230–31.

## Interlude

The epigraphs are from Wallace Stevens, "On the Road Home," *Parts of a World* (New York: Knopf, 1942), p. 26; Barthes, *Roland Barthes*, p. 170; and Jabès, *The Book of Questions*, p. 160.

1. T. S. Eliot, "Little Gidding," *Collected Poems, 1909–1962* (London: Faber & Faber, 1963), p. 222.

2. Hegel, quoted in Mark C. Taylor, *Journeys to Selfhood: Hegel and Kierkegaard* (Berkeley: University of California Press, 1980), p. 263.

3. Stevens, "July Mountain," *Opus Posthumous*, p. 162.

# Biblio Graphy

Abrams, M. H. "How To Do Things with Texts." *Partisan Review* 46 (1979): 565–88.

———. *Natural Supernaturalism: Tradition and Revolution in Romantic Literature*. New York: Norton, 1971.

Adams, Robert. *Nil: Episodes in the Literary Conquest of the Void during the Nineteenth Century*. New York: Oxford University Press, 1966.

Adorno, Theodor. *Negative Dialectics*. Translated by E. B. Ashton. New York: Seabury Press, 1973.

Albright, Daniel. *Representation and the Imagination: Beckett, Kafka, Nabokov, and Schoenberg*. Chicago: University of Chicago Press, 1981.

Allison, David B., ed. *The New Nietzsche: Contemporary Styles of Interpretation*. New York: Delta, 1979.

Altizer, Thomas J. J. *The Descent into Hell: A Study of the Radical Reversal of the Christian Consciousness*. New York: Seabury Press, 1979.

———. "Eternal Recurrence and Kingdom of God." Pp. 232–46 in D. B. Allison, ed., *The New Nietzsche*.

———. *The Gospel of Christian Atheism*. Philadelphia: Westminster Press, 1966.

———. "History as Apocalypse." Pp. 147–77 in Altizer et al., *Deconstruction and Theology*.

———. *Mircea Eliade and the Dialectic of the Sacred*. Philadelphia: Westminster Press, 1963.

———. *The New Apocalypse: The Radical Christian Vision of William Blake*. East Lansing: Michigan State University Press, 1967.

———. *Oriental Mysticism and Biblical Eschatology*. Philadelphia: Westminster Press, 1971.

———. *The Self-Embodiment of God*. New York: Harper & Row, 1977.

———. *Total Presence: The Language of Jesus and the Language of Today*. New York: Seabury Press, 1980.

Altizer, Thomas J. J., et al. *Deconstruction and Theology*. New York: Crossroad, 1982.

Artaud, Antonin. *Theatre and Its Double*. Translated by M. Richards. New York: Grove Press, 1958.

Auerbach, Erich. *Mimesis: The Representation of Reality in Western Literature*. Princeton: Princeton University Press, 1973.

Augustine. *Confessions*. Translated by R. Warner. New York: New American Library, 1963.

Babcock, Barbara, ed. *The Reversible World: Symbolic Inversion in Art and Society*. Ithaca: Cornell University Press, 1978.

Bachelard, Gaston. *The Philosophy of No: A Philosophy of the New Scientific Method*. Translated by G. C. Waterson. New York: Orion Press, 1968.

Bakhtin, Mikhail. *Rabelais and His World*. Translated by H. Iswolsky. Cambridge, Mass.: M.I.T. Press, 1968.

Barthes, Roland. *Critical Essays*. Translated by R. Howard. Evanston, Ill.: Northwestern University Press, 1972.

———. *Empire of Signs*. Translated by R. Howard. New York: Hill & Wang, 1982.

———. *Image-Music-Text*. Translated by S. Heath. New York: Hill & Wang, 1977.

———. *A Lover's Discourse*. New York: Hill & Wang, 1978.

———. *The Pleasure of the Text*. Translated by R. Howard. New York: Hill & Wang, 1975.

———. *Roland Barthes*. Translated by R. Howard. New York: Hill & Wang, 1977.

———. *S/Z*. Translated by R. Miller. New York: Hill & Wang, 1974.

———. "From Work to Text." Pp. 73–81 in J. V. Harari, ed., *Textual Strategies*.

———. *Writing Degree Zero*. Translated by A. Lavers and C. Smith. New York: Hill & Wang, 1968.

Bataille, Georges. *L'Expérience intérieure*. Paris: Gallimard, 1954.

———. "Hegel, la mort, et le sacrifice." *Deucalion* 5 (1955): 21–43.

Beckett, Samuel. *Company*. New York: Grove Press, 1980.

———. *Endgame*. New York: Grove Press, 1958.

Benveniste, Emile. "Le Jeu comme structure." *Deucalion* 2 (1947): 161–67.

Blake, William. *The Illuminated Blake*. Edited by D. V. Erdman. New York: Doubleday, 1979.

Blanchot, Maurice. "The Limits of Experience: Nihilism." Pp. 121–27 in D. B. Allison, ed., *The New Nietzsche*.

Blondel, Eric. *Nietzsche: Le 5ᵉ Evangile?* Paris: Les Bergers et les Mages, 1980.

Bloom, Harold. *The Anxiety of Influence: A Theory of Poetry*. New York: Oxford University Press, 1973.

———. *Kabbalah and Criticism*. New York: Seabury Press, 1975.

———. *A Map of Misreading*. New York: Oxford University Press, 1975.

———. *Poetry and Repression*. New Haven: Yale University Press, 1976.

Bloom, Harold, et al. *Deconstruction and Criticism*. New York: Seabury Press, 1979.

Borges, Jorge Luis. *Labyrinths: Selected Stories and Other Writings*. Edited and translated by D. Yates and J. Irby. New York: New Directions, 1964.

Boudot, Pierre, et al. *Nietzsche aujourd'hui*. Paris: Union générale d'éditions, 1973.

Brown, Norman O. *Closing Time*. New York: Random House, 1973.

———. *Life against Death: The Psychoanalytic Meaning of History*. New York: Random House, 1959.

———. *Love's Body*. New York: Random House, 1968.

Burke, Kenneth. *The Rhetoric of Religion: Studies in Logology*. Berkeley: University of California Press, 1970.

Cage, John. *Silence*. Cambridge, Mass.: M.I.T. Press, 1966.

Casey, Edward. "Imagination and Repetition in Literature." *Yale French Studies* 52 (1975): 250–66.

Cavell, Stanley. *Must We Mean What We Say?* New York: Scribner's, 1969.

Chipp, Herschel. *Theories of Modern Art: A Sourcebook by Artists and Critics.* Berkeley: University of California Press, 1968.

Cochrane, Charles Norris. *Christianity and Classical Culture.* New York: Oxford University Press, 1957.

Collingwood, R. G. *The Idea of History.* New York: Oxford University Press, 1956.

Cox, Harvey. *The Feast of Fools.* New York: Harper & Row, 1969.

Crites, Stephen. "The Narrative Quality of Experience." *Journal of the American Academy of Religion* 39 (1971): 291–311.

———. "Unfinished Figure: On Theology and Imagination." Pp. 155–83 in Mark C. Taylor, ed., *Unfinished: Essays in Honor of Ray L. Hart.*

Crossan, John Dominic. *Cliffs of Fall: Paradox and Polyvalence in the Parables of Jesus.* New York: Crossroad, 1980.

———. *Raid on the Articulate: Comic Eschatology in Jesus and Borges.* New York: Harper & Row, 1976.

Culler, Jonathan. *On Deconstruction: Theory and Criticism after Structuralism.* Ithaca: Cornell University Press, 1983.

———. *Ferdinand de Saussure.* New York: Penguin Books, 1976.

———. *The Pursuit of Signs: Semiotics, Literature, Deconstruction.* Ithaca: Cornell University Press, 1981.

———. *Structuralist Poetics: Structuralism, Linguistics, and the Study of Literature.* Ithaca: Cornell University Press, 1975.

Cullmann, Oscar. *Christ and Time: The Primitive Christian Conception of Time and History.* Translated by F. V. Filson. Philadelphia: Westminster Press, 1950.

Daly, Mary. *Gyn/Ecology: The Metaethics of Radical Feminism.* Boston: Beacon Press, 1978.

*Deconstruction and Criticism.* See Bloom, Harold, et al.

*Deconstruction and Theology.* See Altizer, Thomas J. J., et al.

Deleuze, Gilles. "Active and Reactive." Pp. 80–106 in D. B. Allison, ed., *The New Nietzsche.*

———. *Différence et répétition.* Paris: Presses universitaires de France, 1968.

———. *Logique du sens.* Paris: Editions de Minuit, 1959.

———. *Nietzsche et philosophie.* Paris: Presses universitaires de France, 1962.

———. "Nomad Thought." Translated by R. Cohen. Pp. 142–49 in D. B. Allison, ed., *The New Nietzsche.*

———. "Pensée Nomade." Pp. 159–74 in P. Boudot, et al., *Nietzsche aujourd'hui.*

———. *Proust and Signs.* Translated by R. Howard. New York: Braziller, 1972.

Deleuze, Gilles, and Félix Guattari. *Anti-Oedipus: Capitalism and Schizophrenia.* Translated by R. Hurley, M. Seem, and H. R. Lane. New York: Viking, 1977.

De Man, Paul. *Allegories of Reading: Figural Language in Rousseau, Nietzsche, Rilke, and Proust.* New Haven: Yale University Press, 1979.

———. "The Crisis of Contemporary Criticism." *Arion* 1 (1967): 38–57.

———. "The Rhetoric of Temporality." In *Interpretation: Theory and Practice,* edited by Charles Singleton, pp. 173–209. Baltimore: Johns Hopkins University Press, 1969.

———. "The Timid God." *Georgia Review* 29 (1975): 533–58.

Derrida, Jacques. *The Archeology of the Frivolous.* Translated by J. P. Leavey. Pittsburgh: Duquesne University Press, 1980.

————. *La Carte postale de Socrate à Freud et au-delà*. Paris: Flammarion, 1980.

————. *Dissemination*. Translated by B. Johnson. Chicago: University of Chicago Press, 1981.

————. *Glas*. Paris: Editions Galilée, 1974.

————. *Of Grammatology*. Translated by G. C. Spivak. Baltimore: Johns Hopkins University Press, 1976.

————. "Limited Inc abc . . . ." *Glyph* 2 (1977): 167–251.

————. "La Loi du genre/The Law of Genre." *Glyph* 7 (1980): 176–233.

————. *Margins of Philosophy*. Translated by A. Bass. Chicago: University of Chicago Press, 1982.

————. *Positions*. Translated by A. Bass. Chicago: University of Chicago Press, 1981.

————. "The Purveyor of Truth." *Yale French Studies* 52 (1975): 31–113.

————. "Signature, Event, Context." *Glyph* 1 (1976): 172–97.

————. *Speech and Phenomena and Other Essays on Husserl's Theory of Signs*. Translated by D. B. Allison. Evanston, Ill.: Northwestern University Press, 1973.

————. *Spurs: Nietzsche's Styles*. Translated by B. Harlow. Chicago: University of Chicago Press, 1979.

————. *La Vérité en peinture*. Paris: Flammarion, 1978.

————. *Writing and Difference*. Translated by A. Bass. Chicago: University of Chicago Press, 1978.

Descombes, Vincent. *Modern French Philosophy*. Translated by L. Scott-Fox and J. M. Harding. Cambridge, Eng.: Cambridge University Press, 1982.

Detweiler, Robert. *Story, Sign, and Self: Phenomenology and Structuralism as Literary-Critical Methods*. Philadelphia: Fortress Press, 1978.

Donoghue, Denis. *Ferocious Alphabets*. Boston: Little, Brown, 1981.

Douglas, Mary. *Natural Symbols: Explorations in Cosmology*. New York: Random House, 1973.

Ehrmann, J., ed. *Game, Play, Literature*. Boston: Beacon Press, 1971.

Eliot, T. S. *Collected Poems, 1909–1962*. London: Faber & Faber, 1963.

Ellison, Ralph. *Shadow and Act*. New York: Random House, 1953.

Fabro, Cornelio, *God in Exile: Modern Atheism—A Study of the Internal Dynamic of Modern Atheism from Its Roots in the Cartesian Cogito to the Present Day*. Translated by A. Gibson. New York: Newman Press, 1968.

Feuerbach, Ludwig. *The Essence of Christianity*. Translated by G. Eliot. New York: Harper & Row, 1958.

Fish, Stanley. *Is There a Text in This Class?* Cambridge, Mass.: Harvard University Press, 1980.

————. *Self-Consuming Artifacts*. Berkeley: University of California Press, 1972.

Foucault, Michel. *The Archaeology of Knowledge*. Translated by A. M. S. Smith. New York: Harper Torchbooks, 1972.

————. *Language, Counter-Memory, Practice: Selected Essays and Interviews*. Translated by D. F. Bouchard and S. Simon. Edited by D. F. Bouchard. Ithaca: Cornell University Press, 1977.

————. *Madness and Civilization: A History of Insanity in the Age of Reason*. Translated by R. Howard. New York: Random House, 1965.

————. *The Order of Things: An Archaeology of the Human Sciences*. Translated by A. S. London. New York: Random House, 1970.

————. *Power/Knowledge: Selected Interviews and Other Writings, 1972–1977*. Translated by C. Gordon, L. Marshall, J. Mepham, and K. Soper. Edited by C. Gordon. New York: Pantheon, 1980.

————. "What Is an Author." Pp. 141–69 in J. V. Harari, ed., *Textual Strategies*.

Frei, Hans. *The Eclipse of Biblical Narrative: A Study in Eighteenth- and Nineteenth-Century Hermeneutics*. New Haven: Yale University Press, 1974.

Freud, Sigmund. *The Complete Psychological Works*. Standard Edition. 24 vols. Translated by J. Strachey. New York: Norton, 1976.

Frye, Northrop. *Anatomy of Criticism*. Princeton: Princeton University Press, 1957.

Funk, Robert. *Language, Hermeneutic, and Word of God*. New York: Harper & Row, 1966.

Gadamer, Hans-Georg. *Truth and Method*. Translated by G. Barden and J. Cumming. New York: Seabury Press, 1975.

Gasché, Rodolphe. "Autobiography as Gestalt in Nietzsche's *Ecce Homo*." *Boundary 2* 9 (1981): 271–94.

————. "Deconstruction as Criticism." *Glyph* 6 (1979): 177–215.

Geertz, Clifford. "Religion as a Cultural System." In *The Religious Situation*, edited by D. Cutler, pp. 639–88. Boston: Beacon Press, 1968.

Genette, Gérard. "Boundaries of Narrative." *New Literary History* 8 (1976): 1–13.

Girard, René. *Desire, Deceit, and the Novel*. Translated by Y. Freccero. Baltimore: Johns Hopkins University Press, 1965.

————. *Violence and the Sacred*. Translated by P. Gregory. Baltimore: Johns Hopkins University Press, 1977.

Gombrich, E. H. *Art and Illusion: A Study in the Psychology of Pictorial Representation*. Princeton: Princeton University Press, 1972.

Goodman, Nelson. *Ways of Worldmaking*. Indianapolis: Hackett, 1978.

Grene, Marjorie. "Life, Death, and Language: Some Thoughts on Wittgenstein and Derrida." *Philosophy in and out of Europe*. Berkeley: University of California Press, 1976.

Guthrie, W. K. C. *The Greeks and Their Gods*. Boston: Beacon Press, 1951.

Habermas, Jürgen. *Knowledge and Human Interest*. Translated by J. Shapiro. Boston: Beacon Press, 1971.

Hamilton, George. *Nineteenth- and Twentieth-Century Art*. Englewood Cliffs, N.J.: Prentice-Hall, n.d.

Harari, J. V., ed. *Textual Strategies: Perspectives in Post-Structuralist Criticism*. Ithaca: Cornell University Press, 1979.

Harr, Michel. "Nietzsche and Metaphysical Language." Pp. 5–36 in D. B. Allison, ed., *The New Nietzsche*.

Hart, Ray L. *Unfinished Man and the Imagination: Toward an Ontology and a Rhetoric of Revelation*. New York: Herder & Herder, 1968.

Hartman, Geoffrey. *Criticism in the Wilderness: The Study of Literature Today*. New Haven: Yale University Press, 1980.

————. *Saving the Text: Literature/Derrida/Philosophy*. Baltimore: Johns Hopkins University Press, 1981.

————, ed. *Psychoanalysis and the Question of the Text*. Baltimore: Johns Hopkins University Press, 1978.

Hassan, Ihab. *The Dismemberment of Orpheus: Toward a Postmodern Literature*. New York: Oxford University Press, 1971.

————. *The Literature of Silence*. New York: Knopf, 1967.

Hawkes, Terence. *Structuralism and Semiotics*. Berkeley: University of California Press, 1977.

Hegel, G. W. F. *Early Theological Writings*. Translated by T. M. Knox. Philadelphia: University of Pennsylvania Press, 1971.

————. *Lectures on the Philosophy of Religion*. 3 vols. Translated by E. S. Haldane. New York: Humanities Press, 1968.

————. *The Logic of Hegel*. Translated by W. Wallace. New York: Oxford University Press, 1968.

————. *Phenomenology of Spirit*. Translated by A. V. Miller. New York: Oxford University Press, 1977.

————. *Philosophy of History*. Translated by C. J. Friedrich. New York: Dover Publications, 1956.

————. *Philosophy of Nature*. Translated by A. V. Miller. New York: Humanities Press, 1970.

————. *Science of Logic*. Translated by A. V. Miller. New York: Humanities Press, 1969.

Heidegger, Martin. *Being and Time*. Translated by J. Macquarrie and E. Robinson. New York: Harper & Row, 1962.

————. *Discourse on Thinking*. Translated by J. M. Anderson and E. H. Freund. New York: Harper & Row, 1966.

————. *The End of Philosophy*. Translated by J. Stambaugh. New York: Harper & Row, 1973.

————. *Identity and Difference*. Translated by J. Stambaugh. New York: Harper & Row, 1969.

————. *Nietzsche*. Vol. 1. *The Will to Power as Art*. Translated by D. F. Krell. New York: Harper & Row, 1979.

————. *Poetry, Language, Thought*. Translated by A. Hofstadter. New York: Harper & Row, 1971.

————. *The Question Concerning Technology and Other Essays*. Edited and translated by W. Lovitt. New York: Harper & Row, 1977.

Heller, Erich. *The Artist's Journey into the Interior*. New York: Random House, 1965.

————. *The Disinherited Mind: Essays in Modern German Literature*. Cambridge, Eng.: Bowes & Bowes, 1952.

Herrigel, Eugen. *Zen in the Art of Archery*. Translated by R. F. C. Hull. New York: Random House, 1971.

Hoy, David. *The Critical Circle: Literature, History, and Philosophical Hermeneutics*. Berkeley: University of California Press, 1978.

Hyppolite, Jean. *Genesis and Structure of Hegel's "Phenomenology of Spirit."* Translated by S. Cherniak and J. Heckman. Evanston, Ill.: Northwestern University Press, 1974.

————. "Hegel's Phenomenology and Psychoanalysis." In *New Studies in Hegel's Philosophy*, edited by W. E. Steinkraus, pp. 57–70. New York: Holt, Rinehart, Winston, 1971.

Iser, Wolfgang. *The Act of Reading: A Theory of Aesthetic Response*. Baltimore: Johns Hopkins University Press, 1978.

Jabès, Edmond. *The Book of Questions*. Translated by R. Waldrop. Middletown, Conn.: Wesleyan University Press, 1976.

———. *The Book of Yukel, Return to the Book*. Translated by R. Waldrop. Middletown, Conn.: Wesleyan University Press, 1977.

Jameson, Fredric. *The Political Unconscious: Narrative as a Socially Symbolic Act*. Ithaca: Cornell University Press, 1982.

———. *The Prison-House of Language: A Critical Account of Structuralism and Russian Formalism*. Princeton: Princeton University Press, 1972.

Jaspers, Karl. *The Origin and Goal of History*. Translated by M. Bulloch. London: Routledge & Kegan Paul, 1953.

Joyce, James. *Finnegans Wake*. New York: Viking Press, 1976.

Jung, C. G. *Psyche and Symbol*. Edited by V. S. de Laszlo. Translated by C. Baynes, and R. F. C. Hull. New York: Doubleday/Anchor, 1958.

Kafka, Franz. *Penal Colony: Stories and Short Pieces*. Translated by W. and E. Muir. New York: Schocken, 1961.

Kant, Immanuel. *On History*. Translated by L. W. Beck. Indianapolis: Bobbs-Merrill, 1965.

Kaufman, Gordon. *Relativism, Knowledge, and Faith*. Chicago: University of Chicago Press, 1960.

———. *The Theological Imagination: Constructing the Concept of God*. Philadelphia: Westminster Press, 1981.

Kaufmann, Walter, ed. and trans. *The Portable Nietzsche*. New York: Viking Press, 1980.

Kemp, Peter. *Døden og Maskinen: Introduktion til Derrida*. Copenhagen: Bibliotek Rhodos, 1981.

Kermode, Frank. *The Genesis of Secrecy: On the Interpretation of Narrative*. Cambridge, Mass.: Harvard University Press, 1979.

———. *The Sense of an Ending: Studies in the Theory of Fiction*. New York: Oxford University Press, 1967.

Kierkegaard, Søren. *The Concept of Anxiety*. Translated by R. Thomte. Princeton: Princeton University Press, 1980.

———. *The Concept of Irony*. Translated by L. M. Capel. Bloomington: Indiana University Press, 1968.

———. *Concluding Unscientific Postscript*. Translated by D. F. Swenson and W. Lowrie. Princeton: Princeton University Press, 1968.

———. *Either-Or*. 2 vols. Vol. 1 translated by D. F. and L. M. Swenson. Vol. 2 translated by W. Lowrie. Princeton: Princeton University Press, 1971.

———. *Fear and Trembling*. Translated by W. Lowrie. Princeton: Princeton University Press, 1970.

———. *Philosophical Fragments*. Translated by D. F. Swenson. Princeton: Princeton University Press, 1967.

———. *Repetition*. Translated by W. Lowrie. New York: Harper & Row, 1964.

———. *The Sickness unto Death*. Translated by W. Lowrie. Princeton, Princeton University Press, 1970.

Klossowski, Pierre. "Nietzsche's Experience of the Eternal Return." Pp. 107–20 in D. B. Allison, ed., *The New Nietzsche*.

Kojève, Alexandre. *Introduction to the Reading of Hegel*. Translated by J. H. Nicholas. Edited by A. Bloom. New York: Basic Books, 1969.

Kristeva, Julia. *Desire in Language: A Semiotic Approach to Literature*. Translated by T. Gora, A. Jardine, and L. Roudiez. New York: Columbia University Press, 1980.

Kurrik, Marie J. *Literature and Negation*. New York: Columbia University Press, 1979.

Lacan, Jacques. *Ecrits*. Translated by A. Sheridan. New York: Norton, 1977.

———. *The Four Fundamental Concepts of Psychoanalysis*. Translated by A. Sheridan. New York: Norton, 1978.

———. *The Language of the Self*. Translated by A. Wilden. New York: Delta Books, 1968.

———. *Speech and Language in Psychoanalysis*. Translated by A. Wilden. Baltimore: Johns Hopkins University Press, 1981.

La Fleur, William. "Buddhist Emptiness in the Ethics and Aesthetics of Watsuji Tetsurō," *Religious Studies* 4 (1978): 237–50.

———. *The Karma of Words: Buddhism and the Literary Arts in Medieval Japan*. Berkeley: University of California Press, 1983.

Laing, R. D. *Knots*. New York: Random House, 1970.

Lawler, Justus George. *Celestial Pantomime: Poetic Structures of Transcendence*. New Haven: Yale University Press, 1979.

Leach, Edmund. *Claude Lévi-Strauss*. New York: Penguin Books, 1974.

Leahy, David. *Novitas Mundi: Perception of the History of Being*. New York: New York University Press, 1980.

Leibniz, G. W. *Theodicy*. Translated by E. M. Huggard. Edited by A. Farrer. New Haven: Yale University Press, 1952.

Lentricchia, Frank. *After the New Criticism*. Chicago: University of Chicago Press, 1980.

Levinas, Emmanuel. *Existence Is Existents*. Translated by A. Lingis. The Hague: Nijhoff, 1978.

———. *Totality and Infinity: An Essay on Exteriority*. Translated by A. Lingis. Pittsburgh: Duquesne University Press, 1979.

———. "La Trace de l'autre." *Tijdschrift voor philosophie* 25 (1963): 605–23.

Lévi-Strauss, Claude. *Identité*. Paris: Grasset, 1977.

———. *Structural Anthropology*. Translated by C. Jacobson. New York: Doubleday, 1967.

Malraux, André. *The Metamorphosis of the Gods*. Translated by S. Gilbert. New York: Doubleday, 1960.

Marx, Karl. *Writings of the Young Marx on Philosophy and Society*. Translated by L. Easton. New York: Doubleday, 1967.

Mehlman, Jeffrey. "The 'Floating Signifier' from Lévi-Strauss to Lacan." *Yale French Studies* 48 (1972): 11–38.

Merleau-Ponty, Maurice. *Phenomenology of Perception*. Translated by C. Smith. London: Routledge & Kegan Paul, 1962.

———. *Sense and Non-Sense*. Translated by H. L. and P. A. Dreyfus. Evanston, Ill.: Northwestern University Press, 1964.

———. *Signs*. Translated by R. C. McCleary. Evanston, Ill.: Northwestern University Press, 1964.

———. *The Visible and the Invisible*. Translated by A. Lingis. Evanston, Ill.: Northwestern University Press, 1968.

Miller, David. *Christs: Meditations on Archetypal Images in Christian Theology*. New York: Seabury Press, 1981.

Miller, J. Hillis. "Ariadne's Thread: Repetitions and the Narrative Line." *Critical Inquiry* 3 (1976): 57–77.

————. "The Critic as Host." Pp. 217–53 in H. Bloom et al., *Deconstruction and Criticism*.

————. *The Disappearance of God: Five Nineteenth-Century Writers*. Cambridge, Mass.: Harvard University Press, 1963.

————. *Fiction and Repetition: Seven English Novels*. Cambridge, Mass.: Harvard University Press, 1982.

————. "Geneva or Paris? The Recent Work of Georges Poulet." *University of Toronto Quarterly* 39 (1970): 212–28.

————. "Narrative and History." *English Literary History* 41 (1974): 455–73.

————. *Poets of Reality: Six Twentieth-Century Writers*. New York: Atheneum, 1969.

————. "Theology and Logology in Victorian Literature." *Religion and Literature: The Convergence of Approaches*. Supplement to *Journal of the American Academy of Religion* 47 (1979): 345–61.

*New Catholic Encyclopedia*. 17 vols. New York: McGraw-Hill, 1967.

Niebuhr, H. Richard. *The Meaning of Revelation*. New York: Macmillan, 1967.

Niebuhr, Richard R. *Experiential Religion*. New York: Harper & Row, 1972.

Nietzsche, Friedrich. *Beyond Good and Evil*. Translated by W. Kaufmann. New York: Random House, 1966.

————. *Ecce Homo*. Translated by W. Kaufmann. New York: Random House, 1969.

————. *The Gay Science*. Translated by W. Kaufmann. New York: Random House, 1974.

————. *On the Genealogy of Morals*. Translated by W. Kaufmann. New York: Random House, 1969.

————. *Thus Spoke Zarathustra*. Translated by M. Cowan. Chicago: Henry Regnery, 1957.

————. *The Will to Power*. Translated by W. Kaufmann. New York: Random House, 1968.

Norris, Margot. *The Decentered Universe of "Finnegans Wake."* Baltimore: Johns Hopkins University Press, 1976.

Palmer, Richard. *Hermeneutics: Interpretation Theory in Schleiermacher, Dilthey, Heidegger, and Gadamer*. Evanston, Ill.: Northwestern University Press, 1969.

Percy, Walker. *The Moviegoer*. New York: Knopf, 1961.

Polhemus, Robert M. *Comic Faith: The Great Tradition from Austen to Joyce*. Chicago: University of Chicago Press, 1980.

Preus, Samuel. *From Shadow to Promise: Old Testament Interpretation from Augustine to the Young Luther*. Cambridge, Mass.: Harvard University Press, 1969.

Raschke, Carl. *The Alchemy of the Word: Language and the End of Theology*. Chico, Calif.: Scholars Press, 1979.

Richman, Michèle. *Reading Georges Bataille: Beyond the Gift*. Baltimore: Johns Hopkins University Press, 1982.

Ricoeur, Paul. *The Conflict of Interpretations: Essays in Hermeneutics*. Edited by D. Idhe. Evanston, Ill.: Northwestern University Press, 1974.

————. *Essays on Biblical Interpretation*. Edited by L. S. Mudge. Philadelphia: Fortress Press, 1980.

————. *Freud and Philosophy: An Essay on Interpretation*. Translated by D. Savage. New Haven: Yale University Press, 1970.

————. *Interpretation Theory: Discourse and the Surplus of Meaning*. Fort Worth: Texas Christian University Press, 1976.

————. "The Metaphoric Process as Cognition, Imagination, and Feeling." *Critical Inquiry* 5 (1978): 143–59.

————. "The Narrative Function." *Semeia* 13 (1978): 177–202.

————. "Narrative and Hermeneutics." In *Religion and the Humanities*, edited by K. Mullikin, pp. 37–56. Research Triangle Park, N.C.: National Humanities Center, 1981.

————. "Narrative Time." *Critical Inquiry* 7 (1980): 169–90.

————. *The Symbolism of Evil*. Translated by E. Buchanan. Boston: Beacon Press, 1967.

Robbe-Grillet, Alain. *For a New Novel*. Translated by R. Howard. New York: Grove Press, 1965.

Rorty, Richard. "Derrida on Language, Being, and Abnormal Philosophy." *Journal of Philosophy* 74 (1977): 673–81.

————. "Philosophy as a Kind of Writing: An Essay on Derrida." *New Literary History* 10 (1978): 141–59.

————. *Philosophy and the Mirror of Nature*. Princeton: Princeton University Press, 1979.

Rosen, Stanley. *Nihilism: A Philosophical Essay*. New Haven: Yale University Press, 1969.

Said, Edward W. *Beginnings: Intention and Method*. New York: Basic Books, 1975.

————. "The Problem of Textuality: Two Exemplary Positions." *Critical Inquiry* 4 (1978): 673–714.

Sartre, Jean-Paul. *Being and Nothingness*. Translated by Hazel E. Barnes. New York: Washington Square, 1968.

————. *Nausea*. Translated by L. Alexander. New York: New Directions, 1964.

————. *No Exit*. Translated by L. Abel. New York: New Directions, 1959.

Scharlemann, Robert. *The Being of God: Theology and the Experience of Truth*. New York: Seabury Press, 1981.

————. "The Being of God When God Is Not Being God: Deconstructing the History of Theism." Pp. 79–108 in Altizer et al., *Deconstruction and Theology*.

Scholes, Robert, and Robert Kellogg. *The Nature of Narrative*. New York: Oxford University Press, 1966.

Schwartz, P. W. *Cubism*. New York: Praeger, 1971.

Silverman, Hugh. "For a Hermeneutic Semiology of the Self." *Philosophy Today* 23 (1979): 199–204.

Sontag, Susan. *Styles of Radical Will*. New York: Farrar, Straus & Giroux, 1969.

Spanos, William. *Toward a Post-Modern Literary Hermeneutics*. Bloomington: Indiana University Press, 1980.

Steiner, George. *Language and Silence: Essays on Language, Literature, and the Inhuman*. New York: Atheneum, 1967.

Stevens, Wallace. *Collected Poems*. New York: Knopf, 1981.

————. *Opus Posthumous*. Edited by S. F. Morse. New York: Random House, 1982.

Strauss, Walter. *Descent and Return: The Orphic Theme in Modern Literature*. Cambridge, Mass.: Harvard University Press, 1971.

Streng, Frederick. *Emptiness: A Study in Religious Meaning*. Nashville, Tenn.: Abingdon, 1967.

Sturrock, John, ed. *Structuralism and Science: From Lévi-Strauss to Derrida*. New York: Oxford University Press, 1979.

Suleiman, Susan, and Inge Crosby, eds. *The Reader in the Text*. Princeton: Princeton University Press, 1980.

Taylor, Mark C. *Deconstructing Theology*. New York: Crossroad, 1982.

————. *Journeys to Selfhood: Hegel and Kierkegaard*. Berkeley: University of California Press, 1980.

————. *Kierkegaard's Pseudonymous Authorship: A Study of Time and the Self*. Princeton: Princeton University Press, 1975.

————, ed. *Unfinished: Essays in Honor of Ray L. Hart*. Chico, Calif.: Scholars Press, 1981.

Thoreau, Henry David. "Walking." Pp. 251–304 in *The Writings of Henry David Thoreau*, vol. 9. New York: Houghton, Mifflin, 1896.

Tillich, Paul. *Systematic Theology*. 3 vols. Chicago: University of Chicago Press, 1967.

Towsen, John. *Clowns*. New York: Hawthorn, 1976.

Tracy, David. *The Analogical Imagination: Christian Theology and Cultural Pluralism*. New York: Crossroad, 1981.

Turbayne, Colin. *The Myth of Metaphor*. Columbia: University of South Carolina Press, 1970.

Turner, Victor. "Liminal to Liminoid in Play, Flow, and Ritual: An Essay in Comparative Symbology." *Rice University Studies* 60 (1974): 53–92.

————. *The Ritual Process: Structure and Anti-Structure*. Chicago: Aldine, 1969.

Vaihinger, Hans. *The Philosophy of "As If."* Translated by C. K. Ogden. New York: Harcourt, Brace, 1924.

Wellek, René. *A History of Modern Criticism: 1750–1950, The Romantic Age*. New Haven: Yale University Press, 1955.

White, Hayden. *Metahistory: The Historical Imagination in Nineteenth-Century Europe*. Baltimore: Johns Hopkins University Press, 1974.

————. *Tropics of Discourse: Essays in Cultural Criticism*. Baltimore: Johns Hopkins University Press, 1978.

————. "The Value of Narrativity in the Representation of Reality." *Critical Inquiry* 7 (1980): 5–27.

Wilden, Anthony. "Lacan and the Discourse of the Other." Translator's Preface to Jacques Lacan, *The Language of the Self*.

————. *System and Structure: Essays in Communication and Exchange*. London: Tavistock, 1980.

Willeford, William. *The Fool and His Scepter: A Study in Clowns and Jesters and Their Audience*. Evanston, Ill.: Northwestern University Press, 1969.

Williams, William Carlos. *The Collected Earlier Poems of William Carlos Williams*. New York: New Directions, 1938.

Winquist, Charles. *Homecoming: Interpretation, Transformation, and Individuation*. Chico, Calif.: Scholars Press, 1978.

————. "The Subversion of the Subject." *Journal of the American Academy of Religion* 38 (1980): 45–60.

Yeats, W. B. *The Collected Poems of W. B. Yeats*. New York: Macmillan, 1956.

# Index

Aberrance, 12, 158–68
Abraham, 52
Absence, 8, 15, 27, 47, 49, 69, 71, 90, 91, 103, 110 114, 138, 146, 159–60
Absurdity, 8, 117
Adam, 59–60, 70
Adorno, Theodor, 28, 33, 137, 146
Affirmation, 24, 31, 69, 72, 140, 144, 145, 166–67. *See also* Yea-saying
Aggression, 27–29, 31
*alētheia*, 57
Alienation, 23, 151
Alpha, 73, 183
Alterity, 23, 26, 30, 31, 48, 49
Altizer, Thomas J. J., 9, 23, 33, 35, 46, 49, 52, 97, 110, 116, 118, 129, 137, 142, 143, 147, 155, 168, 169
Ambiguity, 12
Anarchy, 109
Anonymity, 15, 34, 129, 135, 140–45, 181
Anthropology, 13, 21, 25, 75
Anti-Christ, 103, 158, 167
Anxiety, 27, 42, 151
Apocalypse, 53
Apollinaire, Guillaume, 19
Appearance, 16, 37, 169, 171–72, 175, 176, 180
Appropriation, 29, 30, 40, 42, 69, 139, 159
*archē*, 64, 70, 86, 175
Archeology, 59, 153
Archetype, 81, 85–86
Ariadne, 61–62, 67, 69, 168
Aristotle, 41
Assimilation, 57–58

Atheism, 6, 12, 13; humanistic, 13, 20–33, 84
A/theology, 6, 8, 10, 12, 15, 20, 98, 104, 155, 158
Auerbach, Erich, 56
Augustine, 34, 38, 43–45, 55, 56
Authentic, 41
Author, 4, 14, 16, 17, 64, 80, 82, 84, 88, 100, 181
Authority, 3, 4, 16, 80, 87–90, 179, 181
Authorship, 77–87
Auto-affection, 30, 38, 46
Autobiography, 35, 44–45, 54, 66
Autonomy, 22, 31, 134, 141

Bacchus, 103, 167–68, 182
Bacon, Francis, 20
Bakhtin, Mikhail, 161, 164
Baptism, 130
Barthes, Roland, 27, 34, 46, 68, 74, 89, 91, 92, 143, 147, 170, 172, 173, 176, 177, 179, 180, 182, 183
Bastard, 88, 90–91, 93
Bataille, Georges, 143, 144, 146, 155, 157, 166
Beckett, Samuel, 70, 105
Becoming, 8, 113, 114, 156
Beginning, 13, 53, 63, 66, 97, 153, 175, 183
Being, 8, 15, 36, 42, 43, 47, 49, 98, 113, 114, 130
Belief, 5, 10, 21
Beyond, 72
Bible, 40, 52, 53, 58, 60, 77, 78, 103, 119, 160

Binary, 8
Blake, William, 104, 151, 176
Blanchot, Maurice, 140
Blank, 92, 182
Blindness, 8
Bloch, Ernst, 5
Blood, 103, 120, 160
Bloom, Harold, 178
Body, 8, 162, 167
Book, 7, 13, 14, 16, 75, 84–93, 98–99, 177–80
Border, 10, 12, 18, 93, 130, 158
Borges, Jorge, 75–76, 87
Boundary, 11, 12, 91, 102, 115, 137, 161, 184
Brown, Norman O., 23, 25, 27, 28, 29, 32, 42, 68, 70, 73, 91, 121, 133, 144, 160, 164–65, 173, 174, 177, 182

Canon, 88, 179
Care, 144
Carnality, 8, 12, 56, 168–69
Carnival, 12, 15, 75, 158–68
Cause, 7, 36
Cavell, Stanley, 73, 155
Center, 9, 14, 26, 33, 36, 45, 54, 63, 64, 81, 85, 91, 135, 139, 142, 156, 158, 179
Certainty, 8, 22, 26, 32, 42, 76, 171, 176, 180
Cézanne, Paul, 122
Change, 8
Chaos, 8
Chaplin, Charlie, 165
Christ, 14, 21, 40, 60, 62, 65, 122
Christianity, 6, 53–55, 76, 88
Christology, 15, 103, 168
Chronicle, 62–64, 156
Chronos, 14, 62, 66, 68, 69
Circle, 18, 61, 70, 78, 79, 88, 183
City, 25
City of God (Saint Augustine), 54
Clean, 41, 162
Closure, 66, 70, 77, 92, 136, 153, 157, 183
Clown, 18, 164–65
Codependence, 118, 135, 154, 161, 180
cogito, 22, 132, 136
Coleridge, Samuel Taylor, 66
Colonialism, 28, 71
Comedy, 12, 15, 158–68
Communication, 100, 142, 174

Communion, 90
Compassion, 142
Confessions (Saint Augustine), 14, 35, 46
Connotation, 173
Consciousness, 22, 32, 39, 55, 69, 86, 105; lacerated, 152, 156, 164; un-happy, 45, 68, 72, 151–52, 156, 164
Consumption, 12, 14, 25–29, 143, 147, 178
Context, 173–74, 178
Contradiction, 13, 37, 100, 161
Conversation, 90
Conversion, 45
Counterfeit, 81
Creation, 54, 61, 65, 118
Creator, 4, 7, 13, 20, 23, 35, 46, 58, 83
Crites, Stephen, 65
Cross, 11, 13, 33, 40, 51, 107, 118, 138, 182
Crossan, John Dominic, 119–20
Crucifixion, 33, 59, 65, 120, 132–43
Cubism, 129
Culler, Jonathan, 63
Cullmann, Oscar, 65
Cure, 69, 71, 87, 91, 118, 144, 157

Daedalus, 61
Dance, 15, 146, 168, 177
Darkness, 8
Death, 8, 12, 14, 15, 16, 23, 29, 32, 47, 51, 62, 68, 73, 91, 102, 121, 134, 141, 145–48, 151, 166, 176; of God, 1, 3, 6, 7, 13, 19–33, 86, 103, 105–16, 140
Deconstruction, 5–6, 11, 13, 92, 112
Deferral, 66, 146–47
Deficiency, 27, 69, 71, 146
Dehiscence, 92
Deicide, 30
Deleuze, Gilles, 13, 23, 27, 97, 113, 114, 156, 164, 167
Delight, 12, 15, 145–48, 176–77
Delirium, 103, 160–61, 167–68
Dēmiourgos, 58
Depth, 9, 56, 59, 168
Derrida, Jacques, 3, 5, 6, 10, 17, 18, 23, 24, 27, 28, 29, 34, 37, 41, 42, 46, 47, 48, 49, 50, 51, 52, 55, 69, 70, 74, 75, 76, 81, 82, 85, 88, 91, 92, 93, 99, 101, 106, 110, 115, 117, 122, 131, 135, 138, 139, 145, 147, 149, 153, 154, 156, 157, 158, 164, 168, 171, 175, 178, 179, 181, 182

Descartes, René, 21, 26, 38, 132
Desire, 12, 15, 26–27, 31, 50, 56, 145–48
Despair, 5, 21, 141, 152, 157
Destruction, 142, 162, 168
Diderot, Denis, 78
*différance*, 55
Difference, 8, 15, 24, 28, 30, 31, 37, 48, 88, 92, 98, 107, 108–11, 112, 117, 133, 138, 155, 172
Dionysus, 103, 118, 121, 144, 146, 158, 167
Dismemberment, 44, 45, 103, 118, 120, 168
Displacement, 47, 156
Dispossession, 12, 14, 23, 29, 30, 46, 48, 122–40
Dissemination, 12, 15, 92, 118–20, 141, 167
Divine, 15, 33, 88
Divine milieu, 15, 16, 112–18, 134, 141, 156, 168, 182, 183
Domestication, 28, 29, 71, 150
Domination, 12, 14, 15, 22, 25–29, 68–69, 133–34
Doubt, 21, 22
Dread, 21, 164
Drift, 98, 132, 140, 143, 156, 181
Duplicity, 9, 10, 12, 16, 18, 24, 49, 110, 166, 171–77

Easter, 164
Ego, 27, 31, 104, 134, 136, 142
Eidos, 85, 86
Eliot, T. S., 183
Ellison, Ralph, 34
Empiricism, 21
Emptiness, 27, 31, 120, 137, 141–42, 147, 159
Encyclopedia, 14, 78–79, 87, 91, 178
End, 7, 13, 53, 63, 66, 99, 153, 175, 179, 183
*Endgame* (Beckett), 71–72
Enjoyment, 26, 29, 42, 69, 90, 147
Enlightenment, 4, 20, 21
Envy, 24
Equivocality, 42, 163, 173
Erasmus, 101
*Eros*, 29
Erring, 11, 15, 88, 91, 93, 114, 143, 149–58, 175, 184
Error, 8, 12, 42, 88
Eschatology, 42, 69, 99, 120, 130

Essence, 26, 37, 86
Eternal recurrence, 113, 119, 158, 166
Eternity, 8, 36, 114–15
Event, 63–65, 70
Evil, 8, 10, 75, 118, 166
Excentricity, 9, 10, 139, 156, 157
Excess, 140, 182
Exclusion, 24
Exile, 15, 64, 71, 153–54
Exorbitance, 157
Expenditure, 93, 143, 144, 159
Expression, 84
Expropriation, 15, 41, 122–40
Exteriority, 9, 18, 51, 93, 110, 138, 144. *See also* Outside

Fabrication, 17, 180–82
Fact, 67
Faith, 3, 25
Fall, 61, 64, 65, 151–54
Family, 28, 93
Father, 4, 5, 20, 23, 25, 27, 28, 30, 81, 87, 91, 104, 106, 117, 143, 156, 183
Fault, 6, 61
Faust, 68
Fear, 23, 25, 27, 32
Feast of Fools, 164
Festival, 15, 161, 168
Feuerbach, Ludwig, 25
Fichte, J. G., 83
Fiction, 45, 67
Finitude, 8, 113–14
*Finnegans Wake*, 146, 164–65
Fissure, 10, 71, 77
Fix, 91–92, 131, 176
Fool, 18
Force, 111, 113, 134–35, 142
Foreplay, 18
Forgetfulness, 144–45, 160
Form, 111
Foucault, Michel, 22, 35, 80, 83, 88, 122, 123, 129, 136, 169, 172, 181
Foundation, 8, 79, 82, 91, 159, 177, 179
Fragment, 99, 111, 151
Frame, 18, 89–90, 129
Freedom, 22, 35
Frei, Hans, 56
French Revolution, 21, 83
Freud, Sigmund, 4, 5, 31
Frivolity, 159
Frye, Northrop, 85
Future, 43, 49, 59, 68, 71, 89, 156

Gadamer, Hans-Georg, 84, 89, 90, 160
Gap, 24, 27, 31, 48, 50, 69, 90, 91, 92,
    147, 162, 182
Garden, 45, 65, 71, 153
Gasché, Rodolphe, 44, 111
Geertz, Clifford, 65, 75
Genealogy, 87–88
Generosity, 143, 144
Genesis, 53
Gift, 61, 145, 167
Gnosticism, 36, 55
God, 3, 7, 10, 14, 23, 25, 26, 30, 35,
    40, 46, 52, 65, 80, 87, 104, 105,
    152, 175
Golgotha, 13, 33, 56, 62
Good, 8
Gospel, 54, 58–59
Government, 28
Grace, 15, 21, 73, 149–69, 182
Grammar, 80, 87, 132, 135
Graph, 63, 107
Grotesque, 162
Ground, 36, 57, 59, 111, 119, 142
Guilt, 8, 152, 155
Guthrie, W. K. C., 167

Hades, 146
Harr, Michel, 177
Hart, Ray, 66, 90
Hartman, Geoffrey, 91, 131–32
Hawkes, Terence, 174
Hegel, G. W. F., 23, 24, 25, 30, 31,
    32, 37, 38, 39, 46, 47, 66, 78–79,
    90–91, 98, 109, 111–12, 113, 119,
    134, 144, 161, 183
Heidegger, Martin, 22, 25, 26, 28, 57,
    144
Helios, 61
Heraclitus, 58, 59
Heresy, 13
Hermeneutics, 4; romantic, 84–85
Hermes, 16, 46, 140, 165, 181
Herrigel, Eugen, 157
Heterodoxy, 88
Heterography, 90–93
Heteronomy, 31
Hierarchy, 9, 10, 108, 161
Hieroglyphics, 97–112
Hinge, 107
History, 4, 7, 14, 52–61, 66, 151–52,
    153–54, 166; end of, 14, 52–73
Holbein, Hans, 101–2

Hole, 11, 27, 28, 31, 50, 69, 90, 91,
    147, 182
Holocaust, 32
Holy Spirit, 88
Home, 29, 45, 150, 154
Homelessness, 156–57, 183
Hope, 43, 50, 151
Horizon, 89
Host, 10, 120, 180
Hostility, 24, 120, 133–34
Humanism, 13, 20, 22, 26, 164
Humor, 17, 163–64
Hyppolite, Jean, 32

I, 134, 140, 142, 181
Id, 121
Ideality, 72, 85, 151
Identification, 24
Identity, 8, 10, 14, 15, 23, 27, 29, 31,
    33–40, 44, 98, 109–11, 116, 130,
    138, 144, 155
Illusion, 8, 37, 155, 164, 176
Image, 34–40, 85, 104, 182; of God, 7,
    35, 40, 48
Imagination, 44, 66, 67, 90
Imitation, 1, 9, 34–40
Immediacy, 37, 138
Imperialism, 28
Impropriety, 9, 10, 41, 122–40
Incarnation, 65, 103–6, 141, 168
Incorporation, 24, 27, 29
Indeterminacy, 174–76
Individual, 14, 15, 21, 26, 41, 44, 86,
    120, 130, 137, 161
Infinitude, 1, 8
Innocence, 65, 168
Insecurity, 160
Inside, 11, 24, 30, 51, 109, 136, 162.
    See also Interiority
Intention, 84, 85
Interiority, 9, 18, 130. See also Inside
Interiorization, 44, 69
Interlude, 16, 183–84
Interpretation, 16, 56, 67, 86, 92, 172, 178;
    figurative, 55, 61, 68; typological, 55
Intersubjectivity, 143
Intertextuality, 16, 178–80
Interval, 11, 107
Inwardness, 31, 44, 130
Irony, 17
Isaac, 52
Iteration, 48, 131

Jabès, Edmund, 33, 71, 91, 97, 101, 153, 176, 183
Jaspers, Karl, 54
Jesus, 15, 55, 65, 103
Joint, 107
Joker, 18, 139, 164
Joy, 146–47, 164, 166, 177
Joyce, James, 163, 176, 182
Judaism, 55
Judgment, 132
Jung, C. G., 85
Justin, 56

Kafka, Franz, 100–101, 149
kairos, 64
Kant, Immanuel, 3, 83
kenōsis, 118, 120, 141, 142
Kermode, Frank, 53, 65, 69, 70
Kerygma, 89
Kierkegaard, Søren, 5, 34, 53, 91, 99, 134, 166
Kingdom of God, 7, 54, 65, 153
Klossowski, Pierre, 23, 134
Knowledge, 16, 22, 26, 46, 54, 78, 83, 98
Kojève, Alexandre, 23, 29, 50, 133–34
Kristeva, Julia, 161, 162, 179–80, 181

Labor, 14
Labyrinth, 61, 71, 75, 168
Lacan, Jacques, 31, 137, 143
Lack, 24, 27, 28, 29, 71, 146, 154–55, 157, 166
Language, 41, 47, 68, 131–32, 135, 162
Laughter, 164, 166
Law, 151–52, 160
Leibniz, G. W., 74, 87
Levinas, Emmanuel, 28
Lévi-Strauss, Claude, 86, 87
Liberation, 5
Library, 75–76
Life, 8, 23, 145–46, 177
Light, 8, 58
Liminality, 10, 50, 93, 143, 150, 158, 164–65, 173
Line, 14, 61, 64, 69, 70, 88, 90, 91, 155, 168
Literalness, 56, 174
Logic, 11, 23, 24, 50, 117, 134, 161
Logocentrism, 14, 84, 91
Logos, 7, 35, 40, 54, 55, 56, 58, 66, 68, 70, 79, 82, 84, 85, 87, 103, 106, 112, 114, 119, 135, 175, 178
Logos Spermatikos, 58, 119
Lord, 23, 25, 26, 31
Loss, 6, 15, 17, 29, 64, 71, 134, 147, 154, 166
Love, 30, 38
Luther, Martin, 21, 38

Madness, 8, 18, 28, 141, 144, 146, 163
Malraux, André, 122
Manichaeanism, 55
Marcion, 55
Margin, 5, 10, 93, 98, 107, 112, 139, 141, 150, 158, 162, 184
Mark, 12, 102, 131–32, 137–39, 174, 181
Marx, Karl, 4, 33
Master, 5, 10, 23, 69, 83, 87
Masterpiece, 14, 87–90, 179
Mastery, 13, 15, 19–25, 30, 68, 87, 89, 91, 145
Matter, 78
Maze, 15, 168–69
Mean, 11, 134
Meaning, 3, 8, 10, 14, 16, 45, 47, 56, 57, 61, 64, 85, 87, 89, 91, 154, 158, 173, 179
Mediator, 115
Medium, 11, 112, 113, 115, 141, 168
Melancholy, 72
Memory, 43, 50
Merleau-Ponty, Maurice, 114, 133
Metaphor, 17, 57, 70
Metonymy, 57, 87
Middle, 7, 11, 18, 53, 63, 98, 115, 138, 153, 183
Miller, J. Hillis, 10, 22, 26, 27, 32, 62, 70, 92, 113, 115, 145, 182
mimēsis, 77–87, 172
Mind, 8
Minos and the Minotaur, 61
Mirror, 7, 19, 23, 27, 29, 31, 35, 76, 129
Model, 65
Modernism, 9, 20, 32
Money, 28
Monotheism, 41, 65, 175
Monster, 9, 61, 71
Morris, Robert, 60
Moses, 59
Movement, 8
Music, 9

Name, 17, 34, 40–46, 104, 130, 138–39, 143, 156–57, 182
Narcissism, 12, 14, 29–33
Narcissus, 29, 31
Nagarjuna, 118
Narrative, 7, 14, 44, 62, 66, 69, 153
Nature, 80
Nay-saying, 68, 72–73, 140, 145, 151–52, 167, 182. See also Negation
Need, 26–27, 69, 146
Negation, 23, 24, 27, 31, 47, 69, 114, 140, 144, 145, 151, 166–67. See also Nay-saying
Negativity, 37, 39, 110
Neoplatonism, 36, 43, 55
Network, 7, 135, 177, 178
New Testament, 56
Newman, Barnett, 129
Niebuhr, H. Richard, 45, 53
Niebuhr, Richard R., 121
Nietzsche, Friedrich, 3, 6, 18, 24, 32, 35, 40, 45, 66, 74, 80, 97, 103, 114, 121–22, 133, 137, 145, 146, 148, 149, 152, 153, 156, 157, 164, 166, 167, 169, 170, 171, 176
Nihilism, 12, 14, 15, 29–33, 92, 140, 144, 145
Nomadic, 11, 13, 71, 156, 165, 175
Nominalism, 21
Nomination, 34
Nonbeing, 15. See also Nothingness
Nostalgia, 16, 72, 85, 151, 155
Nothingness, 27, 31, 62. See also Nonbeing
Novalis, 78
Novel, 67
Now, 46–47, 49

Object, 22, 25, 26, 39, 47, 104
Objectification, 85
Oedipus, 25
Old Testament, 55, 56
Omega, 73, 183
One, 8, 41, 65, 130, 175
Opposition, 9, 11, 15, 93, 117
Order, 8
Organism, 77, 179
Origin, 7, 9, 11, 15, 16, 64, 70, 71, 80, 83, 84, 87, 97, 111, 116, 118–19, 136, 154–55, 168, 179, 181, 183
Orphan, 71
Orthodoxy, 4, 88

Other, 15, 23, 25, 29, 30, 31, 32, 37, 39, 48, 92, 110, 134, 139, 140
Outside, 11, 24, 30, 51, 109, 136, 162. See also Exteriority
Ownership, 27, 42, 80, 130, 143

Paganism, 56
Painting, 9, 77, 100, 122–29
Parable, 17, 119
Paradise, 65, 168
Paradox, 10, 17, 93
Parasite, 10, 18, 92, 116, 140, 165, 170
parousia, 42, 44, 54, 66, 153
Part, 64, 79
Pasiphaë, 61
Passage, 11, 50, 69, 102, 106, 118, 137, 158, 168
Passenger, 112
Passover, 164
Past, 43, 49, 59, 68, 89
Patriarchy, 28
Patricide, 4, 22, 104, 106, 120
"Penal Colony, In the" (Kafka), 100–101
Perception, 47
Percy, Walker, 5
Permanence, 8, 171
Person, 15, 37, 38, 42
Perversion, 10, 161
Phallocentrism, 28
Phallus, 28, 162
pharmakon, 117, 167
Phenomenology, 85
Phenomenology of Spirit (Hegel), 14, 35, 54, 78
Philo, 58, 59
Philosophy, 3, 5, 9, 10, 79
Philosophy of History (Hegel), 78
Picasso, Pablo, 129, 165
Plato, 43, 55, 58, 85
Play, 9, 11, 15, 18, 91, 92, 107, 113, 118, 134, 139, 145, 155, 156, 158
Plenitude, 27, 64, 69, 70, 71, 90, 146, 154, 174, 178
Plot, 45, 53, 63, 65, 73
poiēsis, 77–87
Poison, 91, 117
Polysemy, 163, 173–74
Polytheism, 36
Pope, the, 87
Poseidon, 61
Possession, 12, 22, 29, 40–46, 140
Postmodernism, 3, 13

Power, 28, 37, 87, 99
*Praise of Folly, In* (Erasmus), 101
Preface, 18, 75
Prelude, 18
Presence, 7, 8, 15, 23, 26–27, 29, 36,
    37, 42, 46, 49, 57, 65, 68–78, 98,
    103, 109, 114, 130, 138, 151, 153,
    159, 176
Present, 27, 42, 49, 55, 59, 89
*Pro nobis*, 21
Process, 61
Prodigal, 76, 143, 159
Prodigy, 166
Production, 27, 178, 180
Profane, 8, 162, 165, 169
Project, 89
Projection, 4
Promise, 59
Proper, 9, 12, 40, 48, 88, 130, 138,
    162
Property, 14, 24, 26, 27, 30, 40–46,
    81, 130, 140, 181
Propriety, 10, 15, 27, 40–46, 81, 88
Proximity, 42, 46, 57, 82, 87, 130,
    138, 154
Pun, 17, 182
Purity, 9
Purpose, 21
Purposeless, 9, 15, 157, 158–59
Pyramid, 103

Quotation, 81, 181

Rape, 28
Reaction, 24
Reading, 16, 17, 84, 87, 89, 182
Reality, 8, 67, 72, 91, 151, 175
Reason, 3, 55, 58, 66
Recognition, 23, 38, 134
Recollection, 43, 55, 65, 70, 183
Redemption, 7, 61, 64, 65, 155
Reflection, 39
Reflexivity, 38, 39, 42
Reformation, 3, 20, 26
Relation, 108, 118, 132–33, 138,
    172–73
Relativism, 4, 16, 106, 108, 118, 166,
    173, 176
Remembering, 43
Renaissance, 20
Repetition, 12, 14, 16, 40, 46–51, 83,
    113, 131, 166

Representation, 35, 39, 40, 46–51,
    81–84
Repression, 14, 25, 31, 49, 68, 147,
    155
Reproduction, 16, 30
*ressentiment*, 24
Rest, 8
Revelation, 36, 45, 57, 65, 89
Reversal, 4, 9, 161
Revolution, 4, 9, 26, 32, 83
Rhetoric, 68
Richman, Michèle, 142
Ricoeur, Paul, 30, 45, 57, 58, 61, 64,
    89
Rift, 118, 146
Rilke, Rainer Maria, 145
Rimbaud, Arthur, 140
Road to Emmaus, 102, 103
Robbe-Grillet, Alain, 26
Robespierre, 21
Romanticism, 4, 77, 84
Rupture, 92

Sacrament, 115
Sacred, 8, 118, 165, 169
Sacrifice, 15, 59, 103, 140–45, 181
Saint Paul, 35, 60–61
Salvation, 21, 61, 71
Same, 36–37, 41, 48, 87
Sartre, Jean-Paul, 28, 129
Satisfaction, 27, 28, 31, 39, 50, 69,
    146, 147, 154
Saussure, Ferdinand de, 5
Scatology, 162–63
Scharlemann, Robert, 40, 104
Schelling, F. W. J., 83
Schleiermacher, F., 84
Schoenberg, Arnold, 5
Science, 20, 21
Scribbling, 100–101
Scripture, 7, 11, 13, 15, 56, 57, 100,
    104, 105, 107, 116, 135, 146,
    171–82
Second, 9, 17, 69, 81, 88, 97, 132–33,
    146, 181
Security, 22, 144
Self, 7, 13, 14, 21, 22, 24, 25, 33, 34,
    35, 38, 54, 67, 121–48, 143; disap-
    pearance of, 50, 86, 122–30, 140
Self-consciousness, 7, 23, 25, 26, 33,
    35, 38, 39, 42
Serpent, 157

Serpentine, 13, 149–58
Sex, 28
Shiftiness, 12, 131, 139, 142, 171–77
Sign, 14, 16, 46, 57, 80, 82, 84, 104,
105, 107, 159, 172–73, 178
Signature, 80, 130-31
Signification, 47, 80, 104–6, 172–73
Signifier, 57, 85
Silence, 92
Sin, 65, 152–53, 155
Slave, 15, 23, 83
Slip, 11, 174
Son, 20, 23, 25, 27, 30, 31, 71, 90–91,
106, 183
Space, 11, 27, 36, 46–48, 50, 59, 107
Spacing, 48, 107, 110
Speech, 9, 46, 47, 81, 82, 88
Spending, 15, 140–45
Spinning, 12, 177–80
Spirit, 8
Spivak, Gayatri, 48, 138
Stain, 9, 139
Stevens, Wallace, 62, 70, 88, 108, 112,
113, 170–77, 183, 184
Stoicism, 58, 59
Story, 44–45, 63, 65, 66
Structuralism, 86–87
Structure, 64, 85, 111, 135
Struggle, 24, 27, 90, 104, 133
Subject, 7, 14, 22, 24, 25, 26, 31, 33,
37, 39, 45, 47, 130–33
Subjectivity, 15, 23, 35, 37–38, 42, 49,
142–43
Substance, 37, 44, 58, 59, 133
Substitution, 172, 182
Subversion, 10, 90, 161, 165
Suffering, 72
Suicide, 104
Sun, 19, 22
Superego, 31
Superficiality, 12, 56, 168–69, 171–72
Superstition, 21, 23
Supplement, 48, 83
Surface, 9, 16, 59
Syllogism, 23
Symbol, 57
Syntax, 78, 80, 132
System, 11, 69, 75, 79, 86, 91, 98

Tailor, 180–81
Technology, 1, 25
Teleology, 59, 153
Telos, 7, 64, 70, 86, 155, 157, 175

Terminus, 101–2, 118
Terror, 21, 32
Text, 1, 3, 13, 16, 17, 91, 93, 177–80
Thanatos, 29
Theism, 7
Theodicy, 75
Theology, 3, 5, 6, 8, 10, 11, 13, 25, 41,
54, 79, 91; existential, 5; of hope, 5;
process, 5
Theseus, 61, 168
Thief, 16, 46, 88, 140, 181
Thoreau, Henry David, 50, 149–50
Thoth, 116, 158
Thread, 13, 61, 69, 70, 135, 156, 177
Threshold, 18, 112, 115, 140
Tillich, Paul, 57
Timaeus (Plato), 58
Time, 8, 11, 14, 36, 38, 42, 43, 46–
48, 49, 50, 59, 62, 107, 114, 136,
176
Tissue, 13, 136, 177–80
Tomb, 103
Totalitarianism, 28, 92, 109
Totality, 14, 44, 61, 64, 70, 77, 79, 86,
90, 92, 111, 136, 154, 155, 177, 179
Trace, 13, 15, 50, 71, 107, 137–38,
140, 145, 160
Tracy, David, 89
Tradition, 14, 87–90
Tragedy, 15, 20, 147, 163
Transcendence, 8, 36, 72, 114, 168
Transcendental signified, 16, 81, 84, 85,
105, 159
Transgression, 6, 16, 88, 104, 112, 116,
120, 157, 161
Transition, 10, 16, 50, 64, 111, 115
Transparency, 46, 85, 175
Trickster, 18, 118, 140, 165, 174
Trinity, 38, 43
Trope, 12, 52–61
Tropology, 52–61
Truth, 8, 22, 26, 33, 56, 69, 81, 126,
171–72, 180–81
Turner, Victor, 160
Typology, 14, 52–61

Uncanniness, 10, 29, 47–51, 62, 92,
145, 150
Uncertainty, 8, 76, 100, 175
Unconscious, 31, 85
Undecidability, 16, 143, 171–77
Unity, 1, 14, 36, 54, 91, 92, 175, 179
Universality, 142–43

Univocality, 42, 56, 173
Uselessness, 158–59
Utilitarianism, 26
Utility, 12, 14, 25–29, 147, 159

Vagrant, 11, 150, 157, 174
Vaihinger, Hans, 67
Value, 32
van der Weyden, 122
van Eyck, Jan, 122–23
Velázquez, Diego, 123
Violence, 29
Visibility, 46
Vision, 8, 85, 175
Voice, 45, 46, 65, 84, 88, 106
Void, 24

Waiting, 16
Wander, 11, 19, 71, 93, 98, 140, 149–
    58, 183
War, 28, 133
White, Hayden, 62, 63, 65, 67, 68, 70
Whitehead, Alfred North, 5

Whole, 64, 66, 79, 111
Wilden, Anthony, 137
Willeford, William, 101
Williams, William Carlos, 169
Wine, 103, 117, 120, 142, 144, 167,
    182
Wittgenstein, Ludwig, 5
Woman, 171–72, 180
Word, 7, 15, 16, 59, 88, 100, 103, 104,
    105, 110, 117–18, 119, 135, 160,
    182
Wordplay, 13, 16, 135, 180–82
Wound, 22, 69, 71, 91, 120, 139, 140,
    147, 154
Writing, 9, 11, 15, 33, 46–47, 77, 88,
    97-120, 142, 158, 178, 180–82

Yahweh, 55
Yea-saying, 69, 72–73, 140, 145, 167,
    182. See also Affirmation
Yeats, William Butler, 3

Zeus, 16